Philosophy

Philosophy and Fiction

An Introduction to Thinking Through Literature

Schuy R. Weishaar

McFarland & Company, Inc., Publishers
Jefferson, North Carolina

This book has undergone peer review.

Library of Congress Cataloguing-in-Publication Data

Names: Weishaar, Schuy R., author.
Title: Philosophy and fiction : an introduction to thinking
through literature / Schuy R. Weishaar.
Description: Jefferson, North Carolina : McFarland & Company, Inc.,
Publishers, 2023 | Includes bibliographical references and index.
Identifiers: LCCN 2022048375 | ISBN 9781476688473 (paperback : acid free paper) ∞
ISBN 9781476648446 (ebook)
Subjects: LCSH: Fiction—History and criticism—Theory, etc. |
Fiction—Themes, motives. | Literature—Philosophy.
Classification: LCC PN3331 .W45 2022 | DDC 809.3—dc23/eng/20221011
LC record available at https://lccn.loc.gov/2022048375

British Library cataloguing data are available

ISBN (print) 978-1-4766-8847-3
ISBN (ebook) 978-1-4766-4844-6

Front cover image © Mimma Key/Shutterstock

Printed in the United States of America

*McFarland & Company, Inc., Publishers
Box 611, Jefferson, North Carolina 28640
www.mcfarlandpub.com*

For Brooke Nicol, with all my love.

"Where love rules, there is no will to power…"—C.G. Jung

Acknowledgments

I would like to acknowledge a couple of friends who helped me through the conception, the writing, and the revision process that resulted in the present book. It was in conversation with Randy Carden, during one of our many lunches, that the notion of adapting these lectures and ideas into a book first occurred to me (they originated in developing a course); Randy also read some portions of early drafts. Mark Woods read every book and story I wrote about, and he read a late draft of the manuscript and discussed it with me over several Zoom and in-person conversations. Thank you both; your help was essential. The following friends and colleagues were also helpful to me, in one way or another, during the writing process as well: Kyle Weishaar, Sam Stueckle, Erica Hayden (who let me borrow a book), Laura Hohman (who also let me borrow books and answered some questions), Brannon Hancock, Finn Weishaar, Athan Weishaar, Ben Jorge, Whitney and Joshua Rio-Ross, Jooly Philip, Graham Hillard, Michael Karounos, Eleni Reid, Steven Hoskins, Mark Bowles, Lena Welch, my family, and many others whom I may be forgetting to mention. Thanks to you all. Thanks, also, to Dré Person at McFarland and to the peer reviewers who helped me make this study better. Finally, thanks to Brooke Nicol, who read portions of this text and helped me think through many of the ideas in it, and who married me during the writing of this book.

Table of Contents

Table of Contents

Preface

This book is the result of a rethinking of an Introduction to Literature composition course that I have been teaching for fifteen years. The germ of the idea was to teach a freshman/sophomore literature course that was organized more like a philosophy course, according to a few hastily drafted themes, which, after some revision, became the themes outlined in this book. The result was a new lens through which to read the literature, new templates through which to establish connections among texts, and a fresh perspective on how and what the literature was communicating. The literature, much of which I had been reading and teaching for over a decade, with the help of a philosophical approach, took on new meaning and new depth, but in a relatively basic way. In short, attempting to read the texts philosophically de-familiarized them from the standard (more or less Aristotelian) literary model of analysis, that is, analysis according to plot, character, theme, diction, etc. Approaching the texts through a philosophical mode made them strange to me—and helped me read them *as if* for the first time.

Reading and Writing about Literature

People read literature (for our purposes, short stories and novels) for all sorts of reasons: pleasure, escapism, a palatable way to consider big ideas, a way to interact with concepts and people and characters different from themselves, and on and on. Some of these reasons may have provided useful and enjoyable ways to read and think about literature, but the objective demonstrated in the readings of literature in this book is pretty specific. There are two basic goals that I will be focusing on:

(1) The readings I provide are exercises in critical thinking about writing. This means I begin with the words on the page. I will be bringing in philosophical ideas, psychoanalytic theory, historical context,

and so on, but such "para-textual" ideas and information are only useful, in literary study, anyway, as potential directions through which to better understand and make some kind of meaning from the words this or that author wrote down on the page, that is, to better understand the works themselves. This means that the following chapters are intended not as exhaustively researched dissertations on the works but, rather, as introductions to how to break into how literature makes meaning.

(2) These essays are explorations. They exemplify writing *toward meaning*, toward understanding something about these texts. So while, hopefully, the essays in this book do provide interesting interpretations of the texts they focus on, my hope is that they also let the reader see "how the sausage is made" (as it were), that they demonstrate how the process of reading a text begins, how it pays attention to details, how it gathers ideas together in order to arrive at some sense of the meaning that fiction can take on.

So the essays that compose this book are *essays* in the traditional sense of the term, which has, unfortunately, largely fallen out of use: they are "attempts," experiments with and explorations of how ideas fit together in fiction. We can combine the two aforementioned goals under the rubric of *reading toward interpretation*. Interpretation is, basically, how we make sense of what we are reading—how we make meaning from what we are reading. Reading in this way implies that we are reading actively, that we are reading closely (and probably slowly): we are reading to understand not only what happens (the plot) in a story or novel but also to understand the "whys" of the story or novel. We are reading to understand as much as possible about what the story means. This kind of reading is the first act of interpretation, but it is not the standard model for the traditional "academic essay."

The typical academic essay written for college or university English literature or composition courses begins with an already-developed interpretation. But interpretation requires several aspects of critical reading and writing. It involves (1) making claims about what something means, (2) citing evidence (textual evidence) for those claims, and (3) analyzing how that evidence demonstrates what one is saying the text may be (*really*) saying (so matching up [1] and [2] in a meaningful way).

In other words, when we are writing about literature, we typically have to make choices about what to focus on. This means that we have to develop an interpretive thesis, which is the main idea of an essay. This is the kind of essay I tend to make my students write. These kinds of "academic" essays often require that the thesis, or primary interpretive idea, be stated in specific ways and in a specific location (usually near the end of the first paragraph). An interpretive thesis states an argument, so this thesis must be a debatable proposition about some specific aspect of what or how the literature one is writing about makes meaning. Integrated with this proposition, or following or preceding it, should also be a thumbnail sketch of one's argument, a statement of purpose (disclosing the texts one will focus on; how, generally, the ideas will apply to these texts; and so on)—basically, where one is going with the essay. And then the rest of the essay should stick to that thesis, that interpretation, and that plan or purpose, as the writer works through the interpretive claims that fit within the thesis, quotes textual evidence from the literature, and analyzes how those two things fit together to culminate in a valid interpretation before finally digging into the wider ramifications or implications of that interpretation.

My essays will move, more or less, the other way around, which, in reality, is the way we probably develop ideas that become theses and interpretations. My goal will be to unpack the literature, demonstrating a number of possibilities, but by no means will I be observing all of them. In short, I want to show *how* to read deeply: how to draw connections between various aspects in a story/novel; how to isolate images, symbolism, themes, etc.; how to analyze a character, the setting, the tone, etc.—but all through the lens of philosophy. My goal is not necessarily the same as that of the average undergraduate in a literature or writing class. My goal is to use philosophical themes to make reading literary works fresh, to make reading "strange" again, to demonstrate various approaches to the literature, but also to see where texts take me.

But in order for us to understand one another, we will have to acknowledge some shared vocabulary: literary-critical vocabulary and philosophical vocabulary. So, when I use a specialized word from one of these domains, I will briefly define the term to ensure the concept is clear for those readers who may be unfamiliar with such vocabulary. Literary criticism, cultural theory, and philosophy can be daunting subjects, and my intention is for this book to be accessible even to readers just beginning their journeys into these domains. The most difficult part of beginning this sort of intellectual pursuit is learning the vocabulary—learning to "read the notes," as it were—but, once one becomes conversant in the language, any barrier to entry can be overcome through patience, curiosity, and a little research. Further, while this

Preface

book is intended for those setting out on their intellectual journey into "thinking through" fiction, those with more experience in these pursuits may also find new and interesting perspectives on both the classic texts and those that are more often ignored or overlooked in scholarship and teaching. Whether the reader is a beginner or not, the book is best read alongside the primary sources it engages.

Introduction

"Learned we may be with another man's learning: we can only be wise with wisdom of our own."—Michel de Montaigne

"Philosophy and Fiction" and "Thinking through Literature"

There is an interesting double contradiction in Plato's writing regarding literature. On one hand, in Book x of *The Republic*, Plato says that banning "mimetic poetry" is one of the best moves he has made in designing the ideal city. This literature, Plato suggests through his character Socrates, is destructive to human intelligence and leads people to exercise their worst impulses, both of which lead them away from the truth, and thereby away from wisdom (Urmson 226, 229). On the other hand, as James O. Urmson identifies, Plato, in *The Laws*, allows that poets' works may actually be divinely inspired by the Muses through a connection to ancient myth (224). However, this "authenticity" does not mean that such works are in any way true. After all, the Muses told Hesiod that they were as likely to utter fictions as they were to tell the truth (224). As Urmson puts the matter, "If Plato regarded the poets as inspired or spoke as though he did, this was in no way incompatible with regarding them as a danger to society" (225). Further, Urmson reasons, Plato's term "mimetic poetry," if adapted for our own day, would include the best fiction, the upshot being that our finest authors would be liable to the charge of mistaking the "imitation of a shadow for reality," that they, too, "are prisoners in the cave" and that the "deep truths" of their "imaginative literature are in fact shadows on the wall" (231). But, at the same time, Plato uses imaginative literature to convey his message. Even here, then, near the beginnings of philosophy, it seems, philosophy and literature implied one another in an often-contentious relation.

Introduction

I discovered that this contentiousness intruded into the contemporary world when I was a graduate student. I took a literature-based course in a divinity school in which aspiring "divines" and would-be theologians debated the paradoxes of holding "theology" and "fiction" in their minds at the same time. The claim was that, since theology was concerned not only with truth, but *the Truth* (i.e., God, Jesus, etc.), fiction that purported to do theology or be theological was necessarily abortive—it was impossible! I bristled a little at the self-righteousness at the root of the discussion, but I liked the paradox out of which the debate grew. Some philosophers, too, might have the same kind of objection to binding philosophy to fiction so cavalierly, since philosophy itself has something to do with the pursuit of truth, even if often in less "absolute" terms, of its possibility or our ability to define or perceive it. But I like "degrading" philosophy (and theology, for that matter) by forcing it to live in the slums of fiction. The word "fiction" comes from the Latin word meaning "a shaping or feigning," so fiction is, at least to some degree, "made up." It seeks reality through the shadows, but it knows that its images are shadow-play. Fiction realizes its shaping. The conjuncture of "philosophy and fiction" is fraught, perhaps paradoxical, but ultimately quite natural. Fiction lies in order to tell the truth.

"Thinking through literature" (which is, of course, part of the subtitle of this book), while less paradoxical, is not without its own sense of play. The reader may ask, "Is this supposed to mean that it is *through literature* that I will be taught to think?" I would hesitate to put it in such grand terms, but, yes, one reading of the phrase indicates that, in this book, literature will be offered as a catalyst for thinking. I hope that is the case, anyway; that is indeed part of my intention in writing it. The reader may also emphasize the phrase differently: "Is this supposed to mean that this book will provide an introduction to *thinking-through* literature?" The answer is, again, yes. The book will provide tools and models for how to use philosophy to "think through" literature—that is, to persist in sustained consideration of literary texts from beginning to end and back again. Both emphases of "thinking through literature" will inform the relationship between thinking and literature in the coming pages. This may be a different approach to reading and writing about literature than is typical, but it has proven to be a fruitful one. As is said of dreams, literature takes the often-meaningless banalities of our lives, condenses them, reshuffles them, inscribes them with meaning, and then allows us the proper distance according to which we can reconsider them: fiction shapes and fashions meaning where there may not have been any before, and in reading and writing about fiction, we may come closer to understanding that meaning has everything to do with us.

Modern Fiction

The literature under consideration in this book is modern fiction (beginning in the early 19th century), short stories, and novellas (which are short novels or really long stories). But modern fiction did not emerge out of nowhere; it developed from other, earlier types of fiction. Exactly how this development took place is still up for debate, so perhaps better than thinking of a genealogy that leads, historically, from forms like the parable, fable, tale, etc., to the modern story, we can at least think of these earlier forms of fiction coalescing in the modern fiction, which performs a lot of the functions that these earlier forms do (Gioia and Gwynn 1–2). As we shall see, though, regardless of the era, fiction implies thinking about the "big questions" that philosophy considers its territory.

Like a fable, modern fiction can teach us something, though few modern writers would probably want to discuss their fiction in terms of a "moral" (as we would with a fable), though some may. Instead, we would think of "theme," which is similar to a moral in function but often void of the practical application to life that a "moral of a story" entails. And like a parable, a modern story can be perplexing; it may force us to think from a number of perspectives; it is open to any *valid* (a key word here) interpretation. Modern fiction also operates according to some of the formal features we can discern in tales (which are probably the closest of these earlier forms of short fiction to the typical modern short story, if there is one), such as narrative, plot, characters, etc. So the modern story, in a way, takes from all of these earlier forms of fiction, but it is its own thing as well (Kennedy and Gioia 6). Reading modern fiction requires reading with at least some awareness of this history and relation, but also with an awareness of literature's synthetic tendency, its potential to take what it wants from these forms and combine and utilize them as suits the author or the era. Fiction is, in many ways, "freer" than philosophy tends to be (though that is, of course, a broad generalization).

With these older forms of fiction, we might consider what cultural,

Introduction

social, or even political purposes they might have served. Fables, of course, are built around attempts to deliver morals—life lessons—and these lessons usually reinforce a culture's value system and ideology. The same could be said of certain kinds of folktales, tall tales, etc.: they create exemplary figures for (perhaps, primarily) children to imitate, or they relate situations where someone breaks the "rules" and is punished, again buttressing the community's values or beliefs. Parables do something a little different: they evade clear "lessons" or "morals"; they are more concerned with transporting the hearer or reader into a state of reflection—and sustaining such reflection as a good in itself: parables are a contemplative form of storytelling. These aspects of fiction position readers to feel or think—to respond—in particular ways, so reading deeply means that we are paying attention to our own responses as readers.

We can feel such moments of synthesis in modern literary fiction—where we are prompted or even impelled to make judgements or draw conclusions about certain characters and/or situations. Good writers push us in different directions for different reasons; they mess with our feelings, and paying attention to our feelings as we read, and our ability to analyze why we feel the way we do about certain aspects of a story, can help us understand the effect or impact of the literature. But good writing may also compel us to resist hasty or easy judgements. A pat, simple story is often a bad or boring story. Good fiction seeks a reader willing to offer sustained reflection on the questions it refuses to answer, on its implications. Good reading involves paying attention to how our feelings are affected and for what purpose; deep reading requires us to pay attention to how our categories (whether moral, emotional, cultural, ideological, political, or philosophical) are complicated or problematized or played with. Plato's concerns are, to some degree, justified. Fiction does indeed deal with our emotions and impulses, but in doing so, it affords us the opportunity to pay critical attention to them as well.

Modern fiction can do all of these things—modern fiction *synthesizes* all of these possibilities—or at least it can engage the reader on all of these levels. Literature puts us in touch with moral/ethical questions, with cultural/political/social worldviews, with philosophical questions, and with individual value systems and judgements. But, instead of conveying a clear "lesson," modern literature implicates the reader in the problems it devises. The reader is responsible for contributing to the meaning of the fiction; fiction does not mean anything until someone reads and reflects on it. Stories are worlds waiting for us to inhabit them in order to understand what they mean.

Why Philosophy?

Philosophy is useful at every step along the way. According to French philosopher Luc Ferry, the philosopher seeks wisdom through deliberation of meaning, which cannot be done without (1) "theory," or deep reflection upon "things as they are," on what we take to be reality, and (2) consideration of "what must be or what ought to be," which we call morals or ethics (12–13). But, as English philosopher Simon Blackburn claims, philosophy normally studies the "structure of thought," the "structures that shape our view of the world," which moves us toward figuring out something about how that structure provides (or does not provide) some kind of meaning (*Think* 2). For our purposes in this book, however, philosophy will be employed both to structure the consideration of the literature as well as to aid in our investigation and analysis of how fiction makes meaning through narrative. So we will consider the shape, structure, and meaning of human thought, but we will do so through the "filter" of literature. Such meaning may sometimes trend toward reflection on *things as they are* on the page (the "reality" of fiction as it were) and how these words arrive at meaning, and such meaning may sometimes trend toward investigations of the moral or ethical—or, more broadly, the social domain—whether in theme, character, or some other more properly "literary" aspect, or with regard to historical/cultural context.

This is a broadly ad hoc approach to utilizing philosophy for "thinking through" literature, but such an approach may also offer an interesting, perhaps attractive, change of perspective through which to philosophize about the human experience. In Edward Craig's introduction to philosophy, he suggests that most of us, even people who do not typically think about philosophical issues, walk around thinking we have answers to the following three basic philosophical questions. What should we do? (morality/ethics); What is there? (ontology, or doctrines/reflection regarding being); And how do we know? (epistemology, or doctrines/reflection on knowledge) (Craig 1). These are three basic questions through which philosophy frames human experience of the world. When applied to fictional narratives, these questions may find purchase in satisfying ways: literary texts offer objects of consideration that are finite, or limited in ways that our human existence is not, which affords philosophical interpretation a more manageable "experience of the world" to consider, one that allows sustained reflection on a fixed textual world, but one which is tethered to "the world" as such, one which highlights specific experiences of it, and one whose finiteness analogizes the "human 'finiteness'" at the heart of philosophical reflection (Ferry 13). But fiction may also help readers think through philosophical problems. The relationship between the two disciplines is dynamic and multifaceted. Philosophy does not just "explain" literature: the two implicate one another's picture of the human experience.

I will freely admit that I am not a professional philosopher (and I am sure that fact is already apparent to any philosopher who is reading this book); I am an English professor who reads and is interested in philosophy. My approach to "thinking through" fiction in conversation with philosophy is nonsystematic and driven by simpler questions, which often lead to my explorations ending up in the domains of epistemology, ontology, metaphysics, moral/ethical philosophy, and so on: those questions are the ones that every child asks (and most children do start out with a philosophical inclination), perhaps thousands of times before they even go to school. "Why?" and "So what?"

These two questions, though, are not flippant, and they are not deflections when they are employed with seriousness. These questions are behind the questions Craig refers to; they inhabit the "three dimensions of philosophy" that Ferry outlines; they are at the root of Blackburn's concept of the "structure of thought" that "shapes our view of the world" (*Think* 2). The basic interrogative impulse toward "Why?" is always already seeking meaning, seeking understanding. It emerges from a desire for more and deeper understanding, from the same "love of wisdom" from which the word "philosophy" derives: "*philo*" in Greek is "love"; "*sophia*" is "wisdom" (Ferry 15). And "So what?" is always already seeking to make connections between "this" and "that" and the "everything else," whether these refer to aspects of a story or aspects of our selves or minds or the world.

Further, both questions ("Why?" and "So what?") assume a philosophical position of curious ignorance, which, according to Socrates in the "Apology," approximates the starting place of wisdom (26). Accordingly, "loving wisdom," then, entails the acknowledgment that we do *not* know, that we do *not* understand; philosophy is not "acquiring knowledge" or "increasing intelligence." Rather, to love wisdom, to behave like a philosopher, is to *pursue* wisdom, to be able to say that we want to know—but to be willing to admit that we do not yet know. This relation to wisdom parallels the plea from the father of the demon-possessed boy in the Gospel of Mark, which became a famous Christian prayer: "I believe; help thou mine unbelief" (9:24). The philosopher says, "I want wisdom; help me understand." The stakes may be greater, though, for the philosopher. The philosopher's plea for help is general, and the helpers must be vetted; there is no authoritative "helper" (or divine "Helper") whose answers are beyond reproach. Part of seeking wisdom is skepticism regarding "answers."

Themes and Chapters

Our engagement with literature, fiction in the present case, perhaps, oddly organized according to themes that may be more appropriate for the study of philosophy, allows us to break out of the usual ways of thinking about literature. I will explain.

Typically, when we think about the study of literature, we think about a story, say, as being composed of certain attributes. This probably goes back to the way we were first taught the basics of literature in elementary school: according to this early education (which owes a heavy share to Aristotle's *Poetics*), literature must have a setting, a point of view or perspective, characters, a plot, a tone, style, themes, symbols, and so on. Focusing on these aspects of literature sometimes makes us immune to the "deep" aspects of literature—the aspects of stories that make people interested in seeking to read or write them. This focus on the pieces and parts of literature can make the process of interacting with fiction a little mechanical. In engaging literature through philosophy (even in the limited way in which I am able to do so), my intention is to put us back in touch with the big, deep aspects of literature, not to the exclusion of the "parts of a story," but as a mode by which those parts can come alive again in stories in which we can perceive the big, deep questions about us (humans) and our world—in which we can see even "classic" literature as strange again. Just a cursory sketch of the chapters may give the reader a sense of this strangeness.

The following chapters consider fiction texts according to six broadly philosophical themes. Chapter One gathers together five short stories under the theme of "Nature." It moves from theological disputes regarding the meaning of thunderstorms to the ethics of inhabiting gender roles while killing animals and from cosmic plots to compel people

Introduction

to have sex with one another to cosmic plots to murder those who fail to heed the call to a universal silence. Chapter Two takes "Metaphysics" as its theme; this chapter considers remarkable eyes, undying hearts, walking devils, and selfish giants. In Chapter Three, "Time," we investigate a fourth dimension and fly into the future in *The Time Machine* by H.G. Wells, but we end up discussing the science and politics of the past. Then, in Chapter Four, we consider two homicides, a suicide with extenuating circumstances, the class consciousness of a pestilence, and a love affair between a statue and a bird under the theme "Social Cont(r)acts." "The Life of the Mind," in Chapter Five, features two obsessives, both somewhat mystical in inclination; two forking streams of consciousness that lead almost nowhere; and the childhood trauma that led to the formation of a superpower in an old priest. Finally, Chapter Six, "Love and Death," pulls us into a smutty insurance scandal in James M. Cain's *Double Indemnity*—but also into an analysis of the dueling drives toward civilization and entropy that rage just beneath the surface in every human relationship.

So, all together, the book moves through the space of about a hundred years of modern fiction and its interaction with the world of ideas, from Washington Irving's "The Devil and Tom Walker" (1824) through James M. Cain's *Double Indemnity* (1936). Further, within this century-long conversation between these domains, this exploration examines several "classic" works of literary fiction, a few more or less forgotten stories, and a couple of "popular" novels; it discovers that reading them closely through the lens of philosophy can help us perceive the complexity and richness of fiction as such. But this engaged reading also reintroduces us to the submerged reality in fiction, the pursuit of wisdom just beneath the surface of the words on the page.

CHAPTER ONE

Nature

"Let us permit nature to have her way. She knows her business better than we do."—Michel de Montaigne

Introduction

"*Phusis*" (or "*physis*") is the Greek word used to denote "nature," as referring to "the natural world," as well as to the identifying or essential characteristics of something or someone (Russell 204). It is the word from which our English word "physics" derives. As a philosophical theme that brings together a set of short stories, we will see that the "natural world" looms rather large. Such a focus may, immediately, draw our attention to the settings of the stories, since "nature" (as in "the great outdoors") may be interpreted as the setting for the majority of the stories to follow (but, if we consider that "the great indoors" is almost necessarily set in "the great outdoors," we would have to admit that nature is involved in just about all of literature). But we will also see nature doing things in some of these stories—so, that is, nature taking on the characteristics of a person (which we might call anthropomorphism), one with a point of view, motivations, and so on—nature functioning as a character. We will see nature as something that the characters in these stories are crushed by, reflect upon, contend against, embody, serve, emulate, and overcome. But nature, in its other range of meaning (as the identifying or essential characteristics of something or someone), is also active among these stories: the fiction examines human nature; it portrays parts of human nature set against one another; it questions how animal human nature is; it questions how human nature interprets the natural world, God, morality, and so on. So, while setting, atmosphere, tone, and various other literary-critical terms may evoke the clearest, more or less, literal connections to the theme of nature, we should keep our conception of nature open in order to think about this theme in all of its immensity and depth, and philosophy can be useful for reminding us of this immensity and depth.

Plato, in *The Republic*, during his discussion of imitative arts in Book 10, indicates that everything in nature (and the nature of every specific thing) imitates a "form": that "the god," wanting "to be the real maker" of each thing, conceived of the abstract, perfect form of each thing, and things in nature imitate that ideal form; likewise, craftsmen, when they construct things, also imitate the perfect ideas, the realities, of those things they are making (299–301). So behind or above (or wherever in relation to) nature is a world of forms, a world of the perfections of everything, from aardvarks to zyzzyvas, and things imitate those forms to varying degrees. The more perfect the imitation of the form, the closer to being itself it becomes, the closer it is to the form, that which makes it itself.

Thomas Aquinas develops this idea of imitation in the specifically Christian context of a single creator God. He identifies, not just imitation alone, but love as the active principle of imitation—as the constitutive aspect of the degree to which things are themselves, and the degree to which they resemble God, not just "forms," in being themselves. When certain things are more like God, that is because God loves them better than others, which is, in turn, because they are better at resembling God according to the love God has for them (Aquinas, *Nature and Grace* 84). If this seems confusingly circular, that is only because it *is* circular, but the point of the circularity is to see the primacy of God at every step. God remains the absolute source of being and identity of everything, but there is just a smidge of independence with which one may achieve goodness within one's natural gifts to earn "better" love from God—but only in the sense that one's "nature," nature itself, one's ability to achieve anything, and the whole economy of "earning" all come from God's love and goodness. This is imitation that is covering all of the bases in the way Plato's imitation was not. It is a markedly Christian philosophy of nature, which begins and ends with God. The prime example of, say, a human that God loves "more than the entire human race," which God, admittedly, really, really loves, is Jesus Christ (84). In orthodox Christian theology, Jesus *is* God, and one cannot resemble God more than by being God, so Jesus sets the prime example of imitation and resemblance: he, simply, *is* the fullness of God's love. One cannot do better. Jesus's human nature is deified by his divine nature (by his "God-ness"). But the rest of nature, too, is saturated with God's love;

therefore, we can see God in and through nature; thus, nature can be said to reveal God.

Even non–Christian rationalists, like Thomas Paine, like this idea. Paine had no patience for Christian doctrines about deified human beings, special revelations from God to special individuals, or sacred scriptures. In his book *The Age of Reason*, he trounces all of these ideas. But he holds onto the notion that nature imitates God and that such imitation reveals something about God that humans can understand:

> It is only in the CREATION that all our ideas and conceptions of a *word of God* can unite. The Creation speaketh an universal language; independently of human speech or human language.... [I]t cannot be forged; it cannot be counterfeited; it cannot be lost; it cannot be altered; it cannot be suppressed. [...] It preaches to all nations and to all worlds; and this *word of God* reveals to man all that is necessary for man to know of God [46, emphasis in original].

Nature, which for Paine is still couched in the language of "creation," then, is the only really *free* expression of God, the only media through which we can learn anything about God (not divine humans, prophets, and sacred texts—so, revelation and authority are out). But we do not read the "scripture called the Creation" through love or faith anymore; we read it using our reason: "It is only by the exercise of reason, that man can discover God" (47). Paine's reading of nature discloses to him a creator God that is reasonable, one who has organized the world according to mathematical principles, one who reveals his mysteries to those who employ reason and appropriate methods, to scientists, mathematicians, and philosophers. Therefore, if we want to learn about God, we must imitate God: we must be reasonable, too. Our capacity for reason is something like the "image of God" within us, which, when applied to the reasonable nature around us, allows us to see the character of God. Who could disagree?

Lots of people, apparently, especially after Charles Darwin's theory of evolution through natural selection became popular. Scientist and writer Stephen Jay Gould highlights the problem: Darwin argues that the variation that opens the door to adaptation is random and that evolution is without purpose: "Individuals struggle to increase the representation of their genes in future generations, and that is all" (184). Gould completes the thought when he writes, "If the world displays any harmony and order, it arises only as an incidental result of individuals seeking their own advantage" (184). Further, evolution "has no direction," and "matter is the ground of all existence; mind, spirit, and God as well, are just words that express the wondrous results of neuronal complexity" (184). On this view, nature is just nature; imitation is out. At best, "mind, spirit, and God" are all just metaphors for the ways we have tried to make sense of the complexity of the world and our place in and relation to it. We embody, not God's love, nor imperfect imitations of divine principles, but nature itself—sheer, godless nature. There is no purpose to "theologizing" nature—not just because God is not pulling the strings that make it move—but because there is no God at all, and because nature has no purpose, no goal. It just is. Gould's view is that this "Darwinian spirit" may have a moral though: it is the beginning of a cure for our "Western arrogance—that we are meant to have control and dominion over the earth" (185).

Darwin and Gould really suck the wind out of the sails of a view of nature as creation, which was behind the view of imitation and resemblance all along. Regardless of one's religious views, Gould's point rings true in a fundamental way. If humans are part of nature, and God is behind nature in whatever way, then humans find ways to see themselves as occupying the place of God on earth, whether as "dominators" or as "caretakers": they find ways to elevate themselves above the nature to which they belong. If nature is understood as a complex series of random material events and responses with no ultimate purpose, then, at some point, we have to see ourselves within that worldview, which downgrades us from our lofty, preordained position of control and domination over nature. Instead, we must accept that we are part of the complexity of nature, which means that we must learn how to occupy responsibly our place *in* nature and become more self-aware of its action in us. The exploration of stories in this chapter revolves through these views of nature, from seeing the potential for God's action through nature to human triumph over nature, from perceiving humans as agents of nature to seeing nature over against human agency.

"Travelling during thunderstorms": "The Lightning-Rod Man" (1854) by Herman Melville

Just by way of introduction, it bears mentioning that Melville's works, letters, and even his biography show him to be very interested in nature and nearly obsessed with God. And his obsession with God is often navigated through his interest in the natural world. We can take the example of his most famous work, *Moby-Dick*, which demonstrates both tendencies, and which also demonstrates the theological tendencies of the two characters in "The Lightning-Rod Man" (published just a couple of years after the novel): namely, one perspective that sees nature as evidence of God's rage, punishment, and justice and another perspective that sees in nature God's glory, mysteriousness, and mercy. In both the novel and the story, these perspectives elicit very different views, not only of God, but also of relation to one's fellow human beings and one's role in life. We might also observe at the outset that "The Lightning-Rod Man" portrays a philosophical debate about the nature of God through analysis of the weather (nature), but without entering much into the question of religion. Religion backgrounds the debate, but neither of the interlocutors seems representative of a standard Christianity. And maybe this, partly, is the point.

The language of the story probably seems a little "thick" to the contemporary reader. Melville can be this way sometimes, writing in a "high" rhetorical register that, perhaps, is in keeping with his era (the language of literary fiction in the 1850s can ask a lot of readers), but his themes, if we pay attention, I think, are worth the work.

The story begins with the narrator (who is also one of our two characters), more or less, *appreciating* the grandeur of a thunderstorm that has broken out around his cottage in the mountains. He says,

> What grand irregular thunder, thought I ... as the scattered bolts boomed overhead, and crashed down among the valleys, every bolt followed by zig-zag irradiations, and swift slants of sharp rain, which audibly rang, like a charge of spear-points, on my low shingled roof. I suppose, though, that the mountains hereabouts break and churn up the thunder, so that it is far more glorious here than on the plain [123].

A couple of things will get us started if we read these first sentences carefully.

1. We can observe the elevated diction of the rhetoric (that first sentence is complex!).

2. We can discern some things about this character's point of view based on this description, though we may not be sure what about it to pay attention to until we get to the entry of the second character (the titular lightning-rod man), whose perspective is opposed to the narrator's. But, by the end of that first paragraph, when the lightning-rod man enters and immediately disagrees with the narrator, the reader is given a conflict in perspectives, so we can think back to the beginning of the paragraph and reassess its

importance: the narrator's language regarding the storm attributes words like "grand" and "irregular"; he notes the differences of experience that one might observe from the mountain top, where his cabin is located, from the valley below (which indicates some penchant for relativity, which makes him seem pretty broadminded); he notices the interaction of natural forces involved in the thunderstorm (the rain, the lightning, the thunder, the wind), but he is unafraid. In fact, he is mostly just impressed—he sees the storm as wholly good, even to the point that, when he greets the lightning-rod man, he says, "A fine thunderstorm, sir" (123).

3. As with the stories of Edgar Allan Poe, H.G. Wells, and various others we will consider in this book, this story initiates us to a first-person narrator and one who is an actor, or participant, in the story he is telling. This means that his perspective is likely limited to his own experience (so any observation of what other people are feeling or thinking or whatever is probably conjecture, which makes such observations largely unreliable), and this also means that our narrator may be trying to convince us of something or other. It is important to notice the kind of narration or perspective we are given, the "lens" through which we view the events, because that may have an effect on how we interpret the story.

I will briefly summarize the plot of the rest of the story. The narrator invites the lightning-rod man, who is carrying a lightning-rod, to come in out of the storm. The narrator jokes with the man, calling him "Jupiter Tonans" (123), which the lightning-rod man dislikes and rejects as blasphemous. The narrator asks the wet lightning-rod man to come dry himself by the fire, and this sets off an argument between the two men about where would be the safest place to stand in a house during a storm (and, due to some questionable scientific speculation, the lightning-rod man says one should not stand near the fire). The lightning-rod man explains his lightning-rods to the narrator and tries to interest the man, mostly through fear, in purchasing one or more. The narrator challenges the efficacy of lightning-rods by pointing out some evidence that they do not seem very effective. The lightning-rod man defends his product against these criticisms and becomes more and more alarmed when he hears thunder or when the narrator moves around the room or touches anything that might conduct electricity. Their conversation persists, and as the narrator continues lightly abusing and bullying this salesman, the lightning-rod man seems to become

Chapter One. Nature

testier in explaining his strange, alarmist logic regarding thunderstorms. Finally, the narrator seems to have had enough; he insults the salesman's life's work and tells him to leave. The lightning-rod man becomes angry and turns his lightning-rod against the narrator like a sword. The narrator breaks the rod and flings the lightning-rod man out the door by his elbow. The end.

That is a relatively detailed 250-word synopsis of the story. I summarized it at length for a couple of reasons: (1) to set the sequence of events in order, just in case the language of the story presents an obstacle to understanding it, and (2) (and this is my real reason) to demonstrate the limitations of mere plot summary. Let me carry on with this idea for just a moment. When we are asked to interpret a piece of literature, art, writing, or whatever, summarizing what is there only proves a very superficial interaction with a piece of art, which does not demonstrate a thorough "thinking-through" of the artwork. One can observe from my summary that I have not discussed anything deeper than just what happens, even if my summary of the plot is detailed and accurate. We can now move on to bigger, deeper issues that go beyond the plot (which I can summarize even more succinctly, like this: two guys meet during a storm; they disagree about it; and one guy throws the other out—not a captivating plot).

Perhaps we should back up a little. We can see, even on an initial glance across the conversation that emerges between the men, that their disagreement about the storm is about safety during the storm. If we dig in a little past that, we can see that the lightning-rod man is deathly afraid of the storm (or is at least pretending to be), while the other man is rather flippant about such worries. This fact may give us cause to wonder about the lightning-rod man's underlying motivations. Is he truly afraid, or does he try to stoke fears in people because it helps him sell his lightning-rods? Either way, the narrator does not take him seriously— and he levels his attack of the lightning-rod man on both accounts: he pokes fun at the lightning-rod man's warnings and worries (both about the storm and about blaspheming), and he accuses the lightning-rod man of being a "Tetzel." Both of these objects of derision depend on fear, one of something natural, the other of something supernatural.

This second attack is the more interesting of the two, and the one that the story seems to revolve around, the first one (the nature-based fears and precautions) aiming to make the lightning-rod man look ridiculous and to lead into the more philosophical, or theological, climax of the story. Here we may need some vocabulary assistance. A "Tetzel" is a curiously specific insult. We can see from the context—"Who empowered you, you Tetzel, to peddle round your indulgences from divine ordinations?" (129)—that this has something to do with playing on people's fears. If we do a little research, we shall find that Tetzel is the name of the German bishop in charge of the sale of indulgences before the Reformation, a rather unscrupulous man who was willing to make "scandalous claims," so long as they helped increase the sale of indulgences (Gonzalez 21). So the reference is an explicitly theological one, which we can attach to the following sentences from the narrator: "The hairs of our heads are numbered and the days of our lives. In thunder as in sunshine, I stand at ease in the hands of my God" (Melville, "The Lightning-Rod" 129).

Here, we can see the narrator disclosing the "blessed assurance" that his view of God gives him. He views God as a mysterious "hand" behind all things, who knows him well and knows when he will die, and when it is his time, it is his time, and that is all. Implied here are the ideas that fear and worry about nature's dangers are silly—but the deeper message is that he is not in the least worried about God's wrath. He goes on to allude to the story of Noah, as he points out that the storm has rolled away to reveal a rainbow—the image of the promise that "the Deity will not, of purpose, make war on man's earth" (129). The lightning-rod man sees this interpretation as yet more blasphemy (which means profane speech; actions or ideas that are sacrilegious) and accuses him of impiety and infidelity for not relating to God through absolute fear.

But pay close attention to the words on the page at this moment: "The scowl grew blacker on his face; the indigo-circles enlarged round his eyes as the storm rings round the midnight moon. He sprang upon me; his tri-forked thing at my heart," and as the narrator throws him out, he refers to the lightning-rod man as the "dark lightning king" (129). This description of the lightning-rod man is the second of only two really detailed descriptions of him given in the story, which should make us think back to the other one, from near the beginning of the story: "A lean, gloomy figure. Hair dark and lank, mattedly streaked over his brow. His sunken pitfalls of eyes were ringed in indigo halos, and played with an innocuous sort of lightning; the gleam without the bolt" (123).

We should consider the contrast between the two descriptions. In the earlier one, the narrator frames the lightning-rod man as something like a pathetic fallen god who has dropped from the heavens out of a thunderstorm; and he gives the man the ironic moniker "Jupiter Tonans," or "Thundering Zeus." His eyes have "halos"; his lightning is an "innocuous sort of lightning," like Zeus' lightning bolt, but it is lacking the "bolt"—it has only the "gleam" of lightning. The lightning-rod man is described as a sad, wet god trying, still, to arouse fear in this human. The later description puts a satanic twist on the lightning-rod man, while maintaining the overview of the depiction. But now he "foams" his words at the narrator; his lightning-rod becomes a "tri-forked" thing, like a devil's pitchfork. The lightning-rod man goes after the narrator's heart—he wants to destroy his loving, free relationship to a merciful God and replace it with fear of God's wrath. The narrator's shift in description is instructive: this is no fallen god; this is the fallen angel, the devil, Satan. But notice that the satanic intention is not to get the man to disbelieve in God. Rather, it is to get him to believe in a Divine Punisher, to trade his trust in God for fear. But also look at the confidence and ease with which the lightning-rod man is dispensed with.

This can be a little confusing. Melville is not writing a religious parable exactly—he is not saying that the lightning-rod man *is* the devil or *is* a pathetic Zeus. But this is what stories can do with allusions (which are references to ideas outside the text) and descriptions, metaphors and similes: they can elicit these ideas and *present a character as* this or that, which allows the reader to hold the two things together simultaneously, to judge the one in the light of the other, to sustain a paradox of two dissimilar objects *as if* they were similar.

Consider the last lines: "But in spite of my treatment, and in spite of my dissuasive talk of him to my neighbors, the Lightning-rod man still dwells in the land; still travels in storm-time, and drives a brave trade with the fears of man" (129). Here, the story ends, seemingly, with both things on its mind: the literal story and the philosophical or theological metaphor. The narrator is speaking, here, almost like a sermon about avoiding the devil, but, instead of "devil," he is saying "the Lightning-rod man"; he is resolving the story about a guy selling things, but it, at once, seems to take on grander spiritual significance. This demonstrates the power of a theme. In stating it almost too obviously at the end, Melville is aggrandizing the connection between the literal story and the philosophical theme: perhaps, now we see the lightning-rod man as something quite like the Satan figure, "The Tempter," referred to in the gospels. But in addition to these "biblical overtones," Laurie Robertson-Lorant points out in her biography on Melville that "The Lightning-Rod Man" implies that, "while science has become the new religion, religion has become a form of insurance for individuals who want to feel safe, as well as for clergy who want to corner the market on faith so they can keep their followers in line and themselves in business" (346). Whether religious or not, Melville seems to say, guard yourself against the fear-mongers; be they crackpots or prophets, scientists or clergy, those who peddle fear are your adversaries.

Interestingly, Melville's story, for all it invests in nature, has a very human "message"; the questions regarding whether or not God is *in* nature or active through it or whatever end up as part of the smoke-screen. What nature actually *is* does not definitively emerge; it seems to depend on and grow out of the viewpoint of the individual. The narrator, of course, favors his view, but the salesman's view is, if we are being fair, no worse, logically speaking, than the narrator's. Both perceive divine agency in the operations of nature, but it is precisely where those views touch the human character that we see a clear division: one aims at coercion and manipulation, while the other allows human freedom. So we begin with nature, but we end up in the domain of morality.

"An animal that has a bad reputation": "How I Killed a Bear" (1878) by Charles Dudley Warner

Charles Dudley Warner was an influential essayist, travel writer, and short story writer, among other things, now remembered, mostly, for writing the novel *The Gilded Age* with his friend Mark Twain. "How I Killed a Bear" comes from a collection of stories Warner published in 1878. While Warner's work and biography demonstrate his dedication to the tradition of American liberalism, a close analysis of "How I Killed a Bear" shows other dimensions of the wider (shall we say) cultural unconscious bleeding through.

In our analysis of this story, I would like to explore another approach to "thinking through" literature. In analyzing "The Lightning-Rod Man," we focused mainly on traditional literary-critical aspects (narration, point of view/perspective, tone, setting, symbolism, theme, character, etc.) to demonstrate how to read deeply and how to read for meaning, in light of a philosophical idea, but strictly from within the "closed" world created by the words on the page. One could do the same sort of thing with Warner's story, though, perhaps, to less effect, since the story seems, generally, rather "light" and probably written

22

mostly to amuse a popular audience—and we will get into some of that literary-critical territory—but, for the sake of experiment, we can introduce another interesting way to read literature deeply in conjunction with the traditional literary-critical and philosophical approaches: that is reading literature as a "cultural artifact."

By "cultural artifact" I mean this: any piece of literature emerges at a particular time and place, from a particular individual. This means that, as much as we tend to treat many literary texts as "ahistorical," as works of art that are timeless and independent, which all function according to the same principles, etc.—as objects of ahistorical interpretation (along the lines of plot, symbol, theme, character, and so on)— these texts are finite and delimited within the confines of their moment. They come from a fixed point in a cultural world, and, because of this, they carry that culture with them through time, just like an archeological artifact carries its culture through the ages and into a future that can glimpse that culture, even if that future may not fully appreciate the richness of the older culture (Bate 81). Let me explain the analogy.

Archeologists and anthropologists can and do learn all sorts of things about ancient cultures by studying their trash pits, their tombs, their broken dishes, their ritual masks, and their hunting or war gear— even if there is nothing written by or about the ancient peoples from whom such artifacts derive. What I am suggesting is that we can study literature the same way: we can take a story like "How I Killed a Bear" and understand things about the not-so-ancient author—but even more, about the "spirit of the age," or *zeitgeist*, from which that story emerges. Much of what follows will be a short examination along these lines.

"How I Killed a Bear" is a pretty straightforward story. A man (apparently, Warner himself) tells the reader about his trip to the mountains, during which he encounters a bear while gathering berries; the bear charges him; the man shares the things that reel through his mind in the seconds between first noticing the bear and the bear's untimely demise when the man kills it with a rifle. Finally, the narrator tells us how proud he was of himself for having defeated the bear and how impressed everyone was that he had done so.

Again, a mere summary of the story tells us nothing but the plot, and the plot, in this case, may be thrilling but, for my money, is aesthetically unremarkable. If we go searching for a theme, we may arrive at something to do with "man versus nature," a theme which fits nicely within the topic for this chapter, but one which is probably too general, and one which is definitely overused in literary analysis. But even this gesture at a theme gets us somewhere interesting: it throws the story into more philosophically dramatic territory because it is an existential theme. According to such an idea, this is no longer merely a story about some dumb guy's interaction with a surprised animal in the animal's natural habitat: it is bigger than that. This man, in some way, we might say, can represent *human beings,* as such, at least 19th-century American male human beings (as such?—and more on this stuff in a moment), and the surprised bear, in some way, may represent "wilderness," or Nature, generally. It may be interesting to note at this point that the collection this story comes from is called *In the Wilderness.*

We should investigate the character further. I have already described the man as dumb, from the 19th century, male, and American, so, even in my rather cavalier remarks about him, I have specified quite a lot about this man as a character. We could go so far as to claim that all of these things are *essential* to understanding what the story has to tell us *as a cultural artifact.* Let's work in from the outside: we have "19th century," which limits the man in time; we have "American," which limits the man geographically, but also ideologically, or culturally. I will not go on and on, but we know that the map of America in, say, 1870 was incomplete by today's standards. There were still several "territories" (dare we say vast stretches of nature filled with wilderness?) in the middle-western part of the country. African American men had just been given the right to vote; "officially," anyway, Americans had just become interested in learning something about Native Americans (instead of just trying to annihilate them); and women had begun a suffrage movement (attempting to get their voting rights written into the Fourteenth Amendment along with African Americans') and taking on new roles in post–Reconstruction American society in the labor force, etc. (Du Bois and Dumenil 321–322). As Ellen Carol Du Bois and Lynn Dumenil write in *Through Women's Eyes: An American History with Documents*, by the last couple of decades in the 19th century, "the basis had been laid for an epoch of female assertion and accomplishment unparalleled in American history" (321).

What does this have to do with anything? It gives us an outline of a 19th-century American zeitgeist with which we might be able to integrate this story. It might suggest something about the characterization of the protagonist in the story. He is, literally, in the wilderness, but he is definitely not adept at *being in* the wilderness. He does not fit with the ideal of the "rugged American frontiersman"; instead, he seems to be pretending to be a rugged American frontiersman while on vacation from the city. We might invoke, therefore, the often-comic trope of the "city guy" in "the country"—a kind of "fish out of water" idea. We might also think of him as a bookish intellectual who finds himself out of context in the wilderness, perhaps along the lines of a "man of thought" in a situation more suited for a "man of action."

These latter ideas are dramatized in the protagonist's intellectualized, romantic "kindness to animals" story that he dreams up about "a nice romantic bear" (220). There is also obviously a lot of self-deprecating humor surrounding the various "fish out of water" themes. Thinking of the aforementioned history may also help to explain the obvious racism the narrator invokes when he relays the story about "Aunt Chloe," the "colored cook" (219), a story which makes the Black woman look ridiculous and unappealing—even to a bear—which not only dehumanizes her but positions her as an animal with other animals in nature, unable to communicate anything beyond her own fear. Perhaps there is a tinge, here, of a desire to maintain a clear racial superiority for whites, whom the story elevates above nature and animals, even if African Americans during this era are making strides toward equality. Perhaps the story, consciously or unconsciously, betrays a backlash from a perspective that registers a threat.

All of these characterizations point to the idea that this picture of the floundering American male mismatched with his surroundings, more or less pretending to be a "real man," focuses on a fragile identity of the white American urban intellectual male. His racial supremacy is being challenged by the progress of African Americans; his sexual supremacy is losing ground to the self-assertion of women; further, his traditional masculinity has been degraded by life in the city and work at a desk. Could this be the white American male attempting to reassert his fading identity against all of these cultural and ideological forces? It sure seems like it.

Of these, the idea I would like to develop more fully is what the story relays about what it means to be a man at this point in time (and some of this will connect with some of what I have already pointed out). Once we begin paying attention to this "gendered" aspect of the story, it becomes difficult to see anything in the story that is not related to it, which gives an interesting twist to the "man verses nature" theme, because it makes that theme specifically "man" versus nature—not "man" as "human" versus nature (which is often how the theme is intended).

Even in the first paragraph, which initiates the "statement of the facts" with such a heavy dose of ironized humility, we can see that the narrator is quite proud of killing the bear—that it means something to him, even if he is downplaying its significance a little (218). But the second paragraph begins the process of assuring the reader that the narrator and the bear were equally matched: "The encounter was unpremeditated on both sides" (218). This trend continues throughout the encounter he describes, as he reminds us a few paragraphs later, after telling us a little story about how bad he is with guns: "I mention the incident to show, that although I went blackberrying armed, there was not much inequality between me and the bear" (219). So, in short, he is telling us that, yes, this story does fit a "man versus nature" theme, but he wants to present it as an equal match between the two.

His method for doing so is interesting. Would he not appear more "manly" if he had been more accomplished with guns, especially in the 19th century? Maybe. But look at his rationale for bringing the gun with him to pick berries: "Not from any predatory instinct, but to save appearances, I took a gun. It adds to the manly aspect of a person with a tin pail if he also carries a gun" (218). Here, the narrator acknowledges that manliness does align with toting a gun around, even if one is not very accomplished with using one. Also, this paragraph casts collecting berries as potentially "feminizing," as making him less of a man, which he tries to counteract symbolically by bringing the gun (we shall hold off on psychoanalytic interpretations until a later chapter). Further, as we read on, we see that the "Aunt Chloe" story discloses the two "feminine" responses to a bear that he must resist: running away, like the little girl in the story, and sitting and weeping and screaming (which, though effective for Aunt Chloe, is associated with a Black woman, which are two attributes, Black and woman, the narrator derogates) (219). His course of action must be different. It must be "manly." And this will be difficult, namely, because our narrator is not manly.

Even in the imagined story that follows, the story of the "romantic bear" that nurses a little girl, only to be killed by a gun in the able hands the girl's father, is reframed by the reality of the narrator's situation to confirm that the man with the gun did the right thing, even if the intended moral of the imagined "story-within-a-story" was "kindness to animals": such a moral is proven false (220). Then, after the appearance of the bear in the primary narrative, and the certainty of the threat it poses, the story slows down. The seconds that pass between the threat becoming real and the rifle being fired elongate as the narrator enumerates his thoughts—each of which is punctuated with a jerk back to the immediate situation: "The bear was coming on" (220, 221, 222, 223). This is a clever pacing technique, but also one that highlights the reality that everything in this situation does indeed come down to "Man versus Nature."

Okay, sure, one might say, clever theory. But what about all of the self-deprecating comedy the narrator includes about how he really is not that manly? This is an excellent question. I think comedy serves to accentuate the ideology about what manliness means at this point in time. The outcome is, of course, that the narrator kills the bear—that, in the contest between man and nature, man wins. This means that we need to read the rest of the comic "feminizing" aspects of the story along the way in light of this eventual outcome. Yes, the man is not particularly manly by the standards of manliness that we can perceive as alive in the American culture at this point in time (and here we can line up a lot of the ideas I expressed earlier: the "city guy" is less manly than the rugged frontiersman or rural mountain man; the neurotic intellectual is less manly than the "man of action"; men who do domestic tasks like picking berries are less manly than men who expect women to do those sorts of things; and so on—we may even include here that, according to the presentation in the story, a racist man is manlier than one who is not racist), but, when it comes down to the critical moment, the story suggests, if you act like a man—if you fit yourself into "the manly role"—then you are at least man *enough*: you are man enough to be more than nature. Man so far exceeds and dominates nature that even a feminized man acting "like a man" is man enough to win out against the biggest, meanest thing that nature can throw at him. This fits with the resolution of the story too. The last thought the narrator has before killing the bear is of how humiliating it would be to lose this contest with nature and be eaten by an animal. The narrator's pride in getting the approval of the "real men" (who kill things on a regular basis) in the last paragraph also confirms such an interpretation (224).

So, anyway, this treatment of the story, essentially, begins with the question, "What can this story show me about the culture it comes from?" What I have tried to demonstrate is that it shows a lot. But I have also tried to exemplify that, once one finds at least one major aspect of the culture that shines through, much of the rest of the stuff one finds can be realigned to elucidate further that interpretation.

As for the philosophical theme of this chapter, for "How I Killed a Bear" and maybe for the cultural consciousness of its time and place, that is, in America of the 1870s, Nature presents an obstacle to man's progress, but not a serious one, not when we have technology (in this case, guns) and a clear claim to superiority over and domination of the natural world. It is this sort of mentality that drives ideologies like "Manifest Destiny," a belief or doctrine that, not only centralizes the "American Man" and assumes his dominance and self-assertion over nature, but also makes such domination and self-assertion his preordained right and even his patriotic duty. Interestingly, even in an era where the traditional religious consensus was breaking up, spawning all manner of "salvation-salesmen," offering new takes on God and redemption and God's presence in the world, as we see in "The Lightning-Rod Man," published just twenty-four years earlier, God seems, here, in "How I Killed a Bear," to have all but disappeared from nature (Berthoff 187). If God is anywhere, the deity would seem to have to be on the side of the unlikely bear-killer. Perhaps God is available through nature when it suits our speculations, or when we cannot make sense of the randomness of "natural violence" in, say, weather events, but when it comes down to a clear case of "Nature versus Man," and one or the other has to die, it seems that there is no doubt about whose side God is on: Man's side. God binds Man to him through destiny and duty to civilize the wilderness, to bring order to chaos.

Or maybe the publication of Charles Darwin's *On the Origin of Species* in 1859, just five years after Melville's story was published, had adjusted the view of things by the time Warner wrote his story. Darwin's ideas caught on fast. Roland N. Stromberg remarks in *European Intellectual History Since 1789* that, whereas most "epoch-making books have been greeted in total silence and had to wait years to be accepted as important... , *The Origin of Species* sold out on its first day of publication and made its author immediately famous" (128). Further, American religious historians Jon Butler, Grant Wacker, and Randall Balmer write, in *Religion in American Life,* that the idea that "all natural processes proceeded at random, like the roll of a dice" upset religious belief in America, and, more disturbing than this, Darwin's ideas implied that "the only measure of good and bad actions was survival" (284). Warner's story certainly sees no order or harmony in nature, the way Thomas Paine did some sixty years earlier; in fact, Warner's protagonist mocks the possibility of such a thing in his admission to his daydreaming of a "nice romantic bear," that is, a bear that made sense within such a view, even if only in sentimental terms. So maybe this story provides a view of a godless nature, one ruled by randomness and the "law of the jungle," as it were. On this view, Warner's story portrays a struggle over limited resources (the blackberries). But it makes a comic sketch out of the idea of the "survival of the fittest," the upshot being that, once one species is so advanced as to produce intellectuals who vacation with guns in the wilderness, what in nature can really touch them? The story, then, accepts Darwin's facts but not on his terms: Man may be the result of Nature rather than of God's creation; he may be an animal, but he is a predator like no other. It is according to this reality that the story reverses the relation of Man and Nature: Nature is man's domain; it is there for the taking. The struggle for existence is really only a struggle for nature because, once we arrive at an existential theme as crassly expressed as "Man versus Nature," we are already working on an assumption that "Man" does not belong to nature anymore. Nature, through evolution, the story suggests, has produced modern man, and modern man has, in turn, emancipated himself from nature. He has made the "Nature" which produced him into his adversary, one which can still inspire fear and awe, but one which can be summarily dispatched even by a "Man" who is just barely able to claim the title, insofar as cultural gender ideology goes, and even to that extent mostly just through pretense. The next piece, Kate Chopin's story, "The Storm," presents a very different view of the relation between human beings and nature, one in which God is similarly absent, but in which Nature itself, perhaps like a god, pulls the strings.

"The undying life of the world":
"The Storm" (1898) by Kate Chopin

According to the Kate Chopin International Society, "The Storm" was written by Kate Chopin in 1898 but was not published during her lifetime. The story was eventually published in an edition of her complete works in 1969. And the America of the late '60s was much more sympathetic to the themes of the story than was the America of the late 19th century.

The story unfolds through a related sequence of vignettes, and with each shift from one to the next, the point of view transitions from one character to another. The narration stays in the third person throughout the story, but the character whose mind and point of view the narration attends to shifts from one vignette to the next. This experimentation is highly effective, but it is also nearly invisible; it is experimentation that does not get in the reader's way. It is kind of interesting.

29

Philosophy and Fiction

Chopin is known for depictions of women characters, often that controvert cultural norms and ideological expectations, and this story is no exception. In "The Storm," Chopin tells the story of the impact of an extramarital affair on a pair of lovers and the ripples that it makes in the lives of the people they love. The interesting—and for some people, scandalous—part is that those repercussions all seem to be *good*. We will spend just a moment on this idea, and we will come back to it, but our focus will take us elsewhere as well: to a consideration of nature.

Often, in literature or art, that confirms social or cultural morality, sex between people who are married to other people results in punishment, in families being torn apart, in pain and suffering all around: this is true to such a degree that this sort of trope has become a cliché of melodrama in movies and television. But think about all of the characters in "The Storm": none of them is worse off after the passionate afternoon that Calixta spends with Alcee. In fact, the result is quite the contrary; the story carefully observes that each character is rather pleased with the outcome. Bobinot seems relieved that Calixta is not deferring to her, apparently, typical role as "over-scrupulous housewife," which he has prepared for, and instead finds her affectionate, loving, and fun—certainly not the stressed out, anxious person he was expecting to have to defend against (415). Calixta is not guilt-ridden or regretful; she seems very happy, like she has been refreshed. Alcee is warm, full of "tender solicitude," as he writes a letter to his wife (415). Clarisse, his wife, is having a good time with a little independence from her husband; she finds his letter charming and seems relieved that he is not trying to get her to come back home (416). "So the storm passed and every one was happy," the story ends, and there does not seem to be a tinge of irony in that last line (416). Not your typical "infidelity story."

What does all of this have to do with nature though? Quite a lot, we shall learn, but even nature, in this story, is related to this trickle-down feeling that passes through all of the characters in the story as a result of the affair. In this story, rather than a "Man versus Nature" theme, I think we see something like an inversion of that idea: something like "woman in concert or in harmony with nature," which is not quite as snappy but is accurate. This sort of idea guides the reader's attention toward how nature is encoded in the story so that our attention is drawn to the storm, toward the action of nature itself. We might remember that weather, often organized under "setting" in our literary critical vocabulary, can do some interesting things in literature (if we remember Melville's "The Lightning-Rod Man"). But rather than the storm being the object of human interpretation about God's intentions, as it is in the Melville story, Chopin develops the storm, almost, as a character in its own right—maybe even, if we wanted to push it a little, as the protagonist of the story—as if Nature itself is the main character in this story doing things, developing, and guiding other characters' behaviors and interactions.

Think about the storm's relation to the plot of the story. The storm isolates Calixta. It keeps Bobinot and Bibi away from the house. It drives Alcee to Calixta's house. It pushes Alcee from the porch, where he was going to wait it out, inside the house. And once he's in the house, it seems to drive Alcee and Calixta toward each other and toward the bedroom: "The rain beat upon the low, shingled roof with a force and clatter that threatened to break an entrance and deluge them there. They were in the dining room—the sitting room—the general utility room. Adjoining was her bed room.... The door stood open, and the room with its white, monumental bed, its closed shutters, looked dim and mysterious" (412). And the storm eventually even drives the would-be lovers together. When lightning from the storm strikes a tree just outside the window and thunder booms, "Calixta put her hands to her eyes, and with a cry, staggered backward. Alcee's arm encircled her, and for an instant he drew her close and spasmodically to him" (413). And they go on from there.

Okay, so as far as the plot goes, yes, the storm does seem to have love on its mind. Maybe it forces the lovers together and keeps people away, but how is it connected to Calixta—to the woman from our interpretive thesis, the one who comes to be "in harmony with nature"? Look at the similes and metaphors used to refer to Calixta throughout the description of the lovemaking scene (and this is in keeping with an unofficial interpretive rule about thinking through literature that, when an author takes the time to describe sex, it is really doing something else, something bigger):

1. Her face is "warm and steaming" (a relational comparison to nature—like the storm, she emits moisture into the air) (413);
2. "Her lips were as red and moist as pomegranate seed" (direct comparison to nature, combined with the moisture imagery again) (413);
3. Calixta's eyes are "liquid blue" (we can see the steps here: liquid blue relates to water and all of the other water imagery so far, which relates to the storm itself) (413);

4. Calixta's "flesh ... was like a creamy lily that the sun invites to contribute its breath and perfume to the undying life of the world" (an obvious simile comparing Calixta's "flesh" to a flower—but the unfolding of that simile takes us back to "breath"—water [here, in a vaporous perfume] again—which harmonizes with the "life of the world") (414).

5. Calixta's mouth is "a fountain" (obvious nature metaphor with water imagery);

6. Her passion "was like a white flame" (not quite as clear, but we might see the connection to the sun, and the sun, of course, is nature—and what is more natural than fire, anyway?—and, more importantly, as Alcee is leaving just a few sentences later, the "sun was turning the glistening green into a palace of gems" after the storm; we might also read a connection back to the mention of the sun in relation to the floral image from a moment earlier, and both the "flame of her passion" and her "flesh as lily" are white, so we have some braiding of imagery here) (414).

That is more direct textual evidence than many, much longer stories provide for anything.

What do we make of all of this?

Think about what is *not* referred to during this scene between Calixta and Alcee. Just a short list: thinking, rationality, calculation, laws, guilt, rage, regret, tears (all of that moisture and no tears!). There is no pre-meditation to any of this. We are not told that Calixta and Alcee planned the affair, that they had reasoned through any of it, that they are sneaking around. There is nothing about the lovers second-guessing their responses to one another (which is the sort of thing we get in melodrama: "Bert! No, I can't! What about David, my husband?"). The storm incites feelings in them as it pushes them together, and they respond to those feelings in that specific moment, in that specific situation (all of which Nature seems to be calculating or devising), and they are refreshed, less awkward, less neurotic, and happier afterward. The story demonstrates, then, that such feelings are in harmony with nature/Nature—that they are part of the erotic impulse of the "undying life of the world" (more on this idea in Chapter Six) (414). Second, the story demonstrates the view that nature knows what it is doing, even if the people involved do not. The worried, anxious, toiling Calixta, the Calixta who is trapped in her own head, needed some refreshing passion—she needed nature to burst in and remind her of her feelings and desires—and the story is constantly aligning Calixta, her body, her passion, and her sexual desire with nature/Nature. In not stopping to over-think and second-guess, the story suggests, Calixta is listening to and acting in accordance with nature/Nature, and Nature leads through feelings, through emotions—not, in this case, through reason and logic. The idea is that the same thing that drives Calixta into Alcee's arms is the same thing that refreshes the earth around them with the storm— and more than that: it is Nature acting through the one to do the other. Nature is torrential rain, but it is also torrential passion, and it does what it does. Why get in its way?

Now, just to be clear, I am not recommending in this interpretation that one go out and find her or his way into some extramarital affair or whatever, so do not write about me to your dean or your priest or your congressman or something. I *am saying* that the story, very clearly, offers a theme that shows that sex, desire, flowers, pomegranate seeds, and thunderstorms are all part of nature/Nature, and that Nature will get its way, that, one way or another, Nature pulls the strings. It also suggests that when people let Nature get its way, it may make them happy, and not just whomever is directly involved, but everyone who has to deal with them too. The story depicts a storm that interrupts day to day existence. It refreshes people by inducing them to give in to their nature—to live with the grain of existence, of Nature. And when one does so, the story suggests, everyone is happy.

Chopin provides us with an interesting mess, philosophically, that is. While we have a clear sense of Nature as something like a "will to live" that is "running through life" (as Arthur Schopenhauer or Henri Bergson would have it), as an active force pulling the strings, as it were, in individual human lives, we really have no view of a deity at all (Stromberg 132). And if we wanted to force some deification onto Nature as depicted in "The Storm," what kind of deity would it be? It is certainly no rationalist deity, as we discussed with Thomas Paine's *The Age of Reason*, because Nature, in Chopin's story, interacts through passions, feelings, desire, and the merging of Calixta, through "natural vocabulary," with Nature occurs, precisely, during the height of passionate sex. We can imagine Paine (and perhaps any rationalist) becoming very uncomfortable with such a scene. Interestingly, Chopin's depiction does not seem particularly Darwinian either. The synchronicity of the actions of Nature through the weather and the passions of the lovers with one another is anything but random and purposeless. But this "rhyme" between the storm outside and the "storm of passion" (which *has* to be the title of a romance novel) in the bedroom does comply with the language from Plato and Aquinas of imitation and resemblance (though we can imagine such a sentence making Aquinas now immensely uncomfortable).

Think about it. The idea of living *with the grain* of Nature—the parity of the indoor "storm" with the outdoor storm—it suggests that, when humans live in resemblance to nature, they are most themselves: they are living their *most natural* lives in accordance with their most natural impulses. In a Platonic sense, we even have whatever human essence is within Calixta and Alcee, their "nature," imitating, or participating in, its ideal "form," which is exemplified in the heavens of Nature. If we wanted to be scandalous (and perhaps cause poor Aquinas to roll in his tomb in Toulouse), we could push things even further: the language that binds Nature to human nature—the language through which the one communicates with the other in "The Storm"—is love. Nature loves better and elevates those who love freely, passionately, and with abandon. We could take Aquinas' idea on theological resemblance, that "the better anything is, the more it is like God" (Aquinas 84), and make just one exchange: "the better anything is, the more it is like Nature." This would be pretty close to what Chopin's story suggests, and the outcome would not be so far from Aquinas' either: Nature therefore loves and rewards those who more closely resemble it. And with this turn, we are not far from the transcendental philosophy of Ralph Waldo Emerson.

Emerson, too, is interested in this resemblance between nature and human beings. In one essay on art, he claims that artists portraying nature should omit "the prose of nature and give us only the spirit and splendor" (582). The artist needs to know that

> the landscape has beauty for his eye, because it expresses a thought which is to him good: and this, because the same power which sees through his eyes, is seen in that spectacle.... In a portrait, he must inscribe the character, and not the features, and must esteem the man who sits to him as himself only an imperfect picture or likeness of the aspiring original within ... [582].

This is, perhaps, a different context than Chopin's, but maybe not so different: the impulse of the artist here is an erotic one—one based in desire, in feelings, and emotions. For Emerson, as for Chopin's characters, the transcendent resemblance achieved between Nature and the human experience, whether in art or in passion or both (which is Emerson's point), is transmitted through exhilaration, through powerful feelings that "throw down the walls of circumstance on every

side, awakening in the beholder" a profound "sense of universal relation and power" that is the shared object of Nature itself, the artist, and
the beholder (585). On this interpretation, both Calixta and Emerson's
ideal artist act best by being their truest selves—and they are their truest selves when they allow Nature to transcend them with its unifying
love, a love which transcends, or we might say, using our water imagery,
a love which trickles down and refreshes all those whom it touches.

"A glitter in his eyes which I had often seen in the eyes of wild beasts": "The Leopard Man's Story" (1903) by Jack London

"The Leopard Man's Story" was published in 1903, near the beginning of Jack London's writing career, when he was still in his twenties,
though he died not that long after in 1916, at just 40 years old. While
"The Leopard Man's Story" does not necessarily fit with London's wilderness tales, like *White Fang* and *The Call of the Wild*, for which he became
famous, as even a not-so-attentive reader might assume, ideas related to
nature do inform the narrative in interesting and important ways.

We have not yet discussed the concept of literary genre; "The Leopard Man's Story" often gets categorized as a story in the mystery genre,
and it does indeed have many of those attributes. An inquisitive narrator—a journalist in this case, rather than a detective or investigator,
is asking the questions, mostly just to get a story rather than to solve
a crime, but we do indeed have a crime, a murder, and we have some
degree of stealthy avoidance of culpability for the crime—so, a sneaky
crime. We may also look at the manner in which the story unfolds as a
way that the genre feeds into the story: we do not get the final clue that
explains everything until the very end, and, learning that fact, more or
less, "unlocks" the entire story—it solves the mystery for us. In the mystery genre this sort of plotting device is typical. It entices the reader
with the mysterious event, builds suspense, and then provides a denouement (from the French, meaning, literally, "an untying"; a resolution) at
the last moment, once that final detail is clicked into place.

Fitting the story within this particular genre, though, does not necessarily help us understand that much about it. As the description above
lays out, the generic structures do function to make us pay attention
to the plot of the story in a different way—we might say that the genre
guides the plot in a way that builds suspense and makes the story more

engaging for the reader, but other attributes of the genre we will have to put on hold, at least until we get a clearer understanding of some of the other elements in the story that help us more deeply engage the words on the page.

Let's zoom out to our philosophical theme for a moment. Where do we see it at work in this story? Nature is a big concept, of course, but it obviously includes animals—and we have animals front and center in this story. Our primary character is a "Leopard Man." That is already an interesting, difficult sentence, which may help us dig into the complexity of the story because the Leopard Man is, in fact, a character, and he has a place in the action of the story, but he also functions as a secondary narrator. We should be careful not to pass over the fact that his name, as far as the reader knows, is "the Leopard Man." We should pay attention to this, not least because this moniker, quite literally, combines an animal and a man—leopard and man—so if we are looking for something interesting about nature, then we have already found it in the title. But one thing at a time: let's go back to the issue of the narrative structure for a moment. This story provides a frame-narrative, which is the scene with the journalist trying to get a story out of the Leopard Man. There is a little back and forth between them at the beginning, which helps us get a sense of the Leopard Man as a character and of the world of the traveling circus and the place he occupies within it. But, when the Leopard Man lands on a story, he kind of takes over the story itself; he takes the reins of the narrative for some time, while the frame-narrative only breaks in occasionally to comment on his behavior during the telling of the story.

Okay, sure, one may think. That is interesting in an abstract sort of way, but what does it have to do with something like the themes in the story—the big stuff? This set-up early on in the story (465–466) and the interruption of the narrative (467) serve to highlight nature: animals, but also human interaction with animals. So even a seemingly abstract analysis of the structural components of the story leads us toward this theme. We shall investigate these a little more closely.

Here is the introduction of the Leopard Man to the story in the first paragraph:

> He had a dreamy, far-away look in his eyes, and his sad, insistent voice, gentle-spoken as a maid's, seemed the placid embodiment of some deep-seated melancholy. He was the Leopard Man, but he did not look it. His business in life, whereby he lived, was to appear in a cage of performing leopards before vast audiences, and to thrill those audiences by certain

exhibitions of nerve for which his employers rewarded him on a scale commensurate with the thrills he produced [465].

The narrator spends another paragraph describing the Leopard Man's sweet, gentle nature, and his sweet, gentle sadness. We can look at the first two paragraphs and tally up the descriptors: "sad," "dreamy," "gentle-spoken," "sweet," "gentle," "placid," and "sweet and gentle" again. And yet his occupation is contending with big feline predators in a cage! London seems to enjoy the paradox that the Leopard Man is so calm and gentle and sweet, yet his occupation seems anything but. The Leopard Man, though, seems to see nothing too exciting in any of it. Sure, he suggests, wild animals are vicious, but if one is direct, very sober, and rational in one's methodology and execution of discipline, then dealing with lions and leopards, with wolves and monkeys, just depends on consistency (465). His wounds and scars are many, but he sees no significance in them. The Leopard Man verges on being a disappointment: the balance he strikes between animal and human, between, say, leopard and man, is a little boring—not wild enough to be very interesting. He just always maintains control and discipline. That is all. But what happens when all discipline and control are thrown off?

The Leopard Man tells two versions of the same story: about a man getting his head crunched in a lion's mouth. The first story takes only a paragraph to tell. It is about a man who hates a lion-tamer and waits for fate to punish him in time, and its moral is patience—or, we might add, patience, discipline, and control. The second turn on the old "head-crunching lion" story takes more time for the Leopard Man to develop. This is the story about De Ville, the juggler/sword swallower, and King Wallace, the lion-tamer, and it is this story that becomes the central mystery narrative of "The Leopard Man's Story" (466–68). On the one hand, this narrative is, indeed, about patience, discipline, and control but only insofar as they fit with cunning, and on the other, only insofar as they fit with brutality and bullying.

Interestingly, these two men, De Ville and King Wallace, have very human sounding names (certainly, nothing like "the Leopard Man"). In keeping with the contradiction we get between the Leopard Man's manner and his name, London provides an inversion of the same relationship with De Ville (whose name derives from the French phrase for "the town" or "the village"—denoting, of course, human civilization). De Ville is compared to a tiger and something that eats frogs; his knives "bite" into human flesh (like an animal's teeth might, especially in a story with so many lion/leopard tamers); and he is described as having a "glitter in his eyes," which the Leopard Man says he "had seen often in the eyes of wild beasts" (466–67). King Wallace's character works slightly differently: he is almost above humanity in that he seems to enjoy watching or making other people squirm and suffer, whether human or animal, just as his name denotes. He, the Leopard Man says, "was afraid of nothing dead or alive. He was a king and no mistake" (467). He takes pleasure beating a lion down with his fist when he is drunk; he seems to enjoy dominating the animals; he likes watching other people fight; and he seems to derive much enjoyment from his humiliation of De Ville, in particular, by flirting with his wife, abusing him, and trying to get him to fight (467). Perhaps the clearest picture we get of the relationship between the two men is when the narrator interrupts the Leopard Man's story:

> At an uproar behind us the Leopard Man turned quietly around. It was a divided cage, and a monkey, poking through the bars and around the partition had its paw seized by a big gray wolf who was trying to pull it off by main strength. The arm seemed stretching out longer and longer like a thick elastic, and the unfortunate monkey's mates were raising a terrible din. No keeper was at hand, so the Leopard Man stepped over a couple of paces, dealt the wolf a sharp blow on the nose with the light cane he carried, and returned with a sadly apologetic smile ... [467].

This turmoil between the animals, more or less, approximates a depiction of the turmoil between the two men that we are in the middle of hearing about from the Leopard Man. The major difference is that the Leopard Man is powerless to stop the conflict by popping one of these guys on the nose with a cane. Rather, this story is a demonstration of everything that the Leopard Man is not: it is a story about unruly passions, viciousness, rage, violence, and vengeance. It is a story, we might say, about amoral "nature red in tooth and claw," nature "filled with pain and death," with competition and chance (Stromberg 128–129).

If we think about it in these terms, there is a heavy dose of irony to London's story. The set-up in the first paragraphs is that the Leopard Man has no good stories because animals are really not that exciting; if you treat them consistently and in a disciplined and patient fashion, then even vicious predators behave predictably. The irony consists in the fact that the only exciting story of violence, riskiness, and death that the Leopard Man has is about two humans competing for a mate. Human savagery is complex, not only because humans are animalistic—though that is a part of the story, as the narrative shows the animal side of humanity lashing out in their conflicts—it is complex, too, because it is also unpredictable, conniving, clever; it is bold, daring, and sadistic, but it hides behind a human face.

To come full circle, it is this view of humanity that most fiction in the mystery genre is about: human beings doing terrible things to one another in clever ways. This idea is reminiscent of a quotation from Machiavelli's political treatise, *The Prince*. Machiavelli writes,

> [T]here are two ways of fighting: by law or by force. The first way is natural to men, and the second to beasts. [...] The ancient writers taught princes about this by an allegory, when they described how Achilles and many other princes of the ancient world were sent to be brought up by Chiron, the centaur, so that he might train them in his way. All the allegory means in making the teacher half beast and half man is that a prince must know how to act according to the nature of both.... So, as a prince is forced to know how to act like a beast, he must learn from the fox and the lion; because the lion is defenseless against traps and a fox is defenseless against wolves. Therefore, one must be a fox in order to recognize traps, and a lion to frighten the wolves. Those who simply act like lions are stupid [344].

Consider the way the logic moves in this quotation from *The Prince*. Machiavelli begins by referring to the allegory of training with the centaur to demonstrate that one must learn to fight like a human and to fight like a beast. Then, however, he cannot help but be drawn deeper and deeper into the varieties of beastly engagement. We move from the horse-half of the centaur to the lion to the fox to the wolf: it turns out that the metaphor of the centaur alone is insufficient because humans must master the strategies of a whole menagerie of beasts to face the multiplicity and variety of the onslaught of beastly human attacks. Machiavelli is shining a light on, essentially, the same attributes "The Leopard Man's Story" depends on for its drama and mystery, which are the same attributes that nearly all stories in the mystery genre depend on for their effects: when driven in certain directions, humans are brutal, savage animals; they are also tremendously clever, rational creatures. They are both at the same time. It is not an either/or; the men in this story, just like the centaur, combine both natures. They are beasts and philosophers all at once. Without this combination, De Ville would be unable to conceive of a murder that depends on secret methods for making a lion sneeze at the critical moment. Without this combination, we would not really have mystery stories at all. London's Darwinian circus confirms Darwin's claim from the end of *The Descent of Man* that "man with all his noble qualities," and "with his god-like intellect which has penetrated into the movements and constitution of the solar system—with all these exalted powers—Man still bears in his bodily frame the indelible stamp of his lowly origin" (180).

"The bitterest conclusion": "The White Silence" (1899) by Jack London

"The White Silence" precedes "The Leopard Man's Story" by a few years; it was published in 1899 by a 23-year-old Jack London (quite an achievement for a 23-year-old writer). This story revolves around some of the common aspects of London's writing: it is set in the Yukon, a Canadian territory which borders Alaska, and a favorite wilderness setting of London's; it provides a view of the mysterious anonymity of nature, an alienating blankness, and of the place of humans within it and of the struggle for survival in a silent, icy, dangerous climate; and it may relate to recurrence of the "Man versus Nature" motif that we explored in Warner's "How I Killed a Bear." (There is, of course, much more we will have to say about all of these things.)

If we look at the first page or so with something like "Humans (for, here, we do also have a woman) versus Nature" in mind as a loose organizing principle for thinking through the story, we get a pretty dramatic picture that, maybe, even extends toward a more all-encompassing dynamic between life and lifelessness within which our "Humans versus Nature" concept has to fit. The frigid cold is inimical to life. The picture London gives in the first scene provides a striking image of this: chunks of ice frozen into a foot, the ice clotting, maybe killing its life, immobilizing the dog. We can unpack the associations in the image: feet are used for locomotion; ice may symbolize stasis (or lack of movement): in this one image we have each contending against the other—as Mason attempts to crunch the ice between the dog's toes to allow freedom of movement in this ossified, arctic world. We can extend this relationship a little further: the dogs are animals, of course (and animals are usually associated with nature), but these dogs are used as "tools" for movement through the ice and snow by the humans, though the story is careful to show that these dogs are not fully domesticated house-pets; they are vicious and at least half-wild. So where does this place them in our relation of humans to nature? Maybe somewhere halfway between the two? The dogs are definitely symbolically connected with nature, but, perhaps, nature as (literally) harnessed by humans for the humans' own purposes?

Chapter One. Nature

These sorts of interpretive dynamics are a little crudely drawn at the moment (as most interpretations are at the outset). Let's see if they carry over to the characters. The story is populated by only three people: Mason, the Malemute Kid, and Ruth (an "Indian woman" who is Mason's wife). London draws our attention to names and their significances in the second paragraph: Mason says, "I never saw a dog with a highfalutin' name that was ever worth a rap" (427). The dog in question is named Carmen. According to Mason, the dogs with "sensible names" have "dog-like names," which lets the reader know that, by "highfalutin'," Mason means "human-like names," like Carmen. Perhaps such a conversation so early in the story is something like the author saying, "Hey, Reader, pay attention to names!"

So, if we look at the character names, what do we see? Interestingly, Malemute is a breed of dog, so Malemute Kid is a man with a dog name, which provides an interesting parallel to Carmen, the dog with a human name. Further, a mason is a person who works with stone; more instructive for our purposes is the verb form, "to mason," which refers to the cutting or hewing of stone. Interestingly, it is precisely this sort of action that Mason, the character, is doing with his mouth in the first paragraph of the story: he is breaking with his mouth ice that is clustered between the toes of the dog. And Ruth, though, as we read on, we learn she is a difficult character to get a handle on, is an Indigenous woman. At this point, in the years approaching the turn of the century, Native Americans were often stereotyped as people who were "close to nature," "noble savages" in the mold that goes back, at least, to Jean-Jacques Rousseau; in the words of Kurt Andersen in his book *Fantasy Land,* European Americans saw in the Indians the "romantic collateral damage of manifest destiny" (108). It may also be significant that Ruth in the Old Testament was a Moabite who "marries into" the Israelites, which prefigures and parallels the ethnic transition the character in London's story has made.

So, do these associations with the characters hold up? If our initial interpretation of the humans is on track, it shows that Mason stands out from the rest of them (since Malemute Kid and Ruth are, at least symbolically, more "attuned" to nature—even if only according to the Malemute Kid's name and stereotypes about Ruth's ethnic/cultural heritage). We might gesture at the same thing with the dogs: Carmen stands out from the rest according to her human name. We cannot be too surprised, then, when we see the story putting Mason and Carmen into a fraught intersection with one another, or by the fact that Malemute Kid expresses protective affection for both Carmen and Mason. But Mason seems to have it in for Carmen. From the very beginning, he is betting against her, wagering that the other dogs will eat her before the end of the week (427). When Carmen loses steam going up a hillside, toppling the sled and Mason and the other dogs with it, Mason brutally beats her. Similarly, we should not be surprised that Malemute Kid defends Carmen; the narration describes his relation to the animals almost as if he is the dogs' brother rather than their master: "Strong man, brute that he was, capable of felling an ox at a blow, he could not bear to beat the poor animals, but humored them as a dog-driver rarely does,—nay, almost wept with them in their misery" (429). So, yeah, the characters, their names, and the associations hold up, especially with the two primary characters.

We may want to pause here and articulate more carefully the relation of each man to nature, based on what the story has told us. Mason, as a mason does, gnaws and cuts away at nature; he slices through it. Mason's movement in relation to nature is, in essence, *against* the grain. He crushes ice; he whips and beats the dogs. Even when Carmen fails him, it is because he has driven the team up a hill (so, literally, *against* the grain of the natural geography). He also never stops talking, and in a story with the title "The White Silence," a phrase that obviously connects to the mysterious "passive phase" of Nature, we probably do not see this as a trait that will be rewarded. Generally, Mason relates to nature as something to be overcome, something that must be triumphed over, through brute force if necessary. He is also unreflective, at least until nature makes him still.

Malemute Kid is basically the opposite of Mason in almost every way. He works *with* the grain of nature. In nearly every scene he is helping rather than leading—pushing the sleds to help get them started, working as more of a peer with his dogs (just as his name suggests). More than this, though, Malemute Kid is always in respectful awe of the immensity and power of nature. As a character, he is also almost as silent as nature itself. Most of the writing that comes from his perspective is narration about the contents of his thoughts—his inner and almost religious reflection on Nature (capital N). To Mason, we might imagine, snow, ice, and cold are just the effects of the weather, obstacles which he must overcome. To Malemute Kid, these are attributes of the universe, or at least of some universal character of nature—the "White Silence." Consider this quotation: "The stillness was weird; not a breath rustled the frost-encrusted forest; the cold and silence of outer space had chilled the heart and smote the trembling lips of nature" (431). Here, we see the Malemute Kid attuned to the absolute stillness, not just of the climate so far north, but of the nature of the universe, of "outer space," Nature beyond "nature," in a universe where life is the exception.

The narrator spends a whole paragraph describing this feeling of awe at "the White Silence" in the context of Nature's other strategies for convincing "man of his finity" (and "finity," here, we can loosely define as the opposite of infinity—so "finity" as the absolute limitation, smallness, fixity, the finiteness of human existence) (429). Nature's "tricks" include

> the ceaseless flow of the tides, the fury of the storm, the shock of the earthquake, the long roll of heaven's artillery,—but the most tremendous, the most stupefying of all, is the passive phase of the White Silence. All movement ceases, the sky clears, the heavens are as brass; the slightest whisper seems sacrilege, and man becomes timid, affrighted at the sound of his own voice. Sole speck of life journeying across the ghostly wastes of a dead world, he trembles at his audacity, realizes that his is a maggot's life, nothing more. Strange thoughts arise unsummoned, and the mystery of all things strives for utterance. And the fear of death, of God, of the universe, comes over him,—the hope of the Resurrection and the Life, the yearning for immortality, the vain striving of the imprisoned essence,—it is then, if ever, man walks alone with God [430].

With observations such as these, Mason, as we have described him, is more or less a blasphemer; he has no chance against Nature. Further, if Nature, "in its passive phase," is immense and terrifying, when it becomes active—when it makes a move—the narrator identifies its activity as careful, planned, and intentional. It is as Fate that it moves against Mason:

> Fifty feet or more from the trail towered a lofty pine. For generations it had stood there, and for generations destiny had had this one end in view,—perhaps the same had been decreed of Mason. [...] A pulse sighed through the air,—they did not seem to actually hear it, but rather felt it, like the premonition of movement in a motionless void. Then the great tree, burdened with its weight of years and snow, played its last part in the tragedy of life [431].

Carmen, whom the story has paralleled with Mason, as each is the exception in their group, is also devoured by Nature at almost the same time that Mason is: the pack of dogs picks her off, due to her weakness (she only "clung to her slender thread of life," the narrator says), and her pack devours her completely. Mason, now, has also been shown to compromise the strength of his pack, and, even though they do not want to, they must rid themselves of him, too; and that is exactly what Mason instructs Malemute Kid to do.

The method of "burial," though, is strangely specific, and strikes the reader as rather odd. The Malemute Kid bends some young, springy trees toward the ground, ties them down, and lays Mason across them (the method and rationale for doing this with "Moosehide thongs" is described in some detail). In the last paragraph, London writes that the Malemute Kid "cast one glance about him. The White silence seemed to sneer, and a great fear came upon him. There was a sharp report; Mason swung into his aerial sepulcher; and Malemute Kid lashed the dogs into a wild gallop as he fled across the snow" (435).

We should note the care with this description. We know that the set-up with the trees is designed to fling Mason's corpse high and far into the woods (perhaps this is kind of the analogous thing for these arctic sled-guys to how sailors used to be "buried at sea"). But London does not write that Mason was flung deep into the snowy woods or something. He leaves him at the end of the story in the air—as if he never fell back to earth. Of course, we know he eventually fell back to earth and his body ended up in the snowy woods, but by putting it the way he does, London may be giving Mason a glorified end, almost an image of his soul ascending to the heavens. "Aerial sepulcher" has a religious, holy sort of sound to it. Alternatively, "aerial sepulcher" may allude to Mason's persistent separation from the earth, his resistance to Nature, even in death, and, perhaps, Nature's ultimate rejection of him. And on this interpretation, this last experience with Mason may, in keeping with ancient beliefs regarding the need for burying the dead in the ground, portend evil for the Malemute Kid (Dunston 110). Does Mason in death, in a way, pollute or defile the Kid? It seems possible that he does.

We should also be careful in noticing that the narration seems to back away from the Malemute Kid as he kills Mason off (the "sharp report" conveys a gunshot) and flings him away—almost as if it is too terrible, but also as if it is not really Malemute Kid's doing, like it is another step of fate. The point of view is a close-up on the Malemute Kid until he responds with fear to the sneer of the White Silence. The rest of the narration observes the details as if they just happened rather than describing the Kid doing them: "There was a sharp report; Mason swung into his aerial sepulcher" (435). Malemute Kid is removed from the actions.

Finally, the last line shows the possibility that the Malemute Kid's essential character has changed due to this experience. We know, if we read closely throughout the story, how much Mason meant to him—even to the point that he was a little jealous of Ruth's close relationship to Mason—and how much time they had spent together. And, even though he has cowered in awe and fear before Nature, even though he has respected it and humbled himself in silent reverence before the "White Silence," this horrible, seemingly predetermined and malicious action of Nature (or God?) maimed Mason. But it did not kill him. The situation, if interpreted as destiny, or fate, or God, seems to take a turn *against* the Malemute Kid as well. It has forced him to have to kill his own best friend/father figure. And there is some indication that this changes him. The last line of the story observes him imitating Mason—trying on his audacious attitude *against* Nature. Rather than maintaining his respectful awe of nature and his brotherhood with the animals, he "lashed the dogs into a wild gallop as he fled across the snow," almost as if the antagonism between human and nature, motion and stillness, and life and lifelessness is reshuffled and reanimated—as if the whole thing will start over and play out again (435).

Conclusions

This set of stories forces us into an interesting irony. In Melville's "The Lightning-Rod Man," we are given polar positions of belief in some form of divine agency behind or within the operations of nature: one of them inspiring human fear of punishment under the immensity of nature, the other viewing that immensity as cause for awe at the grandeur of nature, and thereby of God. London's "The White Silence" seems to return us to this same dichotomy. Were it just immensity and extremity, perhaps Malemute Kid would have resigned himself to his customary reverent silence before the Nature behind nature, be that God or Fate or the Universe or the great Whatever, but, the Kid seems to interpret the relationship not as "human versus nature," but as "Nature *against* humans," and, by the end of the story, even more personally, as "Nature *against* me, specifically." But this feeling does not cancel the awe and reverence of the earlier moments. So the London story, kind of, gives us two even more extreme versions of the poles Melville writes into his story, but in "The White Silence," they are nearly superimposed in a very Old Testament-feeling "fear of the Lord," the kind which inspires real awe and real fear, a deity present and active in nature—sometimes for you, but sometimes against you, too.

On the other hand, Chopin's "The Storm" gives us a different point of view. It is possible that, in presenting the story through multiple points of view, there is a hint of the omniscient (that is, all-knowing) narrator having the same purview as the storm itself—perhaps the real perspective is the Nature behind the storm, behind the omniscience, watching it all play out according to plan. Perhaps that sounds a little dumb, but the obvious parallels, as we discussed earlier, between the indoor and outdoor "storms" do indeed suggest some kind of synchronous plan.

In none of the cases discussed here so far, however, does any character *know* anything *for sure* about any plan. Melville's characters speculate, and maybe London's Malemute Kid does too. Chopin's, though, follow an attractive impulsion of nature within them; they do not speculate or theorize; they feel and they act. There is an immediacy to Calixta and Alcee that sidesteps the worries and theories regarding what any of it means. Before we run there as a paradigm of hope, though, we might remember that, when faced with a dramatic situation from nature, Warner's bear-killer acts with relative immediacy as well, but *against* nature, though his story, too, rewards him for it (even if my analysis spun things another way). And "The Leopard Man's Story" gives us characters who speculate and plan and act, resulting in questionable "law of the jungle" sorts of outcomes, so even a blend of both tendencies seems inadequate and dissatisfying.

Terry Eagleton, at one point in his book *Why Marx Was Right*, discusses the need to disavow superstitious, sentimental attitudes concerning nature. The reality of human life is that sometimes it is defined by a "Promethean strain" of imposing "Man's sovereignty over Nature, along with a faith in limitless human progress" (226). After all, "milking cows and building cities mean harnessing Nature to our own ends" (not to mention fighting pandemics!) (226). But this attitude must be balanced by our acknowledgment that Nature "lies at the root of human existence"; Eagleton quotes Friedrich Engels to make the following point: "we, with flesh, blood and brain, belong to nature, and our mastery of it consists in the fact that we have the advantage over all other beings of being able to know and correctly apply its laws" (228). This may strike us as a shockingly realistic position (especially after all of this speculation), but it also simplifies the relationship between humans and nature through a practical sort of wisdom.

Because we belong to nature, we must act responsibly toward it in order to ensure its health, because without it we are nothing (because we will die). Because we belong to nature, too, we must learn to master it, both outside ourselves in order to progress and inside ourselves in order not to fall into antisocial evolutionarily inherited patterns.

Do we resemble nature? Do we imitate it? We belong to nature, so how could we not? Does nature move us to awe and reverence and gratitude? How could it not? Does nature pull us into its plans for the perpetuation of life or toward the certainty of its ending? Of course it does. And the big question: where is God in all of this? Nature, in so far as the literature demonstrates, does not seem to say for sure. But metaphysics develops ideas that extend beyond nature, so we shall carry on thinking-through literature with that theme as the topic of the next chapter.

CHAPTER TWO

Metaphysics

"Nothing is so firmly believed as that which we least know."—Michel de Montaigne

Introduction

Here is a working idea of how we will be defining metaphysics: metaphysics refers to attempts to explore and/or analyze that which *may exist* beyond nature, or beyond the world of experience generally, including investigations of the existence of absolute entities, like those invoked in spiritual and religious questions (God or gods, the Devil or demons, people's souls or spirits, absolute good and evil, and so on) (Childers and Hentzi, 186). Metaphysics is also concerned with the exploration of the nature of time, space, matter, and mind—and whatever meaning such categories may (or may not) have.

The prefix "meta" comes from Greek; it means "after" or "beyond." So, applied in relation to "physics," which comes from the Greek word *"phusis,"* which refers to "nature," the entire word "metaphysics" means, roughly, "after or beyond nature." Interestingly, the term "metaphysics" was coined by one of the first-century editors of the works of Aristotle who titled a group of Aristotle's treatises "metaphysics" because this compilation was organized in the collection *after* the philosopher's writings on physics: these "metaphysics" treatises were Aristotle's writings on "First Philosophy," or first principles for dealing philosophically with any topic, and "Theology," or "Wisdom" (McKeon 238). But the name stuck, and metaphysics became associated with both the "rational analysis of the necessary and universal aspects of Being" and "speculative inquiry into the nature of things allegedly beyond experience" (Harvey 149–150). In a lot of contemporary philosophy, the name "ontology" encompasses much of the domain of the first designation of metaphysics (on being, as such), while "metaphysics" continues to be the

48

branch or mode of philosophy that explores the second, more "specula-tive," area. So this domain of thought includes not only questions that are undiscernible according to reasoning about nature, like speculation about "absolute entities," but also the meaning of the categories through which we perceive nature (time, space, matter, etc.).

The idea is that physical entities are there and operate—and that is the domain of physics and "natural" philosophy—but the mean-ing of these things is of a different order altogether, something that is more based in speculation and theory. Meaning also goes deeper and may have something to do with our tendency to ascribe mean-ing to things through the action of our minds, or our minds may even limit our ability to perceive the world as it really is (more on these ideas in a moment). So metaphysics can be a foggy territory; it can be tinged with mystery. Metaphysics has these qualities precisely because it emerges from the center of a paradox: it catalogs our attempts to understand, precisely, that stuff which is least tangible, the stuff that fits under this heading because it evades our more reliable attempts at understanding things.

In his book *The History of Western Philosophy*, Bertrand Russell writes that "Aristotle's metaphysics, roughly speaking, may be described as Plato diluted by common sense" (162). Russell has a way of writing that can seem a little judgmental or dismissive, but which, on recon-sideration, is often quite elucidating. The key to this particular char-acterization of Aristotle is to take Russell literally. Part of what Russell means by this is that Aristotle is still largely working with his teacher Plato's concepts (some of which we have discussed already), but with an adjusted set of terms. At the same time, however, Aristotle is trying to "dignify" human sense perception and human reason, memory, and lan-guage (Russell's "common sense," as in, literally, those aspects which are common to all humans) with the ability to properly understand the world through the employment of such concepts in a way that Plato was suspicious of (Russell 164–165, Aristotle 243–244). Without getting further into the weeds than is necessary to make the point, we should notice that this sets philosophy, from the beginning of whatever "meta-physics" actually is, within the paradox I observed above: that the object of study is exactly that stuff which is least comprehensible according to our human "common sense" tools (sense perception, reason, memory, language, etc.) for comprehending anything.

The 18th-century German philosopher Immanuel Kant had a solution for this paradox, though it may be an unsatisfying one. Kant acknowledges that the limitations of human perception prevent us from knowing reality as it is in itself, or as it really, objectively is, but we are capable of apprehending the world as it appears to us through our sense perception, which may not be the same thing. In his terminology, the world as it appears to us is "the *phenomenal* world," which is transmitted through human perception in specific ways; for example, this perception is temporal, spatial, and so on, and we experience the world according to particular "categories," like substance (matter and its properties), causality (one thing causes another), number (there are numbers of things which we can count), and so on (Hospers 138–139). This view allowed Kant, to some degree, to blend some aspects from both the tradition of rationalism, which believed humans *could know* certain things without having to have experienced them (in philosophical terms: humans can have "a priori knowledge") and the tradition of empiricism, which believed that humans *only* gain knowledge *through experience* (knowledge of the world is only "a posteriori") (Hospers 138; Stromberg 28–29).

So, to boil all of this down to a sentence, Kant's solution is to say that there is a gap between the world *as it is in itself* and *as it appears to us*, and the way it appears to us may have nothing to do with the way it is in itself: the two are distinct, so it is only the world *as phenomena* that we can "conform to our knowledge" (Hospers 139). The tricky part is that we do not typically recognize this distinction. We tend to mistake our knowledge of the *phenomenal* world (again, the world as it appears to us) with knowledge of the *noumenal* world (which is what he called the world "as it is in itself"). But the noumenal world is completely inaccessible to us, so we can say nothing about it at all. The solution is to say that the world we can know is *not equal to* the All that is out there (objective reality), so we can make no statements about that All; therefore, anything we say about anything that extends beyond the view of the world we can access through our human faculties is pure speculation, which is to say that our beginning definition of metaphysics is precisely that domain about which it is impossible to say anything. If you find this frustrating, just remember that I did warn you that this would be unsatisfying.

But we are not quite finished yet. Notice that where Kant leaves us is not a hopeless situation (and Kant, after all, certainly found plenty to say about thinking with just the phenomenal world): it leaves us with a heavy emphasis on language, the tool we use to say anything about anything. The 20th-century Austrian-British philosopher

Chapter Two. Metaphysics

Ludwig Wittgenstein closes his very terse, early book, *The Tractatus Logico-Philosophicus*, with a recommendation for a silence on metaphysics, reminiscent of Kant's, but in his more mature work, he seems to abandon systematic approaches, finding great depth, richness, ambiguity, and variety in the range and meaning of language. In *The Blue Book*, Wittgenstein recommends that "we destroy the outward similarity between a metaphysical proposition and an experiential one, and we try to find the form of expression which fulfils a certain craving of the metaphysician which our ordinary language does not fulfil and which, as long as it isn't fulfilled, produces the metaphysical puzzlement" (55). This creates an "insurmountable barrier" because it suggests an impossible picture (56). The implication, here, is that, for us to agree on the practices of saying anything, we must deal with the innumerable frames of context and/or points of view that are as much the subject of meaning and understanding as the object of discussion itself (Scruton 289). Such a view of language that results in puzzlement relates to "Wittgenstein's duck/rabbit" (a picture, which, in one way, looks like a duck, and in another like a rabbit): to pose the question "What is it *really*?" does not apply (Palmer 41). This may be something like what is possible with language in fiction, and particularly certain types of genre fiction, for which ambiguity and the blurring of reality with sheer "otherness" or with the logic and imagery of myths, legends, and dreams is intimately concerned with the point (if there is one) of the fiction itself.

Further, the critical upshot may be that the trappings of these genres afford writers the opportunity to write about metaphysical subject-matter—to side-step Kant's ban on "talking out of school," as it were. Consider that science fiction (with its emphasis on "the unknown"), Gothic/horror literature (with its reliance on legend, myth, religion, and spiritual and psychological warfare between good and evil), and children's fantasy stories (which merge, at least to some degree, with fables and folk tales that anthropomorphize inanimate objects and relay moral lessons)—all of these genres provide short-cuts to metaphysics. By transporting the reader away from the expectations of realism, that is, from the usual operations of the "phenomenal" world, they are able to introduce us to metaphysical considerations, to speculations about the All that *may be* out there, that we might otherwise see as out of place or as inappropriate. Fiction, precisely because it is not bound to "the truth," is able to achieve the impossible: it seeks the truth through clearly counterfeited reality.

"The facts ... stand on an altogether different footing": "The Remarkable Case of Davidson's Eyes" (1895) by H.G. Wells

If you have been paying attention at all, by this point you should have noticed the special attention my readings have been paying to the beginnings of short stories. Short stories, before they are anything else, are short. This means that whatever a story is going to do in its brief duration has to get started right away, and whatever that is will develop from this initiation-point. All of this is to say that the beginning of any short story is particularly important.

H.G. Wells' "The Remarkable Case of Davidson's Eyes" is no exception to this rule. We can learn quite a lot by reading the beginning closely. Here is the first line of the story: "The transitory mental aberration of Sidney Davidson, remarkable enough in itself, is still more remarkable if Wade's explanation is to be credited" (358). What do we make of it?

First, we can identify that the narration is mimicking a kind of "high intellectual" rhetoric. "Transitory mental aberration" is the sort of phrase we might expect to see in a scientific or psychological journal. Taken together with the title, the story hits the reader right away as very "science-y." The second clause also contributes to this feeling: the "case" has indeed already been interpreted and an explanation attempted by someone named Wade before we are even being filled in on any of the details (the least of which is who this Wade character is). So, between the title and the first sentence, the reader is pulled into this dramatic situation, which is so evasive a case that, if Wade is correct, it is even more remarkable than the title lets on.

The next sentence: "It sets one dreaming of the oddest possibilities of intercommunication in the future, of spending an intercalary five minutes on the other side of the world, or being watched in our most secret operations by unsuspected eyes" (358). The narrator sees earth-shattering significance in this "remarkable case": there are speculations about the future of communication, about the addition of time "on the other side of the world" to our day-to-day existence ("intercalary" means the addition of something, in this case "five minutes," to a calendar or schedule), about the likelihood that someone is spying on us when we least expect it. The situation, whatever it is, we are likely thinking at this point, must be remarkable indeed.

Wells is using the narrator's tone and speculation, here, to grip the reader, to pull us into the story through the manufacture of suspense. He is also establishing, through the narrator, a reliable source. We learn in the second paragraph that the narrator is some kind of scientist, and in the first paragraph we are reading a seemingly scientific account of the case: he is using scientific-sounding vocabulary; he is speculating, projecting into the future about the validity of a certain interpretation; and so on. As a "science fiction" genre story, this one, even from the beginning, fits the specifications of the genre quite well.

As with a lot of science fiction, Wells relies on new technology combined with mystery to establish his effect. The symptom is relatively well examined in the story (even if it is not well-understood), but the cause is left pretty hazy: whatever happened seemed to have had something to do with electricity from the lightning in a thunderstorm (which is our third storm so far among these stories) interacting with the poles of an electromagnet in a science lab, which, according to Wade's interpretation, given at the end of the story, seems to have cast Davidson through a "fourth dimension" through a "kink in space" because he had been "stooping between the poles" of the magnet when the lightning disrupted things (366). Wade thinks Davidson "had some extraordinary twist given to his retinal elements" which allowed him to see precisely the opposite side of the earth (366). As interesting as Wade's theory is, however, he has not been able to replicate the results; he has only "succeeded in blinding a few dogs" (367). The narrator offers this interpretation with the caveat that he is "no mathematician" and that it all "seems mere nonsense" to him (367).

If you understand anything about quantum physics or something, maybe this all makes sense to you, but, as to its use as a literary device, Wells has made a clever move (one he will also make, as we shall see in Chapter Three, in *The Time Machine*). He devises a narrator who is an intellectual and one who, physically, is in close proximity to the immediate event (a witness), but, we should note, too, that the narrator, though some kind of scientist, does not understand the theory enough to explain it well. This makes him the perfect narrator for such a story because he can relate the dramatic event to a reader in a detailed, captivating way, but Wells does not have to use the narrator to propose a convincing rationale for anything: he can speculate philosophically without being burdened with the truth. All Wells has to do with the narrator is gesture broadly at one crackpot theory that sounds pretty high-minded. So the science is bad because it never gets anywhere and is only incoherently expressed, but as science fiction, this is good, precisely because it never gets anywhere. If we had a good explanation, then the case would be less "remarkable."

Philosophy and Fiction

You will notice that I have already written about a thousand words on this story, yet I have only written about the beginning and the end of the story. I have moved from the set-up at the beginning to a mostly unsatisfactory explanation of the event at the end. We will get to some of the stuff in the middle, but I wanted to establish these bookends to suggest the following interpretive idea: We can view the story, in at least one way, as directly about the domain of metaphysics: it is about the failure of rational explanation. Specifically, it seems to me that the story describes a group of people trying and failing to use the reliable tools of scientific observation and reason to explain something that seems to function outside of those rules. So if that is our working thesis, let's see where it goes.

If we pay close attention, we see the men in the story slowly accumulating information about what is happening, cobbling that information together, and then trying to derive a meaningful conclusion about what is happening. In other words, they are trying to decipher what is true.

The following is a list of explanations:

1. "My first impression was that he was drunk" (359). The narrator heard "a queer sort of laugh, and saw Davidson standing unsteadily in the middle of the room, with a dazzled look on his face" (358–59). He sees him reaching for and trying to grab onto something that is not there (359). Already, we see the narrator using the tools of his trade: physical observations through sense perception: he hears and he sees information, and he pieces it together to draw a conclusion. Davidson is unsteady, has a dazed look, has difficulty with gross motor function: all of these lead our narrator to the tentative conclusion that Davidson is probably drunk.

2. "I thought he was up to some foolery" (359). The narrator speaks to Davidson, who responds by talking about seeing waves on the sea. Tentative conclusion: perhaps Davidson is joking around.

3. "It occurred to me that he must be suddenly struck blind" (359). Davidson continues to look around for the narrator but cannot find him (even though he seems to be looking right at him). Davidson breaks some equipment on accident as he asks Bellows (the narrator) to "show himself," even though Bellows is right there in front of him. Davidson seems to be speaking about things that are not there, and he cannot seem to orient himself in the space around him. The narrator's revised tentative conclusion: Davidson has gone blind somehow.

Chapter Two. Metaphysics

4. "We're both dead" (360). Bellows reaches out for Davidson and touches his arm. This shocks Davidson, who is even more confused because he cannot see Bellows, but he also does not understand where Bellows might be hiding, since he sees only a wide-open beach, and there is no place Bellows could be hiding. Here, we see Davidson trying to put his physical data together to draw some kind of conclusion about what has happened. He knows he was in the laboratory; he knows a flash of some kind came; he knows that now he sees a beach and a ship and waves on the sea, but he cannot see himself or his friend. Davidson's tentative conclusion: his soul is somehow free of its body. He and Bellows must be dead, their souls floating in the ether, and maybe it just takes time to get used to being in spiritual form or something like that (360–61).

5. "Well, everything you see is hallucinatory" (361). Boyce, another colleague, gets involved now, and after a few lines, Wade, their dean, is also called in to help. Boyce and Bellows (the narrator) and Wade now establish a baseline of common experience. So now their interpretation of events trumps Davidson's, three to one. The three colleagues think things over as they try to gather more data: they establish that Davidson can feel Boyce's couch and that he recognizes it by sense of touch, that he recognizes their voices by sense of hearing, that he does not hear or feel anything that he is seeing, that he can orient himself by closing his eyes (which eliminates his visual perception). Revised, generally agreed upon tentative conclusion: Davidson is hallucinating.

None of these explanations, though, is satisfactory. The usual rules for drawing conclusions based on physical observations and sensory perception—something we take for granted—has ceased working because Davidson's physical sensations have become disintegrated: they are working with different data, so they are unable to work together. The colleagues stick with hallucination as their working explanation, but even this, most reasonable, interpretation is shown to be inadequate as Davidson's affliction continues for weeks.

Further, his visual data seems to react to his topographical position, to his physical elevation (and now I am sounding very science-y!). When he goes upstairs, he seems lifted high into the sky above the beach. When he goes to low-lying areas of London, he goes underground or into the sea: as he observes in this quotation from the story, "I drove down into the sea, and the stars went out one by one, and the

55

moon grew greener and darker, and the seaweed became a luminous purple-red. [...] I kept sinking down deeper and deeper into the water" (363–64). This means that, if he were experiencing a long-term hallucination, his hallucination is responding to his physical elevation, which does not make much sense, at least according to my limited knowledge of how hallucinations work.

Davidson's vision finally returns in phases before he fully "heals." Sometime after this, he meets Atkins, who had served on a ship six years earlier on the other side of the world, in the South Seas. Atkins shows a picture of this ship to Davidson over dinner one night, and Davidson recognizes it. Atkins "corroborated, word for word, the descriptions Davidson had given of the Island and the boat" (366). The story concludes that "in some unaccountable way, while he moved hither and thither in London, his sight moved hither and thither in a manner that corresponded, about this distant island. How is absolutely a mystery" (366).

So, we began with a "remarkable case," and we end without solving it. Wells gives us a fun and interesting conundrum in the story, but his rendering of the case is very simple. If you think about it, all he has done here is altered one kind of sensory perception—just vision. But in doing so, he also demonstrates how tenuous the human capacity for explanation is: one variation of sense perception sends even scientists scrambling for an adequate explanation, and they cannot figure it out. This, perhaps better than any story I know of, and certainly more accessibly that other contenders (like, say, the fictions of Jorge Luis Borges) illustrates the difficulty of metaphysics. Change one "rule" about our perception of the *physical* world, Wells seems to be saying, and you have a *metaphysical* problem, which is a real challenge because, as we learned in the introduction to this chapter, the typical solutions (which are necessarily narrowed by the limitations of human perception) are of almost no use in explaining metaphysical problems. We are only left with inadequate speculation. Common sense is just not enough for understanding metaphysical conundrums.

"Oh, I go by various names": "The Devil and Tom Walker" (1824) by Washington Irving and "Young Goodman Brown" (1835) by Nathaniel Hawthorne

These two short stories, "The Devil and Tom Walker" by Washington Irving and "Young Goodman Brown" by Nathaniel Hawthorne, share a lot of common ground, not the least of which is the fact that their authors knew each other, read many of the same European folk literature, and also served as American ambassadors to other countries (Ruland and Bradbury 92, Rollyson and Paddock 78). Hawthorne's story was published about eleven years after Irving's, and we can assume that Hawthorne was familiar with Irving's story. We also know that both authors were inspired by the folk and fairy tales of Europe (we can think, here, specifically, of the tales collected and published by Jacob and Wilhelm Grimm in Germany in the early 1800s). We may also think of the German legend of Faust as providing some ideological background for these stories: the Faust legend may have been the most prominent and famous story of someone striking a bargain with the Devil (among others, the legend inspired literary adaptations by Christopher Marlowe in England in 1604 and by the German poet Johann Wolfgang von Goethe in the early 19th century).

However, the stories by Irving and Hawthorne about dealing with the devil are specifically American tales. We see this, perhaps, most significantly in the social or cultural settings of the stories. Both stories are imagined against the backdrop of early American history in Puritan New England. Irving's story is set in the mid–1700s, while Hawthorne's goes into the center of the era of the witch trials in the 1690s, events in which Hawthorne's own great-grandfather, John Hathorne, took part as a prominent judge in the trials, a fact of which Nathaniel was not proud (Ruland and Bradbury 148).

So, both stories point to something crooked and rotten at the heart of America's Puritan heritage, but we can also identify that the stakes are different for each author: Hawthorne's story is, at least to some degree, dealing with his family's connection to Puritan wrong-headedness or bad-heartedness, or whatever it is that results in a witch-hunt mentality (Ruland and Bradbury 148), while Irving's story takes aim at social ills to do with money-lending, economic immorality, and miserliness. The respective tones evoked in the two stories demonstrate this difference in the authors' attitudes toward their subject matter as well.

Let's think about Irving's story first. "The Devil and Tom Walker" is steeped in legend. Throughout the whole thing, the narrator relays the story to the reader, often appealing to other stories, to gossip, to legend, and so on, which has the effect of both undermining any sense of realism and for the sake of maintaining a Gothic-feeling "legendary" status, and we can consider the following specific references as textual evidence for such a claim:

57

Philosophy and Fiction

1. The first reference to the Devil's involvement is prefaced by the phrase "The old stories add" (14).
2. Tom's wife's disappearance begins with "What her real fate was nobody knows, in consequence of so many pretending to know. It is one of those facts which have become confounded by a variety of historians" (19).
3. Then, near the end of the story, Irving relays a number of key details saying, "Some say" and "so says the authentic old legend" (23).

These qualifications couch the progression of the story in the provenance of local legend, as if to say, "It may not be factually true, but it might as well have happened this way." Ironically, by undercutting the factual reality of a "provable" story, Irving frees himself to move into metaphysical territory of legend and myth, which allows the story to function on another plane, one that is not expected to be factual, or even rational. Or, in other words, he relieves himself of the burden of something like Wells' abortive scientific approach to metaphysics. Irving's reliance on myth and legend allows his story not to have to worry about actual reality much at all; he can move freely into speculative local legend, which comes in handy in a story about pirate treasure, the Devil, and matters of the spirit world.

Further, Irving's story, as much as it is good Halloween fare, with its Gothic setting among the "straggling savin-trees," the "forlorn-looking house," grotesquely skinny horses, and abandoned Native American temples where, the narrator says, Indians "held incantations" and "made sacrifices to the evil spirit," there is also a lot of humor—or things that we imagine must have seemed funny to Irving's readers in the 1820s. Tom Walker's wife, in particular, seems, mostly, to have been included in the story as comic relief (as if the reader is supposed to think, "Wow, how bad is this guy's wife! She's so bad that Tom is grateful to the Devil for getting rid of her!"). Tom himself fares little better. He, too, is a ridiculous character. He is not the sort of figure the reader is meant to identify or sympathize with. He is horrible from the beginning, and he never changes. Even the kindest reader probably feels little else than a vague sense of justice served, and perhaps slight amusement, when Tom is carried off to hell, and everything he owns goes up in flames at the end of the story. We are meant to judge him, to hold ourselves above him, to laugh at and ridicule him. The catch may be that we might laugh a little uncomfortably if we have ever behaved anything like him, lent money with the expectation of interest, exploited another person for our own gain, or (God forbid!) worked in a bank or for a student loan company. Irving's story is a morality tale. The humor undercuts the scary stuff—but both contribute to the reader's moral judgement against the protagonist. The metaphysical aspects of the story conduct the moral instruction through a system of mythic and religious symbolism and association to demonstrate the stakes involved just under the surface of the everyday human moral universe.

Hawthorne's "Young Goodman Brown" requires an adjustment of the coordinates of the genre from Irving's settings. There is definitely the spooky, Gothic tone, and we know morality is involved in this story, too, but it feels more serious, more dramatic. It is interested in the rotten human heart, but Goodman Brown is not *essentially* evil the way Tom Walker is, even if Brown may indeed be experimenting with "his present evil purpose" at night in the dark and dreary forest (55). Goodman Brown loves his young wife, Faith, whom he tenderly kisses goodbye as he leaves her at the beginning (54). And we can think, here, of the contrast with Irving's depiction of Tom Walker's marriage. The Browns are obviously in love, but Goodman Brown is keeping secrets; he has secret sins, and he is afraid that maybe her dreams have warned her about what he might be doing in the woods this night: he concludes, "Well, she's a blessed angel on earth; and after this one night I'll cling to her skirts and follow her to heaven" (55). Two things here: first, he is rationalizing whatever "evil purpose" he has in leaving her; second, he is putting her on a pedestal, seeing her as perfect and holy—a "blessed angel" (55). Let's pause for a moment and think about what other purposes Faith serves in the story.

Faith, as a character, is utilized in an interesting way. Hawthorne seems to invest her with wider, almost allegorical, significance at the beginning, though her character does not always work this way. An allegory is a type of fiction in which certain aspects (characters, events, etc.) in the fiction correspond uniformly to a set of meanings outside the fiction. In "Young Goodman Brown," perhaps we see something like this with Goodman Brown, whom we may see as something like an "Everyman" character, and Faith, whom we may see as something like Goodman Brown's "faith" in God or religion or something like that. This relation seems most obvious when the dialog and narration explicitly emphasize it, as it does at the beginning of the story, where Hawthorne portrays Goodman Brown's intention to, literally, *leave Faith behind* to do something she would not approve of, only to return to her in the future. Allegorically, the meaning is pretty clear: that he is leaving his innocent faith (the pink ribbons, perhaps, signifying innocence or naiveté) behind—setting it aside—to gain some experience with the "dark side" of the spiritual world. The corresponding meaning seems so clear, and intended even, that we cannot overlook it, but Faith, the character, also does not only convey the allegorical stuff, as a strict allegory would; she is more than what she represents, and so is Goodman Brown. So, as tempting as the allegorical interpretation is, we cannot say that the story is *just* an allegory, even if we can say that there are *allegorical aspects* to the story which inform its meaning. In fact, Hawthorne seems to use this "loose" allegorical correspondence, so he can, kind of, call it in when it best serves his purposes, as it does here at the beginning of the story and in the middle, when he has Goodman Brown shout, "My Faith is gone!" (61) or "But where is Faith?" (63). It is as if Hawthorne can call in the allegorical aspect as needed for effect by appealing to the proper rhetorical register.

Without drawing out this analysis forever, I do at least want to examine a moral or religious—but a very human—theme in "Young Goodman Brown." We can get there by, first, contrasting its depiction of the Devil with Irving's in "The Devil and Tom Walker." Irving's Devil figure is straight out of the world of medieval legend and folk tale: he is a "great black man," but "neither negro nor Indian"; he has "a pair of great red eyes"; he dresses in "rude half Indian garb" (16). He carries a large axe and has cloven hooves (like a demonic goat-man or a satyr) (20). The character seems like a repulsive cousin to the otherworldly Green Knight from the medieval/early modern poetic romance *Sir Gawain and the Green Knight*. "Young Goodman Brown" portrays the Devil much differently: he "was about fifty years old, apparently in the same rank of life as Goodman Brown, and bearing a considerable resemblance to him"; "they might have been mistaken for father and son" (55); this latter observation is confirmed in the story by Goody Cloyse (58). Both stories grant the Devil special, supernatural powers, and both stories associate the Devil with Indians, with the wilderness, with persecutions of the Puritan's "enemies," and with what we might call "crimes against humanity" (like slavery, war crimes, etc.). For as much as these depictions share, though, they aim in opposite directions: Irving depicts the Devil as a supernatural "other," as something weird and mysterious, as something scary but also comically grotesque in a way; Hawthorne depicts the Devil as just like everybody else—and maybe a little worse because he so much resembles the protagonist that he could be Goodman Brown's father. In keeping with this idea, after Hawthorne invokes the initial Puritan notion that Indians are associated with the Devil, he immediately flips it on its head and associates the Devil also with the holiest Christians Goodman Brown knows, and, at the end of the story, with everyone in the world of the story, the good, the bad, the Indians, the Puritans—everyone is in league with the Devil. If someone were to ask me which is a more terrifying depiction of the Devil, I would have to say Hawthorne's. If Satan is a weird guy who seems like a person who is altogether "unhuman," sure, that is freaky, but if Satan looks like my dad, and everyone I know is secretly under his power, that is terrifying.

Some of the immense existential heaviness of Hawthorne's story may have something to do with its personal, even familial, connections to his life. Hawthorne definitely seems to be dealing with some matters of "inherited" guilt or shame, but he is also, perhaps, trying to dig into the theological and ideological complexities that feed into the running astray of religion, generally, and of the Puritan religion, specifically. More directly, we might come back to the question of what we see in "Young Goodman Brown" that has to do with something like a "witch-hunt mentality" as an interpretive idea, based on the exploratory analysis we have already done.

In the Satanic sacrament in the woods, Hawthorne shows that everyone shares the stain of "secret sin," which is the "communion of [their] race" (63): church members, deacons, reverend pastors, grave and reputable people of all kinds, but also "men of dissolute lives," "women of spotted fame," wretches, "Indian priests or powwows," and on and on (62). Even Goodman Brown's dear wife, Faith, shows up to be welcomed to this dismal collective. Not only this, but the whole world itself seems to sing in harmony with the Devil's chorus: Goodman Brown

> heard the swell of what seemed a hymn rolling solemnly from a distance with the weight of many voices. He knew the tune: it was a familiar one in the choir of the village meeting-house. The verse died heavily away, and was lengthened by a chorus, not of human voices, but of all the sounds of the benighted wilderness pealing in awful harmony together [62].

Worse yet, Goodman Brown cannot escape finding himself contributing to the harmony: even as he cries out in misery and desperation, "his cry was lost to his own ear by its unison with the cry of the desert" (62). So now even our protagonist, who, unlike Irving's Tom Walker, *is* a sympathetic character, who seems only to be experimenting with an abstract evil at the beginning (it is never made absolutely clear what his reasons are for his trip into the wilderness). Now, even as he wants to turn away, ultimate evil seems to be his fate, and he cannot help but to contribute to its pattern in the world.

But Hawthorne is not done. The scene gets more uncomfortable for religious people, and definitely for Puritans. The "sacrament" to which Brown and Faith are to be introduced comes into focus: they are in the wilderness, one not unlike the wilderness of the Garden of Eden in the story of The Fall in Genesis. Further, what the Devil promises them is knowledge, just like in the Biblical myth. And, here, we might consider the allegorical significance of Faith again. The meaning works on both levels: on the literal level, the lovers fear "what polluted wretches" the next moment may show them, as each is promised to see the secret sin of the other; on the allegorical level, Brown is promised knowledge of the fallen corruption of his faith (65). And when he returns to the village—and for the rest of his life—he sees people's secret sin, or at least he knows that it is there. He spurns his former friends and mentors and spends the rest of his life in bitterness, until the "day of gloom" he dies, his dear Faith outliving him, probably embarrassed by his memory (both the literal Faith, his wife, and symbolic faith, his Puritan religion) (66).

So, what does it all mean? On one reading, we can say maybe Goodman Brown is justified. All people are really the fabled "wolves in sheep's clothing," evil people hiding beneath the public practices of religious devotion. But if this is true, then is Goodman Brown not now the one crying "Witch!" Surely, it is not Hawthorne's point that the religious people are the *true* witches—along with everyone else in the world, *except* for Goodman Brown. Plus, this would put Brown, and maybe Hawthorne with him, in the position of the self-righteous, "holier than thou" person, which seems like a position Hawthorne, given his family history, would want to avoid. The lesson seems more difficult, deeper, and more existential than a simple turn-about.

More than deciding who is right and who is wrong, Hawthorne seems to be casting the whole of the religion into the mix: there does seem to be the basic Calvinistic idea that evil is real, and humans—all humans—have a fair dose of it (the "total depravity" of Calvinistic theology), but in another way, Hawthorne is calling the Puritans to task for assuming only "somebody else"—anybody else—is capable of evil. But he is careful not to stop there. Hawthorne is also interested in what we do with this knowledge. If we use it as a cudgel to beat everyone else, then we are no better than anyone who cries, "Witch!" and points a finger at another. We might see the "moral" theme of the story as something like this: once we really see into ourselves and find corruption, it does give us a view into the rotten intentions of others, but it also logically precludes us from seeing ourselves as, in any way, "above" them—and this is the point Goodman Brown is missing, which we can perceive at the end of the story. Seeing the common moral failures that bind us—that we are all, to some degree, "polluted wretches"—is to recognize our common "fallen nature," a nature that no one is "above." This is something like the idea that "total depravity" is only "total" if it includes me, too.

We see Brown recognize this nature in everyone but himself, but the story shows that he has not escaped it either. Hawthorne ironizes Brown's moral naiveté at the end of the story: *"Young* Goodman Brown" may indeed be titled this way to emphasize the persistence of his spiritual immaturity, even at the end. Brown has this experience—whether it was a vision, a dream, a hallucination, or even if it was real—but he does not learn from it. He begins and ends the story seeing only in black and white. At first, Brown perceives Faith and the upstanding members of his village as beyond reproach; he has put them on a pedestal, so he can only be dejected and disappointed when he sees evidence that they do not belong there. Then, by the end of his metaphysical experience in the woods, after seeing evidence of their sin and perceiving the likeliness of the sin even in Faith, he elevates himself to the position of witch-judge. He has learned nothing from the experience; he just utilizes it to invert his system of judgement: what was "white" is now "black," and what was "black" is now "white." On this line of reasoning, Brown's greatest failure is his failure to grow up and recognize that the moral universe is filled mostly with shades of gray.

Both of these stories, "The Devil and Tom Walker" and "Young Goodman Brown," create metaphysical worlds that blend with or emerge from phenomenal reality. But both stories, interestingly, seem to utilize metaphysical speculations in order to lend gravity to their moral reflections. This is a trend that Oscar Wilde's "The Selfish Giant" continues, but with far less doom and gloom and considerably more hope.

"Who art thou?" "The Selfish Giant" (1888) by Oscar Wilde

Oscar Wilde's "The Selfish Giant" is a story in the fantasy genre (the fantasy elements are obvious here, and more about them in a moment), and, apparently, Wilde intended the story for children. So the story merges two genres into one, but the genres fit rather comfortably together. Interestingly, we might even suggest that both of these genres of literature seem built for metaphysical exploration. Fantasy and children's literature are both able to achieve their effects by customarily leaping over reason and rationality and realist expectations just as a matter of course. By doing so, these genres are able to explore "literary" topics and features without having to abide by "the rules" of "serious" literature (Bate 2–4). Children's fantasy literature, then, is capable of going deep, of affording readers opportunities to explore difficult subject-matter (loneliness, death, class, change, and so on) through the inversion of social traditions, through the coalescence of "reality" with the myth-logic of fables and tales, and by anthropomorphizing animals and deifying human beings (Bate 8–12).

Wilde's "The Selfish Giant" does not shy away from these sorts of strategies. The story is as simple and straightforward as any children's story, but it also offers some surprises. The title gives away that the story is going to reach past reality, since "Giant" already puts us in the well-trodden territory of the Old Testament and "Jack and the Beanstalk"; it also primes us to expect some kind of "moral" to the story, as "Selfish" probably hits the reader as just the type of vice on which a children's story should offer some moral instruction.

The beginning of the story draws our attention to the perfection of the Giant's garden when the children are there: "It was a large lovely garden, with soft green grass. Here and there over the grass stood beautiful flowers like stars, and there were twelve peach-trees that in the spring-time broke out into delicate blossoms of pink and pearl, and in the autumn bore rich fruit" (300). The narration sets out a beautiful symmetry between the earth and the sky ("flowers like stars") and between the spring-time and the autumn; it primes us for the biblical allusions in stating the number of the trees. And maybe, if we catch the Eden-like beauty of the garden and the happy innocence of the children, we are not surprised by their banishment.

But already, Wilde is offering us some interesting paradoxes. If we think about the logic of events in the opening paragraphs of the story, we might be left scratching our heads. The banishment of the children from the garden is not a punishment for some sin they have committed (as we might expect in such an allegory). If anything, it is the other way around: it is the Giant who sins in banishing the children. Some legal-minded reader may push back by saying that the Giant is within his rights to banish the children from his property. Maybe so, but the logic of the narrative identifies the Giant with the sin, since the punishment he inflicts on the children hurts him most of all, the moral logic being something like, "sins against others hurt the sinner most of all." The children do not like being kept from the garden, we might conclude, but they are not made to endure eternal winter, loneliness, and confusion, and the Giant is. In banishing the children, the Giant banishes beauty from his garden, for when a linnet returns and sings outside his window, "it seemed to him to be the most beautiful music in the world" (301). Spring returns with the children. He helps a boy onto a tree, and the Giant's heart melts as he recognizes his sin, which is, unsurprisingly, selfishness. It seems pretty straightforward: a little morality tale.

Some readers may be taken aback, though, when the little Jesus boy shows up at the end of the story. My response to this is simple: if one is that surprised, then one is just not paying close enough attention to the rest of the story. First, we have the titular Selfish Giant, who kicks the playing children out of his garden and builds a high wall around it to keep them out; the absence of children in this garden causes eternal winter—and not only that, but winter is composed of wintery people:

> The only people who were pleased were the Snow and the Frost. "Spring has forgotten this garden," they cried, "so we will live here all the year round." The Snow covered up the grass with her great white cloak, and the Frost painted all the trees silver. Then they invited the North Wind to stay with them and he came. [...] So the Hail came. [...] He was dressed in grey, and his breath was like ice [301].

Obviously, anything is possible in this story, so we should not be surprised when a little boy with the wounds of Christ, "the wounds of Love," shows up and banishes winter and returns spring to the garden, especially if we recognize the mythic/biblical garden of Eden imagery combined with the twelve trees, and so on (303). The questions to ask, instead, are these: Why does the Jesus boy show up *again* as a Christ figure? Why is it necessary? These questions seem even more appropriate when we remember that, at this point, the Giant is no longer selfish.

The first appearance of the boy (who just appears as a helpless boy earlier in the story, so far as the reader knows), along with the return of the rest of the children, has already caused a change of heart in the Giant and has already brought redemption through the re-emergence of spring in the garden. The Giant has already learned the error in his ways; he has learned to love the children, which he calls "the most beautiful flowers of all" (303). So why does the story need the Jesus boy to return? We have already got a moral, do we not? Something like "When you are selfish, you cut yourself off from those whom you may love best," perhaps, would be the tentative moral the story is seeking to teach.

If we pay attention to the conversation between the Jesus boy and the Giant during the boy's second coming, we may find a more satisfying answer:

> "Who hath dared to wound thee?" cried the Giant; "tell me, that I may take my big sword and slay him."
>
> "Nay!" answered the child; "but these are the wounds of Love."
>
> "Who art thou?" said the Giant, and a strange awe fell on him, and he knelt before the little child.
>
> And the child smiled on the Giant, and said to him, "You let me play once in your garden, to-day you shall come with me to my Garden, which is Paradise" [303].

In this conversation, we see at least two allusions. An allusion is a reference to something else, something outside the text, that an author expects a reader to know about. The purpose of an allusion is to provide an artful shortcut to a whole other world of meaning. Allusions are helpful because they, essentially, superimpose the other world of meaning onto their occasion in literature. The two allusions we can perceive here are to the Bible: the first is to the scene during the betrayal of Jesus, while he was praying with his disciples in the garden, specifically, when Peter draws his sword against the men who have come for Jesus (see John 18:10, Matthew 26:51, and Mark 14:47); the second allusion here is to Jesus's words to the "good thief," one of the two thieves who are being crucified next to him (see Luke 23:39–43). Jesus says to the Good Thief, "Truly, I say to you, today you will be with me in Paradise."

These allusions provide a new lens through which to see the whole story: the Giant's garden now takes on more meaning (not only the Garden of Eden, but, now, the Garden of Gethsemane in the New Testament gospels, too, seems to have something to do with all of this); the change of the seasons can also now be seen in new context (perhaps as we might think of the movement from winter to spring as the movement from death to resurrection, from something like the dark and cold of Good Friday night to the new dawning light of Easter morning). Okay, but we still have not answered why this particular end is necessary.

Forcing the Good Thief and Peter into one character (the Giant) is interesting—the meaning must be something about the Giant's display of both of their (the Thief's and Peter's) essential attributes during those moments to which the story points the reader—indeed, the good and/ or bad associated with each man. Like the Good Thief, who rebukes the criminal being executed next to him, the Selfish Giant has shown that he is capable of mending his ways, that his change of heart indicates that he is, literally, redeemable, but, like Peter, he still shows a lack of understanding what else love demands of him. The story suggests that both Peter (and, perhaps, the Good Thief) and the Giant love impulsively and passionately, but they still love selfishly. They lash out at anyone who would threaten the object of their affection: but a Christ that is protected against sacrifice is being kept from his mission to the world. The Thief, Peter, and the Giant must allow their love through Christ to perfect them—even if it means that they, too, must die (and it does, as both the Thief and the Giant die almost immediately, and as Peter is later crucified upside-down). This means that they must give up control over him and allow Jesus to bless them on his own terms. It means that the love between them must be free.

Perhaps one other question goes unanswered in the story. The Jesus boy never answers the Giant as to whom it was that "dared to wound" him. The boy just says that his wounds are "wounds of love" (303). But the story may imply who wounded the boy, which may also imply why he does not respond to the question with a direct answer. After all, it was the Giant who put the boy on the tree.

Maybe this is not just a story for children after all. "The Selfish Giant," too, embraces genre fiction's metaphysical possibilities. While the story does require moral reasoning, it also invests in a magical fantasy world stripped of the limitations of "common sense" reasoning, even if that world does hold onto a symbolic, mythic logic to make the sense that it does. Edgar Allan Poe's "The Tell-Tale Heart" demonstrates a metaphysical separation from reality through madness, and, while the story is concerned, to some degree, with morality (if only by negation), its methods break the theological trend that has emerged in the three previously analyzed stories so far. The story is concerned, however, with the human heart.

"What you mistake for madness": *"The Tell-Tale Heart" (1843) by Edgar Allan Poe*

It is hard not to think of a transition from "The Selfish Giant" to "The Tell-Tale Heart" as rather crass and abrupt, but I think I can do it

Philosophy and Fiction

smoothly enough. In an odd way, perhaps, we are moving from a death in "The Selfish Giant" that is full of meaning to one in the "Tell-Tale Heart" which seems random and meaningless. We are moving from a sweet story about an old (giant) man learning the meaning of self-less sacrifice to one in which an old man is sacrificed to satisfy his mad roommate's narcissistic obsession. Further, "The Selfish Giant" provides a deep, complex contemplation on morality, while "The Tell-Tale Heart," quite brazenly, sidesteps morality almost completely. Instead, the narrator of Poe's story pulls us into his delusion, into his mad logic, according to which an old man becomes collateral damage in the annihilation of an Evil Eye that seems to peer into the narrator *through* the old man, his roommate. We take the narrator, certainly, to be "mad," but it is also precisely his madness that serves as the context for the metaphysical attributes of the old man's eye and heart, and of the narrator's compulsions, as if everything in the story lives at least two separate lives simultaneously. Everything in the story bends to this effect of locking the reader into the mind of the narrator.

Poe wrote an essay that outlined his theory of establishing such an effect; it is entitled "The Philosophy of Composition." Poe's essay explains his literary pursuit of what he calls the "unity of impression" (Poe, "The Philosophy" 743). This theory consists of the teleological (when something is "oriented toward its end or aim," "*telos*" meaning "end" or "aim" in Greek) strategy in writing by which an author aims everything in the story toward achieving a particular outcome (the *telos*) in the reader's experience (744). In other words, Poe is suggesting that the most important aspect of a story is for it to achieve its intended impact on the reader, and that everything that goes into the story should contribute to that effect. We might consider "The Tell-Tale Heart" a concrete illustration of his theory. For one thing, the story is brief, which heightens the effect, or, rather, concentrates the effect by disallowing any distraction of the reader during the short duration of the narrative (743). Further, we can use just about any concept from our vocabulary for critical approaches to literature (character, theme, tone, style, genre, narration, and so on) and see it in harmony with what seems like the intended impact of the story, and that effect (whether we want to call it an "experience of madness" or "a sense of heightened anxiety") is appropriate to the genre (crime/horror) the writer has chosen.

Especially with literature I have read several times (and I first read this story when I was like twelve, so about thirty years ago), I try to read *as if* the literature is new to me. The first thing that strikes me about

68

"The Tell-Tale Heart" as I am writing this is its intensity. The narrator is beside himself with excitement as the story begins: "True!—nervous—very, very dreadfully nervous I had been and am; but why *will* you say that I am mad?" (Poe, "The Tell-Tale" 83). He is essentially screaming at us about his nerves, about the fact that he is always nervous, but he is also playing with the reader. He is daring the reader to call him mad, but he is also putting the idea that he is, in fact, mad in the reader's head. He explains further: "The disease had sharpened my senses—not destroyed—not dulled them. Above all was the sense of hearing acute. I heard all things in heaven and in the earth. I heard many things in hell. How, then, am I mad?" (83). Surely, any sane reader taking the narrator at his word assumes that this is a trick question. "How are you mad?" the reader might say, "Perhaps because you cannot finish a thought without interrupting yourself with exclamations? Perhaps because you hear things in heaven and in hell?" Then, after accosting the reader with his defensive exclamations, he wants to impress the reader, so he changes his approach: "observe how healthily—how calmly I can tell you the whole story" (83).

Poe gives us so many things to pay attention to: potential madness, maybe some kind of weird disease (or at least the madman's claim to have such a disease), healthiness, heightened sense perception, heaven and hell, nervousness, his goal of staying calm. This narrator is all over the place. In a fascinating way, though, Poe is able to lead the reader in all these different directions, yet the narrator's peculiar lack of focus is so consistent in its inconsistency already that we are probably beginning to feel the effect—the spasmodic leaping in a hundred directions of a man with so little self-awareness, indeed, feels like madness from paragraph one. Poe grips us already by directing all his faculties at this one effect. And this kind of madness is useful because it can navigate toward metaphysical questions without being expected to offer explanations.

The contradictions continue to pile up as we read on as the narrator reflects on the past, on "the whole story":

> It is impossible to say how first the idea entered my brain; but once conceived, it haunted me day and night. Object there was none. Passion there was none. I loved the old man. He had never wronged me. He had never given me insult. For his gold I had no desire [83].

As we read, we do not yet know what "the idea" even is that "entered his brain" (83). We learn that it has something to do with the old man.

But look at the way the information is given. The idea referred to at the beginning of the paragraph is kept vague. Even if we know the rest of the story, I would suggest that "the idea," as yet, has nothing to do with the eye. I think he is searching himself for an explanation as to why he murdered the old man—that "the idea" that he is searching for the beginning of is the idea of murdering his roommate. It is only after eliminating all of the other possible reasons he can think of for murdering someone (objects or reasons, like passion, hate, vengeance, justice, gold) that he arrives at the eye, as if he has just plucked the idea out of thin air—he is even surprised by it: he says, "I think it was his eye! Yes, it was this!" (83) It is as if he is now trying to convince himself, too, that this was the reason. But, once he latches onto the eye, he runs with it as his rationale for murdering the old man, as if it is a good reason. But if we think about it from a sane, outside perspective, we might come up with something like this: the man has murdered his roommate, but he is not sure why; he has been obsessed with doing so, and, though he had no reason, he did it anyway, and now he is coming up with a reason on the fly—and the reason is surprising to both the narrator-protagonist and the reader. His reasoning seems backward, corrupted somehow. In his book, *Crime Fiction*, Richard Bradford highlights Poe's interest in "the problems of epistemology and reasoning" (9). Poe also often sacrificed familiarity and believability in his stories to his "perverse meditation on our capacity to comprehend other human beings" (Bradford 10). And "The Tell-Tale Heart" is no exception.

We may also wonder, why the eye? I think we already have an answer. Even in the first several lines of the story, the narrator is "dreadfully nervous" about what we think of him, what we know of him, to what degree we are judging him, to what degree we can *see into* him. Perhaps he settles on the eye because he thinks an otherworldly eye can see into him, into his depths, his soul—it is the perfect projection of his paranoia. This object of focus provides perfect corruption of the logic of Jeremy Bentham's panopticon (an "all-seeing eye" that Bentham thought would be useful in reorganizing prisons by centralizing a guard tower, giving prison officials the ability to see everything from one location; the idea was taken up later by French philosopher Michel Foucault) (Bertens 150): instead of an external, all-seeing eye gazing in on his secrets, the protagonist projects his secrets onto an external eye and invests it with metaphysical omniscience. So of course it is the man's "Evil Eye" that compelled him to murder; he just was not aware of it at the time. But in retrospect, it is this that he settles on because, he discovers, it so perfectly suits his feelings. Further, it introduces another metaphysical wrinkle into the story: according to the mad logic of the narrator, if the Evil Eye really is this otherworldly, metaphysical entity, how can he think that he can kill it? On this line, his horror at the beating of the heart might be his recognition that the Evil Eye has shape-shifted and returned in another form.

Readers often focus on how the old man became inured, through the madman's methodical operations, to someone creeping into his room while he slept. But we should keep in mind that this methodical plan just accentuates the madman's failure: even with so much practice, he ends up ruining his plan by too noisily adjusting his lamp. Anyway, instead, I would like to consider the madman's observations and interpretations of the old man's behavior, once he is in the old man's room. After the madman startles his roommate by making noise with the lamp, the old man cries out and remains sitting up in bed listening. After some time, the old man groans. In both cases, the mad narrator draws rather striking comparisons to himself: "He was still sitting up in the bed listening;—just as I have done night after night, hearkening to the death watches in the wall," and a few lines later, "Presently I heard a slight groan, and I knew it was the groan of mortal terror" (Poe, "The Tell-Tale" 84). He goes on at length:

> It was not a groan of pain or of grief—oh, no!—it was the low stifled sound that arises from the bottom of the soul when overcharged with awe. I knew the sound well. Many a night, just at midnight, when all the world slept, it has welled up from my own bosom, deepening, with its dreadful echo, the terrors that distracted me. I say I knew it well. I knew what the old man felt, and pitied him, although I chuckled at heart [84–85].

He goes on and on, talking about how the man must have been comforting himself with explanations for the noise, *"All in vain;* because Death, in approaching him, had stalked with his black shadow before him, and enveloped the victim" (85). Then he hears the heart, "a low, dull, quick sound, such as a watch makes when enveloped in cotton" (85). "I knew *that* sound well too. It was the beating of the old man's heart" (85). Everything in the preceding paragraphs begs us to question this last statement, which offers us an interpretive plot key to the end of the story. Why does the madman still hear the dead man's heart? Because it was his own heart he was hearing the whole time. This is a nice trick for the end, and one that we are prepared for by the narrator's over-interpretation of the old man's behavior, that is, by his tendency to project his own feelings and experiences onto the old man's behavior.

More than being the magic key to the ending, however, Poe may also be leading us into the deeper question with which the story begins. Why did he kill the old man? He says it was the eye, but can we believe this literally? The narrator contradicts himself at every turn. He often interrupts himself with things that seem to strike him as he is telling the story. Yes, the eye draws out the madman's dread and fury, but so does the sound of the old man's heart, the sound of a heart which, as it turns out, is probably the madman's own. Could it be that he hates the eye so much because it, too, turns the madman's focus toward himself in the form of paranoia, guilt, shame, despair, and anxiety? Is it possible that the madman kills his friend because he is, for whatever reasons, unable to kill himself—to annihilate the Evil Eye within himself? Is it possible that he has not become fully aware of how far his projections go? The accusing eye still haunts him, even after he has done the deed. He says, after dismembering and hiding his unfortunate friend's body, "I then replaced the boards so cleverly, so cunningly, that no human eye—not even *his*—could have detected any thing wrong" (86). And he continues to parallel himself with the old man, too, as he does when he explains to the policemen that "[t]he shriek" of the old man, when the madman attacked him, "was my own in a dream" (86). And, as he unravels at the end of the story, it is as if the Evil Eye has moved deeper and deeper into his mind, has overtaken his soul, has eclipsed his heart: he hears the heart, of course, his own heart—the one he wanted to stop all along, the one that drove him furious—but it is the accusing, paranoiac logic of the Eye that outlasts the old man, the perception that whatever the horrible truth about the narrator is, it will come out, that everyone will see what It sees. Killing the old man to eliminate the Evil Eye can only fail. The madman has just made it stronger because now he has nowhere to project it. Now, like any negative feeling without an outlet or another person on whom to project it, his accuser moves back inside him, which is where it emerged from in the first place: it has been within him all along. And killing everyone in the world would not rid him of its accusing gaze.

Conclusions

Fictional explorations of metaphysical questions provide us with novel ways for thinking through philosophical problems that touch, not just the speculative domain or God, the Devil, Being as such, and so on;

they also provide connections between the "why" behind these domains in human thought. We see some interesting groupings form, even among the small selection of stories we have considered in this chapter, as we have used these fictions to think through the truths of metaphysics. On one hand, we have seen stories that invoke religious, specifically Christian, metaphysical imagery. Interestingly, though, none of the stories takes its Christian imagery "whole cloth" from the Christian collective consciousness. Irving, Hawthorne, and Wilde use religious imagery and symbolism in their fictional worlds, but they also use their fictional worlds to recontextualize the significance of the metaphysical possibilities in the religious imagery and symbolism they borrow. Irving's tale demonstrates the moral stakes of giving in to one's lowest impulses and of thriving parasitically on others' suffering through embodying evil in an otherworldly Devil straight out of medieval folk legend. But, at the same time, the form limits the reality of the characters. We understand the metaphysical stakes, but the Devil in the story is more amusing than frightening, which makes us read any connection between the metaphysics in the story and the "real world" as strictly metaphorical, as figurative. Neither the author, nor the reader *believes* in these metaphysics, but that does not necessarily hurt the transmission of the moral theme.

Interestingly, Hawthorne trains his convicting gaze on the righteous themselves, breaking into everyday reality with an inexplicable otherworld that emerges, whether through a dream, a vision, or for real. This conceptual "fuzziness" between reality and the otherworld lends more credibility to his story. His metaphysical functionaries blend into the real world, their evil deeds and sick hearts hiding within pious acts and recognizable faces. He depicts righteousness/morality/goodness and sin/immorality/evil as identical opposites of one another, showing that the distance between them is almost negligible, that one slips into the other before the moral agent can even identify having moved at all. While perhaps not realistic, Hawthorne's metaphysical world is "believable" because we can see ourselves in it, and it is disturbing because we can also see the universal logic by which its lesson is almost inescapable.

Wilde's "The Selfish Giant" is softer and less morbid, but his metaphysics are no less universal than Hawthorne's. In a way, his moral message is more ambitious than the other two: his story demonstrates not just the wages of sin, nor just its universality and persistence in the human heart; but he is also interested in redemption. He is able, through the metaphysics of children's fantasy, to incarnate in his fiction both something like the fatal flaw of original sin (selfishness), its ability to persist among those who have mended their ways, and the stakes of a kind of holiness that transcends human ability—and even human life. Wilde's almost total abandonment of realism for fantasy makes his story more compelling in a way. Rather than grounding his metaphysics in reality, as both Irving and Hawthorne do to varying degrees, Wilde playfully turns the tables and grounds his reality in the logic of his fantasy metaphysics. Winter is caused by "wintery people"; spring is brought on through the play of children; and Jesus even cares for ogres.

The other two stories, Wells' "The Remarkable Case of Davidson's Eyes" and Poe's "The Tell-Tale Heart," problematize metaphysics. They do so by highlighting the unreliability of human "common sense," that is, of both sensory perception and the consistency and reliability of our minds to do anything meaningfully with it. Wells interrupts the usual logical chain linking experience and understanding by ever so slightly changing the rules through the introduction of a metaphysical operation into physical reality. Poe's strategy is a little different. Poe uses madness to problematize the metaphysical worldview by demonstrating that even phenomenal reality is up for grabs. In "The Tell-Tale Heart," madness sabotages the relationship between the mind, sensory perception, and phenomena of experience, which results in the madman assuming that this discontinuity signals his special perception of something metaphysical—of his special powers of perception, of his access to heaven and hell, of his helplessness under the accusing gaze of an otherworldly eye. According to our philosophical terms from Kant, both stories portray something like the intrusion of the noumenal into the phenomenal reality, but unlike with the other group of stories (Irving, Hawthorne, Wilde), the world of the fiction is the "real world"; these are not tales, myths, legends, or fantasies, and the relation of the events comes with dire real-world consequences. They push past moral issues into disruption that loss of predictability of phenomenal reality causes, whether through inexplicable events or mad delusion.

Wells' story explores an exception to the usual experience-based knowledge of empiricism (a posteriori), while Poe exposes the holes in rationalism by demonstrating a logical mind gone awry with a corrupted a priori epistemology (that is, "a theory of knowing"). Each of these stories, is, in its own way, a "duck-rabbit," a picture that shows more than one thing at the same time, no "picture" necessarily exhausting or erasing the meaning of the others. But each story also demonstrates that metaphysics, as grand as the aim of such a domain of thinking is, never gets away from the humans who invented it. This chapter also highlights the usefulness of fiction for thinking through metaphysics: fiction does not have to play by philosophy's rules, but that does not mean that it cannot play with philosophy's categories—and find interesting and compelling ways to describe the world, to speculate narratively about philosophy's problems. After all, people have been using stories to explore the unknown and unknowable aspects of existence, probably, since human consciousness first emerged.

CHAPTER THREE

Time

"We are never 'at home': we are always outside ourselves. Fear, desire, hope, impel us toward the future; they rob us of feelings and concern for what now is, in order to spend time over what will be—even when we ourselves shall be no more. 'Calamitosus est animus futuri anxius.'"—Michel de Montaigne

The Time Machine (1895) by H.G. Wells: "I shall controvert one or two ideas...."

Philosophically, the concept of time can lead us in several interesting directions. French physicist and philosopher Étienne Klein, in his book *Chronos: How Time Shapes Our Universe*, offers a number of questions that initiate such moves:

Did time appear "at the same time" as the universe, or did it precede it? How did it start? Who initially flicked the switch? Is it of the world, or does it contain it? What does time consist of, this time that passes but is always there, that doesn't change but changes all things? What is its real relationship to things? Does it exist independently of all that appears, changes, wears down, ages, and dies? [...] What are the points of convergence between physical time and lived time? [xii].

We can consider the phenomenology of time, which is a way organizing questions about the human experience of time as apart from objective, or cosmic, time: so, in other words, how do our minds conceive of what time is and means? We can consider the ways in which time is related to Being itself (what we might call an "ontology of time" or a "temporal ontology"). For German philosopher Martin Heidegger, being is "thrown" to time similarly to how beings are "thrown" to Being: the life of *Dasein* ("to be there," human being, being human) "involves time more crucially than space" (Inwood 67). Such observations may

76

lead us to speculations about the nature of relations of things (and people) and events within time or to time. As Klein remarks, "Time for us is a sort of familiar evidence, an obvious being, a reality that goes without saying. We always take it to be there around us, secretive, silent but constantly at work" (1).

Here, already we are drawn in a number of directions, just by imagining a couple of possibilities. What happens when time stops, if that is even possible? Does that void events and people happening/acting within time? What does time mean if indeed it is merely something like a "fourth dimension" (as the "Time Traveler" suggests in *The Time Machine*)? (2). According to the novel, this means that people are capable of traveling back and forth in time, just as freely as they can travel here and there in space, which would mean, too, that time stretches out in a way analogous to space (Wells, *The Time Machine* 3–4).

According to the logic of this analogy, time is as definite as space, which means that what is in the future is already just as certain as things that have already occurred. The only difference is our proximity to them on the "timeline" as it were. This invites speculation about ethics/morality in relation to time. Does it make any difference how I behave or what I do if the future is already set? If the future already exists, then how free are we? This is analogous (another analogy!) to theological questions surrounding whether God knows the future. The argument, here, is that, if God knows the future, how is that different from God predetermining the future? For, after all, God's knowledge cannot be wrong, right? In either case, whether the question is put in the metaphysical terms of time or in the theological terms of providence or predetermination, the result is deterministic, or fatalistic. The implication is that we have no freedom, that all of our future choices, acts, feelings—that future human events, or even cosmic events—are all as concrete and determinate as anything in the past.

Or is it possible that the future is "open," fluid, indeterminate? If this is the case, then, if time travel were possible, what future would one be travelling into? And would such a time traveler know the difference? We could push this further, and, perhaps, into more depressing territory: what if we combine these sorts of abstract philosophical speculations with the definite scientific stuff we know about "planetary health," about the life and timeline of a star, for we can imagine that a planet, like ours, can only handle so much before it becomes no longer able to support life, and we know that stars, like our sun, at some point "decay" and die. These pose rather stark questions to us about an "end" to the human timeline anyway (and we may not be comforted by the idea that such an end may not have a large impact on the multi-billion-year timeline of the universe).

Under the impact of these sorts of realizations, even if our future is "open," "fluid," and "free," we may still suffer from some kind of fatalism, from the suspicion that our lives and choices, though free, are limited— that we are bound by time because we, our planet, and our solar system all have an expiration date, even if we perceive that date to be in the distant future. On this interpretation, though the future is largely indeterminate, there are at least some aspects of it that are determined, some aspects that are set and unchangeable, regardless of our individual freedom, free will, or free choice. How or where do we find meaning if we are bound by time, if our individual timeline is so limited in comparison to the timelines of the world around us?

The Time Machine explores, to some degree, the gaps between and convergences of these timelines through the combination of how "physical time and psychological time" exhibit "the present instant" (Klein 133). Klein states that physical time is always concentrated on one point—the present—which separates the "infinity of the past" from the "infinity of the future," while psychological time "mixes a little of the recent past and a little of the imminent future in the very heart of the present": in short, physical time never allows the coexistence of two instants, while psychological time depends on the merging of the past into the present with the anticipation of the future in order to make sense of the present (133). Physical time takes the perspective of the universe, while psychological time takes the perspective of a limited individual consciousness, of a limited point within the universe. Part of what makes time travel interesting in *The Time Machine* is the filtering of discontinuous instants in physical time, some of them separated by hundreds of thousands, or even millions of years, through the limited, individual perspective of the time traveler.

The novel also allows for broader narrative timelines, like an evolutionary timeline or a cosmic or planetary timeline—those which are not exactly Klein's "physical time," but also which are not exactly "psychological time," to converge within the "psychological time" of the limited individual perspective of the Time Traveler. Conceptually, this is a fascinating prospect because Wells gives us an immediate human witness to timelines that extend, not only beyond the possible span of a human life, but indeed those which extend beyond the span of human life itself. So, in a way, Wells is using fiction to break the rules of time (which is expected in a science fiction story) and human subjectivity itself (which may be unexpected): the freedom from time removes some of the limitations of the human perspective, which affords the individual human witness the ability to speculate more broadly about the meaning of his own age and about the significance, or insignificance, of human life, generally, in ways not possible before, in ways that must meet head on the fact of the end to which all life is headed.

"Social triumphs": Politics, Time, and the Limits of Subjectivity

While there are, of course, many other directions time, as a concept, can take us, especially if we are really good at physics, interested in quantum theory, or if we want to dig further into the *grund* covered by Heidegger, H.G. Wells' *The Time Machine* entertains at least everything we have discussed up to this point, but as imaginative as it is, the book was published in 1895, before electricity was even widely available (as we can see in some of those candle-lit dinner conversations in the first chapters). And as much fun as the book has with technology (and the Time Traveler's time machine is indeed a very 19th-century time machine), with scientific and philosophical speculation, and with the genre trappings of science fiction, the heart of the book finds its rhythm with, not physical, geological, or even applied sciences, but with something closer to social science (maybe combined with political philosophy and evolutionary biology). So the interpretive idea I want to highlight, just to help us crack the book open a little, is Wells' strategy for showing how social/political arrangements create conditions within which adaptation and natural selection continue to function as, according to Darwin, they do in "nature"—because all of these things require time, or more precisely, because they develop over a span of time. The fiction of time travel allows a 19th-century aristocrat (or a man who is, at the very least, quite well off) to zoom off into the future 800,000 or so years to see a world very much affected by his own, and it is not a pretty picture.

Wells constructs the novel very carefully, so as not to hit us with all of this at once. The Time Traveler is a man of science, a clever, but reasonable man, but also one who is thrown into situations without any context but the one with which his own 19th century has provided him. So, when he ends up in 802,700, he must quickly orient himself by making observations and drawing conclusions based on those observations and experiences—that is, by induction. The risk of inductive reasoning, however, is that one who employs it is more likely to be wrong, or not completely correct, in his initial conclusions. It is this aspect of the novel that creates the pacing that engages the reader. As the Time Traveler relates his story, we know only that he came back—so that he survived. Everything else he relays to us in a narrative that progresses according to the chronology of his own experience (with a few bits of foreshadowing about how this or that impression that he had turned out to be wrong, incomplete, or only half correct). Cleverly, Wells positions the reader in two ways: (1) as part of this dinner club (we are one of the people fortunate enough to hear this wild story, just like the narrator, Filby, the journalists, and so on), and (2) as the Time Traveler himself (when the Time Traveler kind of highjacks the story and becomes the narrator from chapter three through most of the rest of the novel). So we are kept from knowing anything more than the narrators or the characters know at any given point: we are piecing the story together, just like the rest of them, which means the Time Traveler's incomplete understandings become our incomplete understandings, and we take his feelings and impressions, almost without questioning them (which is something we will come back to near the end of this chapter).

When the Time Traveler first comes to a crashing halt in the future, almost the first face to greet him is one belonging to "something like a winged sphinx" with a "faint shadow of a smile on the lips"; this statue was "greatly weather-worn, and that imparted an unpleasant suggestion of disease" (Wells, *The Time Machine* 25). Already, the attentive reader will recognize in the sphinx, a mythical creature, one known for its violence and riddles, and its smirk betrays that whatever the Time Traveler is going to discover is also likely to pose a kind of riddle—a problem that the Time Traveler must figure out. This should cue to us that the Time Traveler's initial conclusions are likely to be undermined—that the situation he finds himself in will have the logic of a riddle, as indeed it does.

The Time Traveler pieces things together a little at a time. First, he meets the Eloi, slight, frail, diminutive humanoid creatures with curly hair, who are too stupid to be afraid or curious about anything, but who, more charitably, resemble gentle, docile children (Wells, *The Time Machine* 26–27). They think that the Time Traveler has come from the sun through the thunderstorm (29). He examines the nearby buildings, observes the common living arrangements, and these, among other things, lead him to the initial conclusion that in this future communism has won the day: they all dress the same; they all essentially look the same; even sexual differences seem to have been largely eradicated (34–35). He also identifies that this future shows "no signs of proprietary rights," yet all had plenty to eat; pests had been eliminated; "diseases had been stamped out" (36–37). "There were no signs of struggle, neither social nor economical struggle" (37), yet the Time Traveler refers to this as a time of "humanity on the wane," the "sunset of mankind" (36). These people of the future, the Eloi, seem to have been the evolutionary result of a humanity without needs—so, accordingly, their intellectual and physical powers had declined because the improvements made by their ancestors had perfected their existence: they wanted for nothing (38–39). Even the impetus toward creativity had disappeared (39). So, in all, the Time Traveler's initial induction leads him to the conclusion that humanity had succeeded, perhaps, too well—so well that it had created a common life of ruinous ease. But the sphinx's smile signals to the reader that such a view is just the beginning of the riddle, which the beginning of chapter five also signals, for, by this point, the sphinx, it seems, has "swallowed" the time machine—or, rather, someone had taken it and hidden it, apparently, behind the doors of the sphinx's pedestal (40).

And this is the first indication of some other species of human descent lurking under the surface in this new world: the Time Traveler says, "I remember running violently in and out among the moonlit bushes all round the sphinx, and startling some white animal that, in the dim light, I took for a small deer" (Wells, *The Time Machine* 42). We think nothing of this line on the initial reading, but this is our first indication of a Morlock. The Morlocks slowly materialize into the story with all the genre trappings of a ghost or a monster in horror. They come in glimpses; they drift into the story in moments between wakefulness and sleep, through mysterious footprints, and with disturbing laughter (45). It is about at this point when the Time Traveler discovers the "extensive system of subterranean ventilation," and, just a paragraph or two later, his mind wanders to what the Eloi do with their sick, their aged, and their dead (48–49). The Morlocks, it seems, are even haunting his thoughts in such questions. That night, they inspect him while he sleeps: "I had been restless, dreaming most disagreeably that I was drowned, and that sea-anemones were feeling over my face with their soft palps. I woke with a start, and with an odd fancy that some greyish animal had just passed out of the chamber" (52). Near sunrise, after meeting Weena, he sees a "solitary white, ape-like creature running rather quickly up the hill," then another group of them "carrying some dark body" (53). Confirmation: the Eloi are not alone.

It is not long before the Time Traveler tries out another, revised theory on the social politics of the future, one that includes the Morlocks: they are an underground race of human descendants of an exploited working class, and it was "in this Under-world that such work as was necessary to the comfort of the daylight race was done" (Wells, *The Time Machine* 57). The Time Traveler develops this theory in light of the class conflicts of his own 19th century, during which the "Capitalist and Labourer" classes are locked in an economic model that depends on the exploitation of workers, and the increasing separation of the two classes into almost completely divided worlds (58). The Time Traveler reaches a further revised conclusion, which he states in his narration:

> So, in the end, above ground you must have the Haves, pursuing pleasure and comfort and beauty, and below ground the Have-nots, the Workers getting continually adapted to the conditions of their labour.... [T]he survivors would become as well adapted to the conditions of underground life, and as happy in their way, as the Upper-world people were to theirs. [...] I saw a real aristocracy armed with a perfected science and working to a logical conclusion the industrial system of to-day. Its triumph had not been simply a triumph over Nature, but a triumph over Nature and the fellow-man [59].

We end up with something like a Darwinized, roughly Marxist view, here, of the total exploitation of the working class (though Wells repeatedly disagreed with Marx's ideas about class hostility as an "analytical category")—but the Time Traveler's conclusions are still only tentative (Huntington 224).

"An altogether new relationship":
Class, Species, and Survival

When he ventures into the underworld, the Time Traveler finds evidence that the Morlocks, unlike the Eloi, are not vegans. He slowly arrives at a new conclusion: his Darwinized Marxism was, maybe, more correct than he thought, for the subterranean Morlock workers at some point in the past had formed a quiet revolution: they were now in charge (Bergonzi 192–193, Cantor and Hufnagel 237). And not only were they a ruling revolutionary class, but they, quite literally, had begun to eat the rich: "These Eloi were more fatted cattle, which the ant-like Morlocks preserved and preyed upon—probably saw to the breeding of" (Wells, *The Time Machine* 76). The Time Traveler waxes on about the state of future humankind: "Man had been content to live in ease and delight upon the labours of his fellow-man, had taken Necessity as his watchword and excuse, and in the fullness of time Necessity had come home to him," for it was Darwinian "Necessity" that had driven the Morlocks back to the surface for meat when they had been starved out underground, and now the new system was in play (76). Wells has effectively turned class differentiation into species differentiation (Huntington 76).

That is about as complete as the Time Traveler's theory of social relations in the future gets, but I would like to suggest a further interpretive move. The Time Traveler's sympathies are obviously with the Eloi. As he says, "the Eloi had kept too much of the human form not to claim my sympathy" (Wells, *The Time Machine* 76), whereas the Morlocks are terrifying horror monsters who haunt, mumble, nip, grab, and feel; they are compared to animals and insects: apes, lemurs, and rats, as well as spiders and ants (Bergonzi 198). But we should also examine the situation the Time Traveler is in for a moment. He has ended up in a remote and distant future but in one that, in many ways, resembles the remote and distant past—mostly, if we are considering the Morlocks. These ape-like humanoid creatures, for example, are probably closer to our remote human ancestors than the Eloi are; the Morlocks are quite accomplished with tools; they are the ones still driven by necessity to solve their problems; they are still creative and hard-working. They may not seem intelligent, but the Time Traveler never really attempts to learn their language, so he is not sure what their intelligence level is. In fact, his only interactions with them are hostile and violent. All of this to say, on nearly all accounts, the Morlocks hold onto most of the "human" features that he chides the Eloi for having lost; they are just not as pretty. Sure, they eat the Eloi, but which of the two is really more human? Perhaps Wells is suggesting something to us about the Time Traveler himself. The picture we get of him is that he is independently wealthy (perhaps an aristocrat); he travels in elite circles; he is a property owner with servants. Perhaps these are all aspects of his character that we should consider in deciphering the direction of his sympathies. On this sort of reading, we might conclude that, of course, he will side with the Eloi against the Morlocks: the Eloi are, after all, the descendants of his own ruling class, and if they are the "lesser gods" that their name suggests ("Eloi" comes from the Hebrew word, used in the Old Testament, for the "lesser gods"), that makes him one of the "greater gods" (Luckhurst 256). Doesn't it? So perhaps his sympathies for the Eloi are self-serving in some measure.

Seeing the Time Traveler in this light may make us question his repulsion at the Morlocks (whose name may refer to "Moloch," or "Molech," a Canaanite god associated with child sacrifice in the Old Testament), who have proven to maintain at least as much that is human as our own pre- or proto-human ancestors did (think of homo habilis and the rest). Is it possible that the Time Traveler fears, more than anything, the loss of the position of his class in civilization, the topsy-turvy socio-economic conditions of the future age, where brute worker politics have flipped the power structure upside down, but, in doing so, have also turned the world toward meeting their needs after hundreds of thousands of years of exploitation—but also of separate evolution? Sure, they dine on the Eloi, but would they have begun doing so if they had not been forced underground, exploited, and ultimately forgotten, forced to eat rats, and then starved to the desperate point of creeping up after the Eloi for food? Perhaps it seems like I am reading "against the grain," but I do not think I am. Wells' own socialist politics might have led him to come up with similar questions—or at least to leave open the possibilities of such questions. Perhaps the Time Traveler is an earnest supporter of the Eloi, but, as for Wells himself, I think he is more of a Morlock man. I think he leaves some room for irony in our interpretation of the human descendants of future. That hovering sphinx keeps smirking about its riddles from the very beginning until long after the Time Traveler has run away back to his own time and disappeared again.

Conclusions: Status, the Future, and the Irony of Social Darwinism

One final thought on *The Time Machine*. We may also be seeing Wells, in this novella, using Darwinian theory to criticize Social Darwinism, a major school of thought that developed Darwin's ideas in the decades leading up to the end of the 19th century by applying them to the shrewd capitalist social and economic political ideas driving the industrial age, some of which, as the ideas of Herbert Spencer demonstrate, may, indeed, have preceded Darwin's theories (Stromberg 124). According to the Social Darwinist perspective, "It was biology that wanted the rich to be rich and the poor to be poor," the philosopher

Alain de Botton says in his book *Status Anxiety* (68). He continues, "The Social Darwinists, furthermore, insisted that the sufferings and untimely deaths of the poor benefited society as a whole ... [because] the weak were nature's mistakes and must be allowed to perish before they could reproduce and thereby contaminate the rest of the population" (68). If anything, this use of "Darwinian survivalism" leads to a politics that defends exploitative labor practices and poor treatment of the underclasses with the logic that, if they cannot persist under such conditions, then so much the worse for them.

The picture of a future in which shrewd capitalist social and economic ideas have forced the classes further and further apart and adapted social conditions to affect the context within which Darwinian adaptation and selection persists, *The Time Machine* shows a nightmarish future in which Social Darwinism has largely driven class relations. The catch, here, though, is that the ultimate outcome results in the opposite of what the 19th-century Social Darwinists had in mind: yes, the strong did survive among the poor workers; the lines of exploited humans that became the Morlocks did, in fact, adapt to their squalid conditions. But the ease of the "good life" built on the backs of the Morlocks also ruined the Eloi. They, too, adapted to their conditions and became dependent on the life of ease sustained by the labor of the underworld.

The irony here is that Social Darwinism can conceivably favor anyone: sure, it seems great when you are the one who is doing well, the one who is on top, but fortunes change, and humans, like all animals, adapt to fit their conditions, whether those adaptations are progressive or not. And when you base social/political relations on such ideas, you are also removing any reason to see those people belonging to a contending class as your siblings, which, according to the future sketched in *The Time Machine*, thereby removes any real moral hurdle to using them for food, if it comes to that. The message here is this: the Eloi (according to the quasi-Marxian analysis) had robbed the Morlocks of their humanity by treating their class as less than human (according to the Social Darwinist inflection), and this results in the Morlocks, over time, having forgotten the Eloi's connection to them, making the Eloi welcome replacement for the Morlocks' waning food supply. "You want Social Darwinism and survival of the fittest?" Wells seems to ask. "You want to exploit working people, while you enjoy the fruits of their labor? Well, this is the future to which it may lead. Bon Appetit!"

CHAPTER FOUR

Social Cont(r)acts

"We are entirely made up of bits and pieces, woven together so diversely and so shapelessly that each one of them pulls its own way at every moment."—Michel de Montaigne

Introduction

What makes the theme of "Social Cont(r)acts" interesting is the way it makes us focus on aspects of relation among people and people groups (as constructions) in fiction. It makes us pay attention to the story in a particular way—or with a particular lens in place. Philosophically, concepts related to how people understand themselves as connected with what they perceive to be *their* group, position, or identity become important in ways we might not otherwise focus on when reading a story for a theme or just to be able to understand the plot. This takes us toward reading literature in the context of the ideologies that it explores or interacts with. Ideology points to the, often unconscious, "process of representing ideas and beliefs in signifying systems, of making meaning in a social context," whether that context is specifically located in laws, social classes, media, religion, politics, or some other form of belief in or identification with a set of related representational ideas (Castle 314). So, essentially, ideology points to the things people (individually and as groups) think and do and participate in, often without realizing why. This idea is the driver behind my combination of words in this expression: Social Cont(r)acts.

Social *contact* points to our shared social reality. It points to the mere fact that, as soon as there is social contact, something changes: we make different judgements about how to interact; we may perform our own identities in different ways; we may compare ourselves to the other, wonder what that other can do for us, try to get something from the other (and what we want may range from wanting only not to be hurt by the other to wanting some acknowledgment, like eye contact, a nod, or a wave, to wanting what that person has). The point is, as soon as we have combination, or *social contact*, we find ourselves in need of *social contracts*, rules for engagement, whether spoken or not. This puts us in the realm of ethics and morality, concepts that govern how we should behave and what is right and wrong—our responsibilities (which are always constructed within the context of some ideology or other). The problem is that, often, these concepts get in each other's way. Our identities are not singular. We play different roles in different contexts, even if the conceptual layout of the roles may be similar.

The 18th-century Genevan philosopher Jean-Jacques Rousseau observed something like the outline above in *The Social Contract, or Principles of Political Right*. Interestingly, Rousseau says that the family itself is "the most ancient of all societies," and, thus, forms the conceptual foundation of social organization (322).

> [T]he children remain attached to the father only so long as they need him for their preservation. As soon as this need ceases, the natural bond is dissolved. The children, released from the obedience they owed to the father, and the father, released from the care he owed his children, return equally to independence. If they remain united, they continue so no longer naturally, but voluntarily; and the family itself is then maintained only by convention [322].

Because, for Rousseau, the "nature of man" (Rousseau writes about "men" and "man") derives from his liberty, his first obligation is "to provide for his own preservation," the means of which "he is the sole judge"; consequently, each man is his own master, but only after he reaches "the age of discretion," adulthood (322). So before he progresses into freedom and independence, each man fits into his place in the society of the family:

> the ruler corresponds to the father, and the people to the children; and all, being born free and equal, alienate their liberty only for their own advantage. The whole difference is that, in the family, the love of the father for his children repays him for the care he takes of them, while, in the state, the pleasure of commanding takes the place of the love, which the chief cannot have for the people under him [322].

This analogy between the politics of the family and the politics of society is important for our considerations of the fiction in this chapter. We will begin with two stories based around relationships of fathers and sons and explore the extent to which the literature coincides with Rousseau's view of the family: with Mérimée's "Mateo Falcone," we will see how ideological conflict between the wider culture, identity and "the love of the father" disturbs the balance of the relation of father to son; in Kafka's "The Judgement," we will examine a father-son relationship in which the achievement of the liberty and independence of the "age of discretion" goes unacknowledged by a father, which corrupts the relationship, leaving the son unable to distinguish himself as an agent free of certain familial obligations.

The beginnings of society that Rousseau imagines in *Discourse on the Origin of Inequality* are not particularly rosy. He poses that, more than equality, "man" is born into a context of "natural inequality," which "unfolds itself insensibly with that of combination," that is, within the frame of social *contact*: some are stronger than others; some are more skillful; some luckier in their property; and so on (452). This means that, in a short period of time, some people rose above the others, economically. This had political and social ramifications, Rousseau says. "It now became the interest of men to appear what they really were not. To be and to seem became two totally different things; and from this distinction sprang insolent pomp and cheating trickery, with all the numerous vices that go in their train" (453). These social and economic complexities began to subject people to one another: "each became in some degree a slave even in becoming the master of other men: if rich, they stood in need of the services of others; if poor, of their assistance; and even a middle condition did not enable them to do without one another" (453). So we have people's social and political ambitions and desires, their growing economic inequality, and their need for economic survival combining to create a socio-political maelstrom in which inequality grows, self-interest is rewarded, and the social "other" is seen as a means to an end—a means one needs, both as a basis for social contrast to oneself ("I am better than you") and as an object of subjection to oneself ("Because I am better than you, you must serve me") (453–454). Rousseau paints this picture:

> [T]he destruction of equality was attended by the most terrible disorders. Usurpations by the rich, robbery by the poor, and the unbridled passions of both, suppressed the cries of natural compassion and the still feeble voice of justice, and filled men with avarice, ambition and vice. Between the title of the strongest and that of the first occupier, there arose perpetual conflicts which never ended but in battles and bloodshed. The new-born state of society thus gave rise to a horrible state of war; men ... brought themselves to the brink of ruin [454].

It is at this point that the social contract comes in, but Rousseau frames this contract as a trick of the rich upon the rest of society. The social contract freezes social relations, locking into place the dominance of the rich over the rest of society, enlisting the state in the protection of their (that is, rich people's) property, and punishing those who would threaten it (455). At the offer of such a deal, Rousseau says, "All ran headlong to their chains, in hopes of securing their liberty; for they had just wit enough to perceive the advantages of political institutions, without experience enough to enable them to foresee the dangers" (455). Political institutions, thus, fix social conditions, but they do not eradicate the social tensions that develop from them. These tensions are pushed down, repressed, or they are written into politics. The other three stories of this chapter will examine flare-ups of such tensions. Dickens' "Nobody's Story" and Wilde's "The Happy Prince" demonstrate these tensions socially in stories that appeal for the reader to look past the social and political institutions that separate people and place this group over that one, while Poe's "The Cask of Amontillado" appeals to a higher order of justice, beyond typical political order, to settle a score that seems to reach back to the "avarice, ambition, and vice" that originally, according to Rousseau, brought men "to the brink of ruin" (454).

Fiction is useful in imagining such social tension because it can play out these conflicts with little actual risk—but in ways that can have deep insights for how conscious of ourselves as social beings we can become. One might even argue that reading fiction with an attunement to, or through an interpretive lens of, "the social" allows us to become more self-conscious of our own ideological presuppositions and the tensions associated with them because the literature helps us examine those aspects in the lives of fictional characters in fictional worlds who are stand-ins for us and the worlds we inhabit.

"Father, father, don't kill me!"
"Mateo Falcone" (1829) by Prosper Mérimée

The narration of "Mateo Falcone" gives us a taste of the kind of social world we are in for in this story, even from the first paragraph. The narrator, with a gritty, dispassionate tone, introduces us to at least one social tension right from the start:

> Leaving Porto-Vecchio and heading northwest, toward the interior of the island, you see the terrain rising quite rapidly; and after walking three hours

along twisting paths, obstructed by large boulders and sometimes intersected by ravines, you find yourself at the edge of a very extensive area of brushwood. This brush is the home of the Corsican shepherds and of anyone who has fallen afoul of the law. You must know that the Corsican farmer, to save himself the trouble of manuring his field, sets fire to a certain stretch of forest; it's just too bad if the flames spread farther than necessary ... [25].

So, there is Porto-Vecchio, the closest city, civilization, and then there is this place, the *maquis*, this wilderness of tangled brush, "made up of trees and bushes, mingled and confused as God wishes," a rough and tough refuge that one does not reach by accident, a mountainous region where you can hide out if you happen to have killed a man, and where you will be protected and cared for by the shepherds, like Mateo Falcone, who live in the area (25–26). The narrator imposes this wild world that works according to different rules, and "it's just too bad" if you do not like it, or if you are used to the rules of the civilized world: it is as if the narrator is saying, "This is the world of Mateo Falcone; deal with it." Mateo Falcone's house is the gateway to the *maquis*. He lives there "like a nobleman," though Mateo is only a well-to-do shepherd; the truth is that he is not a nobleman; rather, he has earned respect by what he could do with a gun, by his toughness, by his history of effective violence, and by his family's heritage. Here, on the wild side of the line that marks the perimeter of civilization, as we see in many of the exchanges *about* Mateo Falcone, concepts like "respect" and "fear" are very close together, and they may even have a large degree of overlap (26).

But we soon learn that, as wild as this place may be, there are rules that govern social contact at the gateway to the *maquis*, but we are not given that set of rules all at once. We see them slowly emerge as Fortunato, Mateo's son, flirts with and then finally breaks those rules altogether. The rules are not outlined by the narrator; they are just part of the world of the narrative—they are imposed on the readers' experience with the characters, and we are left to piece them together. The story has such power because we can only make sense of it by reinterpreting it through its end—it is a teleologically driven narrative: one oriented toward its completion—its end, which means that we will work backwards, beginning with the end, to figure it out.

Mateo's response, at the end of the story, to his son's "social sin" probably strikes readers as very extreme, especially considering that this brutal justice emerges from within the relationship between father and son. But this extreme response points to the significance and seriousness of the "laws" that Fortunato has broken. The "justice" Mateo deals out to his son is a death sentence (36). But what Fortunato's sins are the reader may have a hard time identifying. Is it that the kid is just too bratty? Sure, Fortunato seems to take pleasure in annoying nearly everyone he comes into contact with in the story, and he seems to take advantage of the fear his father's reputation puts into people, but just being an entitled little jerk is not a sin that requires death, is it?

If we pay very close attention to the second paragraph of the story, we see the situation set up that Fortunato and Gianetto (the bandit) play out later on: "If you've killed a man, go to the Porto-Vecchio *maquis*, and you'll be safe there.... The shepherds will give you milk, cheese, and chestnuts, and you'll have nothing to fear from the law..." (25). Gianetto comes through, having exchanged bullets with the military men, and begs Fortunato to hide him. The bandit knows Mateo Falcone by name and reputation, and he knows that he will be safe there at the gateway to the *maquis* (27). Fortunato, though, first refuses assistance to Gianetto, and, instead, he teases him. It is only after Gianetto pleads with him and offers him money that Fortunato agrees to hide the bandit (28).

We should pause here to ask what social responsibility Fortunato has to Gianetto. According to the "rules" stated earlier, Fortunato is bound to keep him safe, offer him food—make it so that he has "nothing to fear from the law," if we are taking the words of the story seriously (25). We see, after the whole situation plays out, that, under his father's exacting gaze, Fortunato knows what his responsibility is. The story says, "Fortunato had gone into the house on seeing his father arrive. He soon returned with a bowl of milk, which he offered to Gianetto with eyes cast down" (34). Instead of doing his duty, Fortunato extorts money out of Gianetto in exchange for hiding him; he offers Gianetto no food or drink. Then, when Sergeant Gamba comes with the military men, he eventually betrays Gianetto to them for a valuable watch and chain (30–31).

All of this is bad, and we see Mateo reacting to each development after he arrives home and pieces things together. And Mateo does not seem happy. Mateo's first thought at seeing the soldiers was "that they had come to arrest him" (32). This detail speaks to his dodgy past, to the habitual violence that is just a part of life out here in "the wild," but, more than these (for our present purposes), it also identifies him *with* Gianetto, the bandit, and *against* the lawmen, the soldiers, who defend the rule of civilization, a distinction which is consistent with everything about "the social" that we have been saying so far. Mateo is the icon of the wilderness and its laws; the soldiers represent the social order and law of the city, of civilization: the two are at odds. Mateo is especially concerned about Fortunato's cooperation with the lawmen. Mateo becomes enraged when he hears that both father and son will be named in the report to the prosecutor (34). Gamba relays this information to praise Fortunato, but, to Mateo, his son's actions have dishonored the family.

Still, the reader may object. The skeptical reader may ask, "Does this dishonor deserve a death sentence?" We need to unearth two more observations related to the betrayal Fortunato enacts in order to understand the social stakes of the situation.

First, what is it that drives Fortunato to betray the bandit? Greed? Sure. Gamba offers a silver watch "that was worth at least thirty francs" in exchange for Gianetto, and Fortunato wants that watch. As Gamba dangles it in front of the kid's face, the narrator says, "The boy's face clearly showed the struggle being waged in his soul between greed and respect for the laws of hospitality" (31). Here, the narrator tells us that Fortunato knew his responsibility to "the laws of hospitality," and he went with his greedy impulse anyway. Further, this choice is dramatized in the interactions between the soldiers and the bandit in the sequence that follows. After Gianetto is disarmed and captured, the soldiers treat him very hospitably: they dress his wounds; they make a "litter" (a stretcher) to carry him on and pad it with straw; they give him water from their own canteens. The point of these actions is that even enemies keep the laws of hospitality that govern their classes' interaction with others (32).

More than simple greed, however, Fortunato's actions emerge from his sympathies with the "social world" of civilization. Mateo left the boy behind "to guard the home" (26). But when the reader first sees the boy, "Fortunato was peacefully stretched out in the sun, looking at the blue mountains and thinking that, on the following Sunday, he would go and dine in town at the home of his uncle the *caparole*," a man of a near-noble caste who was well-connected in business and politics in the life of the city, of civilization (27). Sergeant Gamba seems to see this, too, when he is trying to convince the boy to give up Gianetto. He says, "You'd surely like to have a watch like this hanging from your neck while you promenaded through the streets of Porto-Vecchio..." (30). The boy replies that, when he grows up, his well-connected uncle (not his father) will give him a watch. He is drawn toward the ease and riches of the upper classes; he is jealous of his cousin, whose father (the *caparole*) has already given his son (the cousin) a watch. Beyond Fortunato's jealousy and greed is something less concrete—something hinted at in the text: that, in his heart, he has already betrayed Mateo Falcone's way of life, his code, his laws, and his caste; Fortunato dreams of leisure and riches. He wants civilization.

The second observation is this: Fortunato does not just overstep a line in Mateo's perspective. The watch, which Mateo only discovers near the end of the story, is evidence of something deeper, more constitutive of his son's complete corruption. Further, the "laws of hospitality," to Mateo, are not just rules for how to be polite. They go to the heart of his family's identity. The justice Mateo delivers at the end of the story is not just his parental punishment; it is not even a punishment for his son's not meeting the cultural expectations. There is divine justice in this moment, too. From Mateo's point of view, Fortunato's sins are not exclusively "social": they are also religious—sins against God. Because Fortunato's sins go against his identity, including all of the ideological strands braided into it, this one sequence of acts composes a sin against his father (family law), a sin against Gianetto (moral law), a sin against hospitality (social/cultural law), and a sin against God (religious law).

The story takes a marked turn toward the religious perspective in the last sequence, as Mateo allows Fortunato to say his prayers, so he may die "like a Christian" (36). But this scene, out in mountains, amid the boulders and ravines, where a father kills his son should remind us of another story. Many literary interpretations built around biblical allusions seem a little forced to me, but I think this one is almost undeniable. After all, surely there are not that many stories where a father prepares to kill his son on a mountainside amid a significant turn toward religious allusions that do not have something to do with the story of "the binding of Isaac" in Genesis 22. But if we take a look at the very end of that story in the Bible, we may see this story, "Mateo Falcone," in a new light. The "Angel of the Lord" says to Abraham, in Genesis 22:16–18, after stopping him from sacrificing his only son, Isaac, to God:

> Because you ... have not withheld your son—your only son—I will indeed bless you.... Your offspring shall possess the gate of their enemies, and by your offspring shall all the nations of the earth gain blessing for themselves.

We can see, in Mérimée's story, almost an inversion of this logic in the Abraham and Isaac story from Genesis. Mateo Falcone's house is set out in the very beginning of the story as, literally, the gateway to safety, where those who seek it "shall gain blessing." Fortunato, Mateo's only son, was put in possession of that gate while his father was gone, but he refused to help a man in need. Whether Gianetto was an enemy or not, he was to be provided for. But, instead, he was sold out, betrayed. Mérimée plays the logic of the Angel of the Lord backwards—it goes something like this: Because your son—your only son—withheld the blessings to this man, who may have even been an enemy (he did steal a goat after all), justice requires the sacrifice of your son. Otherwise, neither you, nor all the nations of the earth, will gain blessing through this gate.

So, we see the various layers of ideological law coalesce in these last moments—especially in the context of this biblical allusion. Further, any time we see a reference to the Abraham/Isaac thing, it is worth looking for a Jesus allusion too (since the two can be understood as functioning according to a similar sacrificial logic), though, since the Abraham/Isaac allusion is a little inverted, our Jesus connection may be inverted as well. What do we see? Well, there is the sacrifice of the "only begotten son" to satisfy the law of the father. Okay, but that is pretty obvious, so maybe not very interesting, unless we consider that the son, Fortunato, is also his own "Judas," his own betrayer. In betraying the bandit for a silver watch (a watch worth how many francs? Was it 30? Isn't that the same number of silver pieces that Judas received for betraying Jesus?), the kid is also betraying his father, his responsibility, and ultimately himself.

Mérimée's "Mateo Falcone" is a starkly captivating, if somewhat disturbing, story that ends up giving us more to think about in terms of the social aspects of philosophy than one quick read-through might afford us, but if we are willing to put in the time and attention, we may find that some of our own ideological commitments, fictionalized in this form, can take rather terrifying directions—certainly directions we would not expect or want to follow.

Further, if we think about the dynamics of the interpretation we have just explored, we also see some interesting traction with "the social" as theorized by Rousseau. In this story, as in Rousseau's theory, the family proves to be the foundation of wider social organization. Here, we might observe that Fortunato attempts to act and think independently of his father's authority, and that within the social/cultural dynamics of the story, this is perceived as an unforgiveable sin. Because independence from the father is betrayal of the father; it assumes equality with the father. Betrayal of the father, accordingly, equals betrayal of the social/cultural order, and betrayal of this social order entails betrayal of the religious order within which it finds its meaning. In short, Fortunato's disruption within the family, his refusal to fulfill the responsibility of his position, is a disruption of the entire ideological superstructure that is built upon it.

"My father is still a giant": *"The Judgement" (1913) by Franz Kafka*

The title of this story, "The Judgement," has also been translated into English as "The Verdict." The German phrase from which the title comes, *"Das Urteil,"* has a range of meaning in English: the judgement, the opinion, the verdict, the sentence, the adjudication; and all of these possibilities are words in the legal domain. Readers will probably not be surprised to learn that Kafka was a lawyer. But, be that as it may, I do like the ambiguity in translating the title as "The Judgement." It prevents a *strictly* "legal" interpretation of the title's significance, especially as we consider the minutiae under Georg Bendemann's consideration in the first half of the story—the judgement he makes concerning the letter to his friend in Russia that becomes the catalyst for the father's verdict or sentence (in authoritative, strictly legal terms) concerning Georg near the end of the story. Further, translating the title as "the judgement" allows for the irony in the reader's recognition of Georg's inability to make proper judgements about what is happening from one moment to the next as his father defies the roles Georg employs as he attempts to judge what or who his father is: pathetic widower, senile old man, weak invalid, aloof crank, failing businessman, wild man, understanding father, brutal father, etc. Georg simply cannot make a sound judgement; he cannot orient himself in the moment. But, as we learn in the first half (or so) of the story, failure to come to conclusions—to adequately make judgements—is characteristic of Georg's personality, or of Kafka's construction of Georg as a character.

Georg probably strikes the reader as at least somewhat neurotic. As he sits on a Sunday morning in the spring at his desk in his room in his family's relatively anonymous house along the river, looking out at the water and at the bridge from which he will, by the end of the story, leap to his death (a river mentioned twice in the first brief paragraph, foreshadowing its significance), Georg reflects on his friendship with a young man who had moved, some years previously, to St. Petersburg

(636). One layer of the story concerns this friend. Georg seems incapable of understanding this man, his friend. The man had moved away and is now failing in business in Russia, yet, in Georg's opinion, he is "wearing himself out uselessly far from home" (636). The man is ill, his face yellowing; he is alone and lonely. But Georg seems unable to decide how he should feel about his friend. He is frozen in this indecision between two contrary attitudes: (1) a feeling of warmth toward and worry for him and (2) a cold, stagnant apathy concerning his ability to make any sort of difference in the man's life from so far away. The first several paragraphs of the story narrate Georg's oscillation between these two feelings; each volley to and from these two positions concludes with a definitive "lose-lose" situation. No matter what, Georg must write to his friend, but, no matter what, he reasons, Georg "could not send him any real news": the result would only be humiliation—or the possibility of a feeling of humiliation—of his friend, regardless of Georg's intentions. "And so Georg confined himself to continually writing his friend about nothing but insignificant events" (638). He stays in touch but only to maintain contact, to continue to be a friend, but at a distance, in order to maintain the relationship by protecting his friend's feelings.

But on this day, Georg finally decisively makes up his mind that he will assert himself and tell his friend about his life, about his recent engagement to a "girl from a well-to-do family" (638): "That's how I am and that's how he's got to accept me"; "I can't remake myself into a person who might be more suited to be his friend than I am," Georg reasons (639). After so much overthinking, second-guessing, and neurotic oscillation, the reader probably also feels a sense of triumph in this small moment. "Yes, Georg," we might think, "just be yourself. Put yourself out there as you are." We understand that Georg is a very sensitive man, that he has been through a lot (his mother has died; he has taken responsibility for his father's business; he has become engaged to this woman), that he wants to be a good and thoughtful friend, that he second-guesses himself, so perhaps we are not surprised that he wants to check in with his father about his decision to be honest and forthright with his friend. Of course Georg is a dutiful son, one who looks up to his father and seeks his opinion on matters of importance: he is too conscientious not to be.

The story moves with Georg from the setting of his bright, sunny room to his father's dark, stuffy room. This physical move accompanies the shift in the tone of the story from this small feeling of personal triumph, a little healthy self-assertion and honesty, to a tense relation to the mysterious father, who sits in a dark room with imposing shadows, holding a newspaper, oddly, very close to one eye (639). Georg's feelings concerning his father are mixed: he moves very quickly from being intimidated by his father's physical size to perplexed by his father's sudden activity in the room to feeling guilty about having neglected his father's health (as he notices that the old man is wearing dirty underwear, that he is not eating properly, that he wastes away in this dark room) (640–641). Further, the father seems not to be making sense.

When Georg explains that he has decided to send news of his engagement to his friend in St. Petersburg, his father's response is confusing. Georg explains the situation with the friend, deferring to the father, saying, "Before I mailed the letter I wanted to tell you" (641). His father's response begins with a faltering, oddly formal preamble:

> You came to me with this matter to consult with me. That doubtless does you honor. But it is meaningless, it is worse than meaningless, if you don't tell me the whole truth now. I don't wish to stir up matters that don't pertain to this. Since the death of your dear mother, certain unpleasant things have occurred. Perhaps the time is coming for them, too, and perhaps it is coming sooner than we think [641].

He talks about his fading abilities at work, how his wife's death took a toll on him, and moves toward a question: "I implore you, Georg, don't deceive me. It's a trifle, it's not worth mentioning, so don't deceive me. Do you really have this friend in St. Petersburg?" (641).

Readers follow the cues for how to respond to this through our relation to Georg, and he is immediately worried about his father's health, weakness, and state of mind, so we assume the father is losing his mind or something (after all, we might think, Georg has just obsessed over writing to this friend for pages, and Georg, if a little neurotic, seems completely rational; we do not think he would dream up an imaginary friend). Georg takes decisive action again: he encourages the old man, offers to make changes in the house for the sake of his health, puts him back to bed, and tucks him in like a little child (641–642). His father keeps repeating that Georg has "no friend in St. Petersburg" as Georg tries to jog his father's memory as he ensures his father that he is all covered up in bed.

Then the father explodes in a tirade against his son. The old man leaps onto the bed, shouting,

> Of course I know your friend. He would have been a son after my own heart. And that's why you have cheated him all these years. Why else? Do you

think I haven't wept over him? Isn't that why you lock yourself in your office, so no one will disturb you—"the boss is busy"—just so you can write your treacherous little letters to Russia. But fortunately no one needs to teach a father how to see through his son. Now that you believed you had got the better of him... , this fine son of mine has decided to get married! [643].

Georg is terrified and confused. And we can understand why this stings him. We just read how carefully and thoughtfully he reasoned through this decision to disclose some real news to his friend. The father's spin gives his questions about the friend's existence a new interpretation: it is not so much a question of having forgotten the young man; it is questioning the existence of the friendship. The father is shaping Georg's careful navigation of a tricky situation with the friend as the worst possible evil that could be done to the poor, lonely man in St. Petersburg. And Georg suddenly sees his friend "lost in far-off Russia" at "the door of his empty, plundered establishment," "standing amid the ruins of the shelves, the mangled merchandise, the falling gas brackets" (643). Georg is struck with pity for the man.

But the father does not stop there. He pipes on with an explanation for why Georg has behaved in so vile a manner:

Because she lifted her skirts and so and so, you went for her, and in order to satisfy yourself with her without being disturbed, you profaned your mother's memory, betrayed your friend and stuck your father in bed so he couldn't move. But can he move or can't he? [645].

Again, Georg had only just allowed himself a tinge of happiness and satisfaction at feeling he was grown up, successful, that he was honoring his parents by taking over the family business, expanding it, making it thrive, that he had become a man just in time, and now he was engaged—he would be married; he would build a home; he had decided he and his new wife would care for his father, and so on. But his father throws it all back in his face. In every development he thought was good, true, and noble, his father refuses to see as anything but baseness, vice, and selfishness. The shock is more than Georg can bear; he becomes disoriented. The father rants on and on, saying that the man in St. Petersburg has been *his* friend for some time now, since Georg betrayed him, that Georg had undercut him (the father) at business, persecuted his staff, kept himself aloof (644). "Do you think I wouldn't have loved you, I who gave you your being?" he asks (644). The father threatens to sweep the fiancée away from Georg (645). He demonstrates that he has known everything that Georg had tried to keep from him, about the friend, about the business—everything; he had only been pretending to be feeble. He finally shouts, "So now you know what existed outside yourself; up to now you knew only about yourself! You were a truly innocent child, but even more truly you were a fiendish person!—And therefore know this: I now condemn you to death by drowning!" (645).

This penultimate accusation is so precise. It is, at once, so accurate but also so unfair. The reader can feel the impact. We read Georg's reasoning through every conceivable interpretation of the possible damage his words could cause. He seems nearly incapacitated by his anxiety, his worry that he will hurt someone, by his fear that he has neglected his father. We have been through all of this with him in the first part of the story. He tries not to embarrass his father, but to honor him, by putting his head down and making the business a success. And every single one of these things is cast back to him by his father, the one person he strives to please, as cuts, as slights against his father's authority, against his mother's memory, against his friend's loyalty. But, we might be thinking, this is all wrong; Georg is just sensitive, a little neurotic, and very introverted. Yes, Georg was kind of "stuck in his own head," but he was only trying to do what he thought his father wanted. He was trying to be deferential and obedient. Georg was trying to rise to the familial and social expectations for an adult son in his situation.

All of this paralyzes Georg (just as it paralyzes us as readers)—all, that is, except the father's verdict, his sentence, or judgement: "I now condemn you to death by drowning" (645). And in the sprint to the end of the story, we see Georg unable to resist his father's condemnation. His father issues a command, but look at the specific way in which the end is narrated: "Georg *felt himself driven* from the room" (646, emphasis mine). He is being acted upon by some unstoppable compliance with the command. "He leapt past the gate and across the roadway, *impelled* to reach the water. Now he clutched the railing as a hungry man clutches food" (646, emphasis mine). We are given, in this narration, two opposite actions in the same man: something is pushing Georg to the river, even as he tries to stop it, to cling to life, but his hands grow weak, and he gives in, only softly calling, "Dear parents, I *did* always love you" (646, emphasis in original).

We are not surprised to learn that Kafka had a very tense, crippling relationship with his father, whom he was afraid of and intimidated by (Grunfeld 182). But beyond the biographical connection, what are we to make of this story? We see some obvious interpretive "rhyme" between "The Judgement" and "Mateo Falcone" in the tragic father-son relationship that each story depicts. But, whereas in Mérimée's story, we can see a string of mistakes in bratty young Fortunato's actions, which, even if we find the punishment excessive, makes it at least logically explicable, in Kafka's portrayal of this relation, there is no course of action that would have been "correct." Georg is simply existentially misfit to his father's expectations, and, maybe, to his society as a whole. There is nothing he really did wrong; in fact, he was more conscientious about the impacts of his behavior than anyone. And it was this, specifically, that seems to have been the flaw.

But even this existential "poor Georg was just not made for this world" interpretation does not cover all of the bases. Why does the father accuse Georg of base sexual fantasies? Why does he insult the fiancée, accusing her of being a "ninny" who "lifted her skirts"? What does that have to do with "profaning" his mother's memory (those items are all condensed into a couple of lines of the father's tirade)? Why can we not get a fix on who or how the father is? He is completely unpredictable. He demands nearly every kind of response from Georg, sympathy, pity, tenderness, perplexity, confusion—and above all, deference and obedience—but none is satisfactory. Georg, as Georg, cannot satisfy his father's unknown demands and shifting expectations.

It may help us to know that Kafka, as he wrote in one of his letters, "of course" had Freud in mind while he was writing "The Judgement" (qtd. in Friedlander 129). And he had his relationship with his own father in mind, too, which he seems to have made some sense of through Freud's psychoanalytic theories (Friedlander 130). Without getting into the weeds farther than we need to in order to make sense of the story, Freud's theory of the "Oedipus complex" may shed some light on the father-son dynamic in "The Judgement." The Oedipus complex describes a cluster of feelings that a child experiences—feelings of desire for the parent of the opposite sex and hostility for the parent of the same sex (Childers and Hentzi 213). In psychoanalytic theory (more generally), the relations among this triad of the father, the mother, and the child take on symbolic importance (beyond the more literal interpretation of Freud's own early theories regarding the idea). Symbolically, then, the father signifies unyielding authority and its demands (the abstract "paternal role"), while the mother signifies the "privileged possession" of the occupant of the "paternal role," which must be protected by the paternal authority (that is, the father); this leaves the child, who loves the mother and desires her love, to be subservient to the "law of the father," which the child can never adequately satisfy because the child can never symbolically "possess" the mother like the father does (Childers and Hentzi 198). I am not suggesting that any of this is (objectively) "true" or "not true"; I am only offering it as a potentially helpful way to interpret the relationships in the story (and perhaps readers are already beginning to make the connections to Georg's situation).

Georg's mother is dead; she is inaccessible—but is still the "special possession" of the father, whose memory he feels compelled to protect. The father also feels that Georg is threatening his paternal role: Georg is taking over the business, preparing to marry, learning mature ways of dealing with childhood friends. Symbolically, then, we might say, there is role confusion between Georg and the father (which we also see in the opposite direction in the father's somewhat infantile behavior surrounding the tantrum, during which he is literally jumping on the bed). The father seems to fear, too, that Georg is replacing the mother with the fiancé, so the father cheapens the relationship, depicting it as profane, coarse, and built only around sexual pleasure. So the father disallows Georg any pleasure, any sense of accomplishment, any sense of independence. He reasserts his authority within the confused coordinates of the triad of the symbolic Oedipal relation by condemning Georg both as an "innocent child" and as a "fiendish person"; the condemnation takes legal form, as if to point to its no longer just being "parental" but now more broadly authoritative, socially and symbolically: "I now condemn you to death by drowning" (645).

And Georg's split roles compete for dominance. Georg's own unspoken wish (from his burgeoning "paternal role") that his father "would only fall and smash himself" (so, essentially, that he would "learn his lesson" about throwing such a tantrum) ultimately comes true as the father collapses on the bed at the end of the story (644, 646). But Georg also appropriates the subservient, deferential role as well when, though part of him resists, he executes his father's final judgement upon him by throwing himself into the river to drown, as the climactic "lose-lose" scenario of "The Judgement" plays itself out.

Though psychoanalytic theories help describe the symbolic significance of this rupture in father-son relations, on a wider view, we are still in the territory Rousseau sets up in *The Social Contract*. Put in these terms, we see, essentially, the same rupture that Freud helps us perceive. In Rousseau's terms, Georg has risen to the age of independence; he has proven himself capable of being an independent equal of his father, and thereby should be "released from the obedience" he owes his father (Rousseau, *The Social* 322). He has reached the "years of discretion," so,

likewise, he should become "his own master" (322). Social-familial custom, however, disallows Georg's independence: its ideological rule is
that Georg must defer to the father's authority, even as he comes into
some degree of independence in adulthood. So he is locked in arrested
development: Georg is unable to grow up, and he is unable to remain
completely dependent; he cannot take over the "paternal role," but he
cannot remain a child. Georg is precluded from beginning his own family with the fiancé, but the father's family (to which Georg belongs) is
being ripped apart. In short, Georg cannot join "society" because his
obligations to family prevent the independence necessary for doing so.
The story demonstrates the power of the family, this "most ancient of all
societies," over against one's ability to mature into "the social" as such
(Rousseau, *The Social* 322). The outcome is that the "rule of the father"
takes on new significance. For Rousseau, the transition from the family
to society entails a shift from rule based on love (in the family) to rule
based on the "pleasure of commanding" (in the state) (*The Social* 322).
In "The Judgement," the father's rule combines these two: he claims to
love Georg, but he also clearly loves commanding him: he speaks in two
contradictory voices; he issues contradictory judgements and interpretations. And, to Georg, his father's authority is total because the father
combines both the familial and the social in one paternal role, and
Georg is ill fit to satisfy the requirements of either.

"The evil consequences of pernicious neglect":
"Nobody's Story" (1853) by Charles Dickens
and "The Happy Prince" (1888) by Oscar Wilde

Oscar Wilde once remarked on Charles Dickens' peculiar tendency toward sentimentality that "one must have a heart of stone" to
read about the death of a Dickens character "without laughing" (qtd.
in Henderson and Sharpe 1396). However, one might observe a similar
sort of sentimentality in a story like Wilde's own "The Happy Prince" or
"The Selfish Giant." Both "Nobody's Story" by Dickens and "The Happy
Prince" by Wilde combine an almost saccharine sentimentality regarding poor and working people with a trenchant critique of the failures
of the social imagination that causes their alienation. The combination of these strategies is interesting because, in order for the fiction to
achieve its "message" (and both of these stories do certainly have such
a message—indeed, almost a "moral"), such a combination is almost

necessary. The stories evoke mental cartoons for the reader in which the innocent, or naïve, and the uncaring, or exploitative, are drawn in absolute, indelible lines. It is as if the necessity of articulating the message requires such clear delineation of the one from the other in order to ensure crisp clarity in communication of the moral theme. These stories do not obfuscate their social meaning, the way we might feel Mérimée and Kafka do, with stories that move from a slow simmer to a violent boil, leaving the reader to try to parse where exactly and how and when the first bubbles appeared. Dickens and Wilde develop stories that seem eager to be understood, eager to go straight to the heart of the reader, eager to change us.

Let's start with Wilde's "The Happy Prince," since its message is more universally applicable, and, then, we will move, within the moral universe "The Happy Prince" establishes, to Dickens' much more specific "Nobody's Story." The first brief paragraph of "The Happy Prince" just provides a picture of the statue of the prince. He stands high above the city on a column: "He was gilded all over with thin leaves of fine gold, for eyes he had two bright sapphires, and a large red ruby glowed on his sword-hilt" (291). The narrator gives us a direct picture, the only context being the city below—just a picture. The next several lines interpret the significance of the statue of the prince from a variety of perspectives. A town councilor, "who wished to gain a reputation for having artistic tastes," compares the beauty of the statue to a weathercock (which tells us something about his artistic sensibilities), hedging that comparison by saying that the statue is "not quite so useful" in order to give the impression that he is not an aesthete (291). A mother asks her crying child, "Why can't you be like the Happy Prince?" He "never dreams of crying for anything" (291). A depressive man gazing at the statue remarks, "I'm glad there is some one in the world who is quite happy" (291). The orphaned "Charity Children" say the prince looks like an angel because they have seen angels in their dreams, only to be corrected by the "Mathematical Master," who "did not approve of children dreaming" (291). We do not recognize the importance of these lines yet, but eventually we will see that each interpretation among the people of the city is wrong, except for the children's. So the story's sentimental logic begins to come through right at the beginning: only the lowliest children, the ones who trust their dream-visions, truly see things as they are. The adults see only what they want, what they lack.

The narration then shifts its attention to the little Swallow, who has been left behind by his friends. The rest of the birds have migrated to

103

Egypt, but the Swallow stayed behind, "for he was in love with the most beautiful Reed" (291). We are told of the complications of this love affair. All summer long, the Swallow had courted the Reed, and she bowed to him when he flew around her, but she never spoke to him, and she flirted with the wind and was unwilling to travel, so the Swallow decides to break things off with her and join his friends in Egypt (292). Before leaving, though, he spends the night at the feet of the Happy Prince.

We should pause here and ascertain the function of this tangent. First, it is fun; Wilde very cleverly and cutely describes the interactions between the Swallow and the Reed, and it is enjoyable to see that the Reed is just a reed, and the Swallow is just a bird—the narration does not go much beyond these details in describing their interaction—but it does frame their courtship, using their particularities to demonstrate why things just would not work out between them. Within developing this relationship, though, Wilde is able to do two other things that drive the story: he is able to show us the *kind* of story we are in for (one where birds fall in love with reeds, but also one where birds are birds and reeds are reeds), a story where anything is possible, but one in which things retain their natural identities, at least to some degree; he is also able to show that the Swallow is a lover, that he loves deeply, but is also uncompromising—he is stubborn. But the Swallow will change.

During the first night at the feet of the Happy Prince, the Swallow notices that the Prince is crying (which demonstrates the error of the "sensible mother" from the beginning of the story). The Swallow feels pity for the Happy Prince (and does not even remark that the statue is alive—after all, he had just broken off a serious relationship with a reed). The Happy Prince is not, in fact, happy; he relates his story to the Swallow: his life (as a real person) had been pleasurable and easy, but now he doubts whether happiness consists in pleasure, for, now, "I can see all the ugliness and all the misery of my city, and though my heart is made of lead yet I cannot choose but weep" (293). And then begins the repetitious cycle at the heart of the story. The Happy Prince can see, all through the city, good, simple people in need of help, a poor seamstress and her sick son, a playwright who is too cold and hungry to write, a "little match-girl" who will be beaten if she does not bring home some money (294–296). The Happy Prince enlists the Swallow's help in taking the jewels from his eyes and sword-hilt and delivering them to the needy, pleading each time, "Swallow, Swallow, little Swallow," "will you not stay with me for one night, and be my messenger?" (there is slight variation, but the refrain stands out clearly; it is repeated three times) (293, 295, 296). Each time, the Swallow puts off his migration to Egypt and stays to help the Happy Prince serve the poor and miserable throughout his city.

Finally, it becomes too late for the Swallow to go, and, now, due to his sacrifices, the Happy Prince is blind, and the little Swallow has come to love the Happy Prince and wants to stay with him and help him by giving him company. He tells the Happy Prince of his travels, but the Happy Prince refocuses the Swallow's attention: "you tell me of marvelous things, but more marvelous than anything is the suffering of men and women. There is no Mystery so great as Misery. Fly over my city, little Swallow, and tell me what you see there" (297). The Swallow finds starving children all over the city, and the Happy Prince has the Swallow peel the golden skin from him to give to the children. When all the work is done, and there is no more to give, the little Swallow confesses his love for the Happy Prince, kisses him, and dies at his feet. The Happy Prince is deemed no longer fit to be a monument in the city. The mayor and city officials have the statue removed and melted down in order for a statue of the mayor himself to be erected in its place. An art professor concludes, "As he [the Happy Prince] is no longer beautiful he is no longer useful" (298). The Happy Prince's broken lead heart will not melt, so it is thrown on the dust heap next to the dead Swallow (299). Then God appears in the story, asking the angels to bring him "the most precious things in the city" (299). Unsurprisingly, the angels bring the dead Swallow and the broken lead heart of the Happy Prince. God concludes the story by confirming the selection; he says, "in my Garden of Paradise this little bird shall sing for evermore, and in my city of gold the Happy Prince shall praise me" (299).

See? Very sentimental. As with Wilde's other story, "The Selfish Giant," though, God seems to come out of nowhere at the end, unless we backtrack a little in light of the ending. Those three refrains from the Happy Prince to the little Swallow ring out; they are familiar. Do they not have a "biblical" resonance? Again, as we saw in "The Selfish Giant," Wilde, here, seems to be condensing two moments from the gospels. First, Jesus' words to the disciples in Gethsemane: "What, could ye not watch with me one hour?" (Matthew 26:40). He asks them to watch and pray with him three times, each time returning to find them asleep. The second is in the Gospel of John, 21:15–19, when Jesus asks Peter three times if he loves him. Each time Peter replies that he does, and Jesus responds: "Feed my sheep." Wilde gives us a mythic coalescence of these moments, where the Happy Prince takes the place of Jesus, and the little

Swallow is his disciple, "my messenger" (the Happy Prince calls him). Why?

Both biblical passages demonstrate humans' weaknesses, their characteristic lack of understanding. But both are punctuated with suffering: the Gethsemane story culminates in Judas' betrayal of Jesus (with a kiss, which Wilde inverts in "The Happy Prince," redeeming the gesture), the scattering of the disciples, and the move toward the crucifixion; the "feed my sheep" moment with Peter culminates in Jesus' prophecy that, though Peter did as he pleased when he was young, when he is old, he will be crucified. There is a dovetailing of these moments in the Wilde story. The Swallow resists; he gets cold; he wants to leave—but he stays and serves the Happy Prince. "The spirit is willing, but the flesh is weak," Jesus says of the disciples in Gethsemane (Matthew 26:41). The same can be said of the little Swallow in Wilde's myth. And like Peter, the little Swallow does not realize what he is signing up for when he agrees to be the Happy Prince's messenger, but the Prince's refrain cues us that the Swallow's service will kill him—that in serving the Prince, he is no longer free: he is a servant of love, and this love requires sacrifice.

Wilde's mythic tale focuses the reader on sacrificial love—but also on the nobility of dedication to a lover. The little Swallow loves deeply. He loved the Reed, but he was unwilling to sacrifice for her. Then why is he willing to die for the Happy Prince? Is it because his love for the Happy Prince is deeper? Yes. But it is deeper because the Swallow's love for and service to the Prince is redirected by the Prince to the needy. After the first good deed, the Swallow remarks curiously that, though it is cold, he now feels quite warm (294). The Prince tells him, "That is because you have done a good action" (the little disciple then falls asleep). Wilde's mythic moral universe aims the reader's attention on the inner transformation needed to help those in trouble. It is a social vision, but one focused on the helpers. The moral theme seems to be that simple love of goodness is enough to transform us into "the most precious things," even if only God will recognize it, even if the powerful in this world go on serving only themselves (299).

Dickens' "Nobody's Story" occupies a similar moral universe to Wilde's, one in which the rich and powerful care mostly for themselves, while the poor workers spend their lives scraping together just enough to eat: it is a "moral universe" that favors the workers—that wants to bend the readers' attention toward their plight in order to demonstrate the social condition of these people, as well as to show its causes and consequences. As much as Dickens does appear to be working in the vein of allegory, with, more or less, the entire working class represented in "Nobody" and his family (a name not ascribed to the protagonist until the story is nearly over) and the rich and powerful represented in the "Bigwig family," his depiction of the interaction of these classes is anything but simple, as we see, especially, once the pestilence is ravaging the city.

But the beginning of the story is a little mystifying to the first-time reader. The unnamed (at the beginning, anyway) protagonist ("He") lives on the riverbank, as the first sentence tells us, but then it goes on and on about the river:

> He lived on the bank of a mighty river, broad and deep, which was always silently rolling on to a vast undiscovered ocean. It had rolled on, ever since the world began. It had changed its course sometimes, and turned into new channels, leaving its old ways dry and barren; but it had ever been upon the flow, and ever was to flow until Time should be no more. Against its strong unfathomable stream, nothing made head. No living creature, no flower, no leaf, no particle of animate or inanimate existence ever strayed back from the undiscovered ocean. The tide of the river set resistlessly towards it; and the tide never stopped, any more than the earth stops in its circling round the sun [111].

All of this seems a little gratuitous, at least until we are somewhere around the middle of the story. What is hiding in this description of the river? Time, perhaps. Moving water often seems connected to the flow of time, the idea that "flow" itself, movement, is the controlling image or concept in play. The other thing that may jump out to us is that the river, which is familiar (the man lives on its banks), which is "a known," flows into a "vast undiscovered ocean." The "he," here, and everyone else around him knows nothing of this ocean beyond their immediate experience. And the narration, specifically, relates this ocean to world-time: "It had rolled on since the world began." It is unknown, but also unstoppable, impenetrable—it is universal: the flow of the river—of everything—moves toward it. It is as natural as the earth circling the sun. This is an eerie description. The biggest influence in nature, the most common aspect of human experience, this outer ocean (and perhaps with it, symbolically, the universal ocean of time toward which every moment and hour flows) is completely unknown (perhaps reminiscent of the relation between the noumenal and the phenomenal, discussed earlier). This is the structure of Nature beyond the small world of the story, the small social world to which the story turns in the second paragraph.

Dickens' little cartoon of the place is clear enough: we understand that the "he" from the beginning, whom we will eventually learn is Nobody, is a worker (some variation of the words "work" and "labour" is mentioned four times in the second paragraph's four sentences), and we understand that, to the narrator, within the moral logic of the story, working gives the man and his family dignity. But the Bigwig Family is another matter. They clamor into the story in a brash, confusing interruption:

> There was over-much drumming, trumpeting, and speechmaking, in the neighborhood where he dwelt; but he had nothing to do with that. Such clash and uproar came from the Bigwig family, at the unaccountable proceedings of which race, he marveled much. They set up the strangest statues, in iron, marble, bronze, and brass, before his door; and darkened his house with the legs and tails of uncouth images of horses. He wondered what it all meant, smiled in a rough good-humoured way he had, and kept at his hard work [111].

We see that the Bigwig family is associated with spectacle, noise, speeches, statues, horses—but just what or who they are, we still do not know. Dickens places us within the same confusion that Nobody feels about the Bigwig family.

The picture of the Bigwigs comes into clearer focus in the next several paragraphs. This stately bunch saves the workers the trouble of thinking for themselves and managing their own affairs. The Bigwigs run things, and they expect workers like Nobody to "fall down and worship" the immensity and grandeur of spectacle they create (112). But Nobody does not quite understand it all. The Bigwigs clarify the meaning: it means "honor and glory in the highest, to the highest merit," and those, of course, who merit all that honor and glory, are the Bigwigs themselves. But who are they? What makes them so special?

Dickens gives us a hint. The Bigwigs, for all of their statues and images of themselves (much like the mayor in "The Happy Prince"), were not the meritorious men "whose knowledge had rescued him and his [Nobody's] children from disfiguring disease, whose boldness had raised his forefathers from the condition of serfs.... Whereas, he did find others whom he knew no good of, and even others whom he knew much ill of" (112). The Bigwigs have "family quarrels" regarding how the working man's children should be educated, but they never actually get around to educating them (112–113). They only spend their time "roaring and raving," "pulpiting and petitioning," "maundering and memorializing"—in short, grandstanding and trying to out-do one another—that they never actually improve the lives of the Nobodies (113). The Bigwigs just keep taking the Nobodies' money and demanding their deference and servitude, while the Nobodies keep working, their bodies breaking down, their imaginations deteriorating, their morality waning, as they sink continually further down in the squalor they live in, as their minds are wasted on unwholesome amusements in lieu of education (112–113).

So, in our allegory, if the Nobodies are the working class, who are the Bigwigs? They are the capitalists, the bourgeoisie. The social commentary, up to this point, is not so far from Dickens' contemporary Karl Marx's critique of the social and political influence of the bourgeoisie in *The Communist Manifesto* (first published in English in 1850, just three years before the publication of "Nobody's Story"): Marx and Engels write,

> We see, therefore, how the modern bourgeoisie is itself the product of a long course of development, of a series of revolutions in the modes of production and exchange. Each step in the development of the bourgeoisie was accompanied by a corresponding political advance of that class. [...] [T]he bourgeoisie has at least, since the establishment of Modern Industry and of the world-market, conquered for itself, in the modern representative State, exclusive political sway. The executive of the modern State is but a committee for managing the common affairs of the whole bourgeoisie [15–16].

The capitalists have achieved, through their revolution in "production and exchange," "exclusive political sway"; therefore, the state is itself the managing committee for the exclusive interests of the capitalist class. In other words, because they have overtaken the state economies and wield the power of capital in the state, they are now able to wield the political power in the state as well—and they do so as suits them best. The workers, in this scenario, become "a commodity" (20). As industrialism increases, work conditions decrease, and as the "repulsiveness of the work increases, the wage decreases," pushing the workers further and further down into poverty (21). The proletarian (working class) "is without property; his relation to his wife and children has no longer anything in common with the bourgeois family-relations": there is no longer even social common ground between the two classes (24–25). The working class, "instead of rising with the progress of industry, sinks deeper and deeper below the conditions of existence," of basic survival (25–26). The capitalist class is "unfit to rule because it is incompetent to assure an existence of the slave within his slavery, because it cannot help letting him sink into such a state" (26). This almost reads like a commentary on "Nobody's Story" or, perhaps, like a revision of Rousseau's *Origin of Inequality* updated for the Industrial Age.

The *Communist Manifesto* is, in many ways, more biting, but the picture is almost the same: the workers have been exploited; they have been pushed through lower and lower wages into poorer and poorer conditions; in the absence of fair wages, even social aid for their well-being and education has been passed off or delayed or deemed unnecessary. The result? The Nobodies are withering, just waiting to be picked off by starvation or disease.

Marx and Engels' answer is revolution: the working class is the vast majority; if they rise up, "the whole superincumbent strata of official society" will be "sprung into the air" (25). "What the bourgeoisie produces, above all, is its own grave-diggers. Its fall and the victory of the proletariat are equally inevitable" (26). But, where Marx and Engels attempt to stoke feelings of indignation, grievance, and injustice toward provoking the workers' revolutionary consciousness, Dickens appeals, instead, to the social conscience of the bourgeoisie. His depiction of the social situation in the second half of the story employs two methods: one is sheer pathos; the other is good old capitalist self-interest.

On one hand, pathos: The Nobodies suffer. Mr. Nobody watches his children misspend their youth and their intellects; their minds, bodies, and consciences are all stunted by work, boredom, and lack of education. When the pestilence strikes, it appears first among the workers (114). People get sick and die, and their "tainted houses" are so small that the dying and dead lie among the living until disease decimates the working class (114). There is simply nowhere else to go, nowhere to escape it. The bourgeois missionaries come and offer their prayers and salvation, but the Nobodies are not interested: "give me my first glimpse of Heaven, through a little of its light and air; give me pure water; help me to be clean; lighten this heavy atmosphere and heavy life, in which our spirits sink...." (114). The indication, here, is this: if your God really wants what is best for us, how about something as simple as good air to breathe and pure water to drink—a world not filled with disease? After all, he concludes, Jesus' "thoughts were so much with the poor," so why will you, his servants, not help us? (114) And when the disease spreads from the workers, the workers themselves are blamed: "The calamity began among you. If you had but lived more healthily and decently, I should not be the widowed and bereft mourner that I am this day," says Nobody's Master (114–115).

And this demonstrates the move into self-interest. Dickens

uncovers the hypocrisy at the root of this sentiment among the ruling classes—the Masters and the Bigwigs. And he does so, using Nobody as his mouthpiece, giving what almost amounts to a social sermon in the final paragraphs of the story. "[M]ost calamities will come from us, as this one did," and "none will stop at our poor doors, until we are united with that great squabbling family yonder," the Bigwigs (115). He goes on:

> We cannot live healthily and decently, unless they who undertook to man-
> age us provide the means. We cannot be instructed unless they will teach
> us.... The evil consequences of imperfect instruction, the evil consequences
> of pernicious neglect, the evil consequences of unnatural restraint and the
> denial of humanizing enjoyments, will all come from us, and none of them
> will stop with us. They will spread far and wide. They always do; they always
> have done—just like the pestilence [115].

The message is something like this: if you want to maintain this capitalist system, which largely benefits you, then you need to perform your role competently by taking better care of us because this is what will keep happening if you do not: the bad stuff starts with us because we are worst off, but it always spreads, and it always will. The good life does not necessarily trickle down, but, just as assuredly as the river that Nobody lives on flows into the immense ocean beyond, the bad will rush resistlessly from the poor to the broad sea of humanity. Even if you do not want to admit it, we are bound together, and because you have good lives at our expense, you have a social—and a human—responsibility to keep us from sinking so low that we become a danger to you, both for your own well-being, and for our survival.

"I must not only punish, but punish with impunity": *"The Cask of Amontillado" (1846)* *by Edgar Allan Poe*

The drama and conflict at the heart of Edgar Allan Poe's "The Cask of Amontillado" revolves around the failure of society in a relation between two of its members, Fortunato and Montresor. Curiously, the wider forces of social order are absent. In "The Tell-Tale Heart" such officials (representatives of society), the policemen, come in near the end of the story, but the narrator of "The Cask of Amontillado" does not even mention such outside influences. Plus, the story unfolds during "the madness of the carnival season" (88), a season traditionally associated with the loosening of the tethers of social order and caste, which permits a kind of jubilant social chaos to reign for the duration of the feast, during which folk traditions and the "popular sphere" take charge (Bakhtin 7–9). This social backdrop causes Montresor's seriousness to stand out considerably from the madness around him (of which, perhaps, Fortunato is typical). Montresor takes advantage of the laxity in social order to execute his personal vendetta against his enemy, apparently unable or unwilling to depend on the social institutions to do anything on his behalf.

We understand that Montresor seeks vengeance on Fortunato—that much is abundantly clear—but we are thrown into the conclusion of this process. Whatever happened between the two men, whatever initiated the response Montresor narrates, is left rather vague. So the story is propelled forward by an odd combination of this vagueness regarding the protagonist's motivations and an absolute clarity regarding what he does about it, and even the calculating logic according to which he executes his plan. "The Cask of Amontillado" is a weird story—perhaps not so weird for Poe—but because of Montresor's preoccupation with this underlying logic of his acts, an aspect that many first-time readers miss, or from which they may be distracted by the gothic atmospherics and the strange methodology for the murder itself. But to understand this, we need to read the first paragraph very closely and unpack exactly what it is that Montresor is saying.

> The thousand injuries of Fortunato I had borne as best I could; but when he ventured upon insult, I vowed revenge. You, who so well know the nature of my soul, will not suppose, however, that I gave utterance to a threat [88].

Okay, we can pause here. The first sentence is interesting because it is at least somewhat self-contradictory. Montresor (our narrator) talks about all of the "injuries" he has suffered from Fortunato, but when it comes to the most serious, most heartless, most inhumane of these injuries—an "almost insult"—he decides he must be avenged. Normally, we would think of an insult, or in this case something apparently very close to an insult, as probably a rather minor injury, which must make the other "thousand injuries" even less significant than that.

What else does this tell us? Why is it significant? This is important because Montresor is disclosing information about himself. And that is important because, unlike what the second sentence says, we *do not* "so well know the nature of [his] soul," but learning that he is very touchy about small things can be useful to us because we, as readers, are indeed people who would like to learn something about what makes this man tick. But we do, later, see the sort of person that Fortunato is, and he seems considerably less reserved than Montresor. Fortunato seems like the sort of person who gets drunk at parties and "runs his mouth" (as it were); he insults Luchesi at nearly every mention of this absent character's name. So maybe we have the perfect scenario for things to go wrong: Fortunato, a man who drinks too much, talks too much, freely throws insults around, a "blow-hard," who crosses another man, Montresor, who is incapable of taking a joke, who takes things much too personally, who takes himself much too seriously.

In the rest of the second sentence, where Montresor introduces us to the confessional quality of the story (we are getting an intimate rendition of his side of the narrative), he is confiding in us as if we were a close friend. But this second sentence also introduces another contradiction: he is pulling us in close in order to tell us a secret, but the first bit of this secret that he tells us is that he is a hard guy to read—that he is not the sort of guy who "gives utterance" to the threats that he harbors toward his most hated enemy. He pulls us in only to push us away, but not without disclosing something essential.

Why is this remarkable? This is significant because this tells us that this man, Montresor, is going to continue to be hard to read, that behind or underneath his words and gestures in the rest of the story that follows, there is a second impulse, a second layer of meaning—there is duplicity. This knowledge gives us a key to many of the bits of humor in the story: the way in which he panders to and pleads with Fortunato, which Fortunato takes as earnest, but which we know has this double-intent; the joke about being a mason, which Fortunato finds confusing, but which, by the end of the story, we understand as also having a double meaning; the mocking way Montresor mimics Fortunato's words; and so on. Montresor's "duplicity" (literally and figuratively) feeds meaning throughout the whole story, and he is letting us in on this fact in these important first lines.

Montresor continues, in the following sentences, by disclosing his intentions concerning his revenge on Fortunato, but at the same time, keeping these intentions private (another contradiction!).

At length I would be avenged; this was a point definitively settled—but the very definitiveness with which it was resolved, precluded the idea of risk. I must not only punish, but punish with impunity. A wrong is unredressed when retribution overtakes its redresser. It is equally unredressed when the avenger fails to make himself felt as such to him who has done the wrong [88].

This is probably the weirdest, most difficult part of the story, but without understanding it, the rest of the story is just a pulpy crime narrative. Why is Montresor telling us this stuff? He wants us to understand in these lines, not why he takes revenge (he has already hinted at that; we already examined that a moment ago), but *how* he must take revenge. His vengeance must be long and drawn out; he must wait for it. Why? Yes, for the opportune moment, but also because this vengeance *needed to happen*. It had to be enacted because it was deserved. "Impunity" means "exemption from punishment or freedom from the injurious consequences of an action." He must punish Fortunato in such a way that he will be exempt from any consequences: his plan must be perfect, so his actions must be definite—because if Montresor is caught and punished himself, the validity of his vengeance would be undercut (and this is important to him—which we know because the rest of the paragraph focuses on other variations of this idea). So there is some outside, objective standard for establishing whether or not his punishment is effectual.

Taking time to plan his revenge also gives Montresor time to calm down. He must be calm and execute his vengeance coolly because, as he says, "a wrong is unredressed when retribution overtakes its redresser," that is, when someone gets caught up in the strong feelings that usually accompany revenge, then said revenge is not effectually executed. This is, then, another requirement of this standard for judging whether or not vengeance is effectual. The logic here goes like this: if something is *actually* wrong, then it is *objectively* wrong, so "payback" (vengeance) must be dealt as objectively as possible. Offenses, he thinks, are not just wrong because they hurt someone or because they are against moral or legal codes; they are *objectively* wrong too—therefore, "payback" for such offenses must also be issued according to the same sense of objectivity, moral and legal codes be damned.

Readers will not be surprised to discover another set of contradictions here. Think about it. Montresor feels hurt by an insult (or a near-insult), but he objectifies this hurt, perceiving it as not just a "personal injustice" but an "objective injustice," so, in order to set it aright, his vengeance must be both *personal* (in that he is the one who enacts it) and *objective* (in that he must enact it without feeling anything but the logical settling of a discrepancy—*as if it were not* personal). Any effectual vengeance must check both boxes, which seems impossible.

But, as he says in the final sentence of the first paragraph, his vengeance will only be successful if he conveys this sense of objective logic *and* the sense of a response to personal affront. This means that, in order for the vengeance to really take effect—to actually be justice—it is Montresor alone who can carry it out, but he must enact it *as if* he is only executing an objective law.

Okay, okay, I know. Readers may be asking, "Why is this guy going on and on about this first paragraph? It's the most boring, least interesting part of the story." It may be the most boring part (that depends on you, dear reader), but it is the *most* interesting: this weird logical/moral paradox controls everything else in the story. Without this rationale, the story would just be telling an oddly creative murder tale. This rationale affects everything: the protagonist's behavior, his strange calm, his interactions, even the method of the murder itself. More than all of these, though, this rationale allows Montresor to see his act of murder within the coordinates of morality and law—not as an immoral and unlawful murder, but as moral because it is both personally and objectively just and lawful according to the highest of all possible laws: objective, rational, divine(?) justice.

Two final thoughts to drive this point home. This logical, moral rationale is how we can make sense of the moment near the end when Fortunato pleads, "For the love of God, Montresor!" (93). Fortunato is pleading for mercy, as in "If you love God, spare me for God's sake, if not for my own!" Montresor, invoking his characteristic duplicity, repeats the same words, "'Yes,' I said, 'for the love of God!'", the meaning, here, being something like, "Indeed, I must carry out this deed for the love of God, the guarantor of objective, rational moral justice." Then, at the very end, Montresor, after walling up the recess in the catacombs and throwing the torch within, says, "There came forth in return only a jingling of the bells. My heart grew sick—on account of the dampness of the catacombs" (94). Here, we see Montresor in one of two ways. Interpretation (1): he is just clarifying that he never broke with his sense of logical objectivity. But on this interpretation, we might question his word choice. Is "heartsickness" even in the top five word choices to describe the effect of dampness on someone? I would suggest that it is not ("My lungs grew heavy"; "I found it difficult to breathe"; "My throat closed up"; "My sinuses filled with mucus"; "I started coughing violently." Any of those would be much more natural, and probably more accurate, ways to describe the physical impact of prolonged exposure to dampness). Heartsickness is gloominess, mournfulness, grief: it is deeper and more emotional than something dampness would cause. I would suggest a second interpretation; let's call it "Interpretation (2)":

115

that what we are seeing here is Montresor breaking out of his objective role as logical punisher; he is feeling something like sympathy for this man who was, after all, his friend. But then he covers for it, steering us away from this conclusion ("um, er, no, I mean, on account of the dampness"). Poe has already primed us to see Montresor's double-meanings, his duplicity. I think this moment is just one the protagonist is trying to conceal, but Poe, of course, wants us to see it, which is why he spent so much time preparing us for this crack in Montresor's emotional armor (which compromises or undercuts his controlling logic).

Poe places Montresor in a curious position. He feels injured to the point that he is willing to take Fortunato's life, yet we must imagine that, were the legal sphere brought in to mediate justice between them, the outcome would be different. Montresor, instead of depending on the legal institutions of society to punish on his behalf, however, not only takes justice into his own hands, but, in order to justify doing so, he also invents a logic which undercuts and outstrips the social order altogether. According to Montresor's reasoning, which we examined in the beginning of the story, the justice must be both completely objective and completely subjective *at the same time*, demands which excise the legal sphere entirely.

Rousseau writes in *The Social Contract* that "all justice comes from God, who is its sole source; but if we knew how to receive so high an inspiration, we should need neither government nor laws" (344). We do have access to the justice of "natural law," the "universal justice emanating from reason alone," but these laws are not meant to function in societies and are "ineffective among men" (344). People need their own "conventions and laws" in order to maintain justice in society (344). Such laws are decrees from "the whole people" for "the whole people": these laws therefore derive from the authority of "the people" and extend to "the people," and even if they do give privileges to some and not others and set up classes that are "above" other classes, the laws cannot identify specific individuals with any such privilege or class identity: the law does not carry over to specific individuals (345). It works the other way around: each specific individual is subject to the laws which pertain to how "the individual" fits into society. According to the law, then, there are individuals in the abstract, but the law decrees nothing about specific individuals per se (345). Such a view of the role and rule of law in a society, then, excludes personal vendettas altogether. The whole point of the legal sphere of society is to prevent such "personal" execution of the law; the point is to remove private feeling and

116

judgement from the adjudication of the law, which is left to the society itself. Even if the story may be set in the Renaissance era or something, the same holds: Fortunato and Montresor both seem to be noblemen, so from the same class; Montresor really has no *legal* recourse against Fortunato.

What we may see here, then, is Montresor's way of requiring the specific execution of justice that only he can visit on Fortunato by defaulting to the "law of nature"—to the justice, which derives from God and is accessible to men through reason, effectively sidestepping the conventional laws of the social sphere altogether (Rousseau, *The Social* 344). Montresor is restoring his own "natural" right to punish. Further, Rousseau writes that, "in order to discover the rules of society best suited to nations, a superior intelligence beholding all the passions of men without experiencing any of them would be needed," an intelligence which "would have to be unrelated to our nature, while knowing it through and through; its happiness would have to be independent of us, and yet ready to occupy itself with ours" (347). Such an intelligence would have to be satisfied with justice done for the sake of an objective, "distant glory" (347). Rousseau concludes that "it would take gods to give men laws" (347). Does this description not, almost too precisely, spell out the logic Montresor devises for his own execution of justice? Montresor holds himself above, not just Fortunato, but civil law and custom generally. He seems both to restore his own private right to punish under the "law of nature" and places himself in an objective godlike position. Accordingly, he becomes uniquely able to satisfy the personal affront (personal vendetta) *and* the objective wrong (act against divine justice), thus permitting (requiring!) himself to satiate his own need for Fortunato's blood and whatever "divine justice" requires—all at the same time. Montresor finds his opportunity to punish Fortunato during a lapse in the social order during the carnival season, just as he makes a conceptual opportunity for himself by ripping a hole in the ubiquity of civil society by weaponizing reason/logic to restore his "natural" rights, satisfy his damaged pride, and correct what he perceives to be an imbalance in the scales of divine, objective justice.

Conclusions

The stories examined in this chapter do, indeed, demonstrate that social contact requires a social contract of one kind or another to address the pernicious effects of social organization. Mérimée's "Mateo Falcone" and Kafka's "The Judgement" problematize the family as a social institution, according to the background of its significance, as outlined with Rousseau's ideas from *The Social Contract*. Mérimée's story demonstrates how fundamental the order established in the family is to the broader social, cultural, and religious laws that revolve around it, even when that "universe" of society conflicts with other such "universes" (as the story demonstrates in the collision of the "social universes" of the *maquis* and the city). Kafka's story exposes a different set of fractures in the ancient society of the family as it relates to the wider social sphere. Here, a young man is not permitted to mature into a social agent. Whether through culture or through paternal authority or both, the primordial social weight of the family disallows the protagonist's development, and, instead, it requires his deference and submission, even as an adult, to his father's demands, which become more and more contradictory, as the father, too, is forced into conflicting roles of authority, both social and familial, neither of which suits his relation to the son any longer. The story portrays the conflict and coalescence of the family and society and its ruinous effects on both father and son.

Dickens' "Nobody's Story" and Wilde's "The Happy Prince" cast a broader view of social responsibility. Both stories rely upon depictions of the suffering exploited classes of society; the authors use fiction to stir the emotions of readers toward sympathy with the poor and working people. Wilde steers readers of his fantasy parable toward social action as a religious duty to sacrifice; Wilde reframes social ethics as holiness and reconceives the imitation of Christ as an ideal of social responsibility. Dickens hits harder and aims specifically for bourgeois readers. "Nobody's Story" uses religious ideology to some degree, but its broader message is social responsibility for its own sake: both because the human dignity of the working classes and the poor demands that they be treated better and because whatever blights the poor will, in one way or another, affect the bourgeoisie as well, the message being that, in a society, no one class exclusively suffers. These stories, in one way or another, acknowledge the pessimistic view of society that Rousseau writes about in *The Origin of Inequality*: that, from the beginning of social combination (social contact), things have been going wrong, and that, even the initial social contract, according to which the rich established their primacy over the rest of the people through social institutions, is part of the ratification of inequality, injustice, and exploitation.

But these stories at least attempt solutions or at least treatments for the social sickness their authors perceive.

Poe's "The Cask of Amontillado" depicts an attempt to get around the strictures of social institutions altogether. Its protagonist employs reason, rhetoric, and cleverness as he seizes his opportunity to evade the social in order to satisfy the vengeance to which he feels entitled but which society would deny him. Montresor finds a way to undo the tethers of society as he aligns his own selfish desires with a novel conception of objective, or divine, justice. For Montresor, the social can be evaded by moving within one's own mind, by reimagining the world from within and then extending it back out to the world around. And it is here, the mind, to which we turn in Chapter Five.

CHAPTER FIVE

The Life of the Mind

"So it is with minds. Unless you keep them busy with
some definite subject that will bridle and control them,
they throw themselves in disorder hither and yon in the
vague field of imagination.... And there is no mad or
idle fancy that they do not bring forth in the agitation."
—Michel de Montaigne

Introduction

The phrase "the life of the mind" has long been associated with
philosophy, literature, and the arts—so much so that it has, perhaps,
taken on some stuffy, academic connotations, associations with eggheads looking down, probably with disdain, from their "ivory towers"
upon the seething mass of humanity. But the phrase itself, for our purposes, is just a way to point to the complexity, difficulty, and importance of the mind—not as way to encode those occupations which
have something to do with critical thinking (the jobs of "eggheads,"
the location of "ivory tower," etc.), but as a phrase that captures the
place or the means through which all human life (or most at least) is
lived.

Plato's famous words from "The Apology" that "the unexamined
life is not worth living" may or may not be true, but what *is* true is that
even the most conscious or intelligent among us have dark corners of
our minds, those aspects of ourselves, of our lives, that go largely unexamined (Plato, "Apology" 41). And, if we are to believe, even a little, in
the theories of psychoanalysis, it is these unexamined, unacknowledged
aspects of ourselves that return to us as symptoms or difficulties (anxiety, depression, delusion, etc.)—as if the mind will, one way or another,
get its due—that those things we are unwilling or unable to acknowledge and examine creep back to the surface in neuroses and pathologies,

120

almost as if they are crying out for attention because they have been left in the dark too long (Myers 20; Homer 3).

We can see this sort of "return of the repressed" in Ottessa Moshfegh's novel *Death in Her Hands.* The novel is, essentially, a character monologue, half revolving around a mysterious letter about a murder that Vesta (the protagonist) finds in the woods near her cabin, and the other half around the construction of her own identity: her reflection on her past, her marriage to Walter, her fading beauty, her regrets, her unlived life, her untapped potential. But readers get the feeling that she is sliding from reality to past traumas to delusions without being able to distinguish one from the next. There are moments when the mere mention of a possibility, a passing thought, or a remembered criticism or worry, emerges as a reality in the present that was not there a moment ago, as if she dreams new realities into existence through the sheer force of her imagination or of her delusions—or through the unconscious workings of her mind, as her heretofore unexamined life is finally resurfacing after all of the years of repression, anxiety, and nervous spinning. Vesta is at the mercy of her mind's unruly and delusional logic, its selective memory, but also its need to make order out of the chaos of her experiences (past, present, or delusional). It is not that she is devoid of reason; it is that her reason has become unmoored from the *real* real.

The Enlightenment elevated the reasoning powers of the mind above social/political authorities and religious revelation and concentrated attention on the rational individual subject, but it was not long before this positive spin put on the mind was challenged by those who saw in it also the germ of human tragedy. The life of the mind can be guided by logic, reason, and rationality, but it can also be driven by impulses, drives, and urges—all of them connected with the mind. The mind is not just one thing, moving in one direction, deriving its commands from one source, from "reason" or "self" or "soul," even though much philosophy has tried to define it in precisely these terms. And it does not just "make sense" of perceptions; it is not as orderly and straightforward as, perhaps, we wish it were. If Sigmund Freud is even a little bit right, then the mind contains an immensity which is, more or less, invisible to us, but which operates within, behind, and underneath our conscious thoughts, decisions, actions, and impulses (Storr 60–61). If Carl Jung is even a little right, then the mind, somehow, puts us in touch with a whole host of mysterious unconscious common templates which suggests that our minds are in some ways connected with

Philosophy and Fiction

the minds of others (Jung 4). If John Watson and B.F. Skinner and the behaviorists are even a little bit right, then our minds are malleable, impressionable, formed and fashioned throughout life in response to experiences and stimuli (Butler and McManus 5–6; "B. F. Skinner").

All of this is to say the mind is complex. It is both connected to the brain—the physical stuff in our skulls, the result of millions of years of evolution—but it is also constitutive of our personhood; it somehow extends beyond that stuff in our heads, transcends that stuff, results in consciousness, in identity, in me being me and you being you. Think of the way we speak about our minds. People can "use" or "lose" their minds. They can "get lost" in their minds. They can have their minds "blown" or "expanded"; some people are deemed "small" or "simple-minded," while others are seen as "broad-minded." Sometimes we are told to "set our minds aside" and "think with our hearts," which is just a metaphor that is really saying something like, "Only think with one part of your mind and not the other one." All of these metaphoric ways of speaking about the mind push us to think about the relationship between the mind, the brain, and the body, or more concisely, about the relationship between the mind and life (a different sort of emphasis on "the life of the mind").

The 17th-century French philosopher René Descartes makes a clear distinction between the body (which contains the brain) and the mind that goes so far as to identify the self with the mind and *not* with the body. The mind/self (the "thinking thing") is "indivisible," yet the body, though divisible, does not, in losing a part, affect the mind/self at all (106). For Descartes, the "mind or soul of man is entirely different from the body" (106). Sensory information communicates with the mind through "the internal parts of the brain" because such relation is useful and because "the goodness and power of God" is manifest in this relation, but the mind/self remains distinct, even from the brain itself (107). This famous "ghost in the machine" dualism of mind and body, of the life of the mind and the life of the body, is, for Descartes, the necessary outcome of the radical doubt the philosopher uses to filter all that might qualify as knowledge (Craig 78). Knowledge of the existence of the self remains, but only as "the thinking thing," that is, only as the mind, which, in order to be properly rational, must doubt the existence of everything else (78). Even the body's sheer existence is subject to Descartes's radical doubt (78). In other words, the life of the mind is certain, even if the life of the body is not. Supposedly, shortly before dying at almost fifty-four years old, Descartes said to his own soul (or mind),

Chapter Five. The Life of the Mind

"This is the time for you to leave the prison and to relinquish the burden of this body. You must suffer this rupture with joy and courage" (qtd. in Critchley, *The Book* 122). The "ghost" of the self lives on; the "machine," or, here, "prison," of the body is left behind.

Philosopher Simon Critchley, in his *The Book of Dead Philosophers*, points to the irony of Descartes's mind-body dualism by highlighting Descartes's "notoriously itinerant" lifestyle, according to which his mind/soul dragged its bodily prison to "no fewer than thirty-eight addresses during his lifetime" (123). And even after he died, his now mindless/soulless body was buried in a graveyard set aside for diseased orphans and unbaptized babies in Sweden (since he was a Catholic in a Protestant nation) (123). According to Catholic thinking at the time, such a burial would banish Descartes's soul (mind?) to limbo, so his body was later exhumed, and it traveled for eleven months before reaching Paris (123). Descartes's ghostless machine was then buried in Paris at the Church of Sainte-Geneviève, and then it was exhumed and reburied two more times before finally being laid to rest at a former monastery in 1819, nearly seventeen decades after his soul left its prison. Russell Shorto's *Descartes' Bones* outlines the story in even more detail, though toward a different thesis. Both Shorto's work and a brief chapter in Bess Lovejoy's *Rest in Pieces* contribute to the irony Critchley identifies, observing that pieces of Descartes's body were made into jewelry and used as corporeal talismans or relics to inspire the love of wisdom in those seeking the life of the mind, and this is not even to mention the fact that the father of rationalism's head went missing for a time and now sits, a few kilometers and across the Seine, from what is left of his body (Shorto 106–107; Lovejoy 180–182).

Critchley's own work in philosophy often drives toward these sorts of ironies regarding the "life of the mind." *The Book of Dead Philosophers* is a compendium of biographical sketches of philosophers that sets "the life of the mind" in tension with the one thing that all philosophers have in common: the death of the body. In *Notes on Suicide*, Critchley argues that the most common reason we humans have for killing of ourselves actually emerges from "optimistic delusions that our death would solve any kind of problem, enact payback, revenge or retribution, save us from ourselves, from others or from the painful commotion of the world" (73). Moving further in this vein, Critchley, in *On Humour*, discovers that cheerfulness and melancholy are two sides of the same coin, both shining through in the locus of sublimity and suffering at the center of the human condition: humor, which is what allows us to see our own ridiculousness, whether in ourselves or others (111). *Faith of the Faithless* attempts to locate theology through politics, and vice versa, again, allowing Critchley's philosophizing to pierce the paradoxes at the heart of the dualisms into which we have become accustomed to organizing our experience of the world. In the novella *Memory Theater,* the philosopher includes himself in the joke, merging philosophy and fiction, autobiography and research, the subject and the object, delusion and knowledge, reason and experience, the mind and the body, the beginning and the end. The life of the mind is, hopelessly, the life of the body. The history of the body's experiences is tied, through memory, to the mind's narrative of itself. The life of the mind is always already caught up with everything else it means to be human. All of our dualisms are really paradoxes.

The ancient Greeks used the word *psyche* to refer to the mind, the soul, or the spirit (Sears 268). In Greek mythology, the goddess Psyche was the goddess of the soul. She was a beautiful, curious wanderer. Zeus allowed her to become immortal in order for her to be wed to Eros, Cupid to the Romans (god of erotic love—much more on Eros in Chapter Six), a marriage which resulted in a great feast that unified the often divided pantheon (268). The Romans "rebranded" Psyche as "Anima," the root of our English word "animate," as in "to give life."

I like the slipperiness of the word *psyche*. It is not limited to the "thinking mind," which our modern conventions separate from feelings and emotions, from spiritual life and religion. Psyche is a richer, fuzzier, more ambiguous concept. The mythological connections, too, bind the mind, which we can think of as abstract, stuffy, and detached, to erotic love—to passion—to those aspects of us which are grounded in the concrete fleshiness of our bodies. It is a union of opposites, a paradox, because it is human. Psyche, in a way, counteracts the dualism of Descartes, as well as his scission of mind from body. We will explore the union of opposites in the stories in this section. We will see "the life of the mind" as a rich, complex, abstract, concrete, free-flowing, isolating, connecting force. We will see connections between the meaning of the life of the mind and "stream of consciousness" writing, as well as in character dynamics (conflict, motivation, etc.) and in narration, point of view/perspective, and so on. Literature of the life of the mind is as rich as the psyche itself because both are concentrated on the imagination, rather than exclusively on reason, and the imagination is capable of entering into the paradoxes of human life and the complexities of its representation in literature.

"Not born for ordinary life": "Looking Back" (1900) by Guy de Maupassant

"Looking Back" is a psychologically rich, but formally very simple, portrait of a French priest, Abbé Mauduit. Part of its beauty is located in its simplicity. The story is just over one thousand words, and it is really more of a character sketch packaged inside of a frame-narrative than it is a full-fledged story. But this economy serves the functions of spotlighting the priest, allowing him the opportunity to tell his story, and then sending him off into the night, and leaving the reader, not with the priest, the story's protagonist, but with his friend, the Comtesse, to contemplate "many things that do not occur to the young" (180). This ending line returns the reader, in a way, to the beginning of the story, in which three young children are running off to bed: it accentuates the chasm between youth and old age. This fact may point us to the priest's story, too, which is about his traumatic youth. Both the Comtesse and the Priest are old: she is the children's grandmother, their caretaker, their parents both having died (another trauma); Mauduit, the priest, is "a tall, white-haired old man," who has been a priest in the community for twenty years (176). So the story seems to tell us that it has something to say, not just about this priest and his psychological complexity, but about age, youth, and trauma, too.

The Comtesse is struck by the fact that Mauduit loves children and that he is not "a mystic nor a fanatic, neither a kill-joy nor a pessimist," and yet he decided at some point to dedicate his life to a vocation that is lonely and difficult, one that forbids him a family of his own (because a Catholic priest is not permitted to marry and is required to remain celibate) (176). She requests of him, "tell me how you made up your mind to renounce all that makes the rest of us love life, all that comforts and consoles us" (175–176). She reverses the roles between priest and parishioner: "it's time for *you* to make your confession to *me*" (176, emphasis in original).

Mauduit is hesitant to share his story, but eventually he does so in one long, uninterrupted monologue, as he stares into the fire in the hearth. He begins with what almost amounts to a thesis statement: "I was not born for ordinary life. Fortunately I discovered it in time and I have very often had cause to know how right I was" (176). His story returns to his childhood and culminates in a specific trauma, which becomes *the* critical moment in his life, the singular event on which the rest of his life depends: this is his origin story. What, perhaps, strikes the reader about the way Mauduit tells the story is that he does so without any drama or emotion, without any self-pity; rather, his origin story is organic, detailed, and somehow even reasonable. He admits that his "excessive sensitiveness" as a child was probably "pathological and dangerous," but he accepts it, and, by the end, frames it as both his burden and his gift.

Before diving into the priest's trauma more thoroughly, it may be helpful to observe that the dangerous pathology Mauduit identifies in himself is not madness, like we have seen, for example, in the stories by Edgar Allan Poe, though it does compare to the madness of both of Poe's protagonists: the young Mauduit's psychological constitution is characterized by peculiar nervousness, and his "disease" did, in fact, accentuate his senses to the point that he "shrank from all contacts, all advances, all the activities of school life" (177). Further, the logic by which his mind works develops from a narcissistic delusion: that "life was a battle, a frightful struggle, in which one received terrible blows and wounds not only painful but mortal" (178). In these two ways, at least, the young Mauduit resembles Poe's protagonists, both the one from "The Tell-Tale Heart" and the one from "The Cask of Amontillado" (the two discussed in this book), but instead of flaring out at others, Mauduit hides himself away; he recoils from and resists any contact with others, his mind "an open wound" that he tends in private (177). His pathology does not invent metaphysical entities that he must resist, trick, and kill; his corrupted logic does not lead to strange speculations that condemn others to death: Mauduit's pathology pits him against himself, an enemy he would never overcome or escape—and one that he projects onto the world as a whole.

And then he makes a friend.

At sixteen years old, the young Mauduit returns home. He remains isolated, alienated from his parents, who did not understand how to love him properly, and friendless until the day he meets Sam, a dog. Mauduit and Sam soon become inseparable, and the significance of the affection between them was not wasted on him, but neither was the fact that it was "exaggerated and ridiculous":

> This was the first living creature I had ever loved passionately, because he returned my affection. My love for the animal was, no doubt, exaggerated and ridiculous. I had the vague idea that in some way we were brothers, both lost in life, both lonely and defenseless [179].

Given the young Mauduit's penchant for projection, we probably are not surprised at this tendency to ascribe his own feelings and anxieties—his own identity—to the dog, but the way he projects himself onto the dog is interesting. It is precisely the inverse of his projection of his woundedness and sensitivity onto the world. On this account, his logic goes something like this: "I am wounded, anxious, and sensitive; the world is full of those who might wound me, situations that might make me nervous, stimuli that I will feel too much." The projection onto Sam, the dog, goes something like this: "This dog is just like me, miserable, sensitive, wary of the world; here is another victim; we only have one another, and he is the only thing that will hold me together." He sees himself in the dog, and he learns to love himself through the dog, but he also fetishizes the dog, as if the dog, because he imagines that it embodies the self that he can love, is his lifeline in the world. (I am, of course, not intending "fetishize," here, in a sexual sense, but rather as the process by which an object is endowed with an "unusual degree of power" or meaning) (Childers and Hentzi 108).

And these ideas are, essentially, confirmed when the dog is ripped in half by a speeding horse-drawn carriage. The moment is viscerally etched in his mind. He relates this trauma with grotesque detail:

> He was almost severed in two; his belly was torn open and his entrails were hanging out, spouting blood. He tried to get up and walk, but he could only move his fore legs, which scrabbled at the ground; his hind quarters were already dead. And he was howling pitiably, mad with pain [Maupassant 179].

According to the analysis we have already done, we cannot be surprised by the young Mauduit's response: he recoils back within himself; he is inconsolable. According to the symbolism of his private emotional logic, all of his fears are confirmed. This dog, this externalized version of himself, was, in fact, torn to pieces by the world, and the wounds were, indeed, "not only painful but mortal" (178). Further, on the "outside" level, the dog-as-fetish-object was ripped away from him, severing from him his talisman, effectively ripping open again his hidden wounds. The effect of the trauma is double: at once he sees both (a) himself split in two, his insides spilling out, and (b) he sees what, in his mind, was the one thing in the world that held him together torn apart: his lifeline is severed.

After the initial response to the trauma, the young Mauduit's logic takes over, and he has an epiphany:

> I realized why little everyday troubles assumed catastrophic proportions in my eyes; I saw that I was so constituted that I felt everything over-keenly and was hyper-susceptible to painful impressions, which were intensified

by my abnormal sensitiveness; and a paralyzing fear of life gripped me [179–180].

And he comes up with a solution, a self-accepting and logical solution.

I was without physical desires or ambition; so I decided to sacrifice the possibility of happiness to the certainty of suffering. "Life is short; I will devote myself to the service of others; I will soothe their sorrows and rejoice in their happiness," I said to myself. "As I shall not feel either myself directly, I shall experience these emotions only with diminished intensity" [180].

His self-awareness is shocking. He returns to his thesis at the end of his monologue: "I was right; I am not made to live in this world" (180). But now the Comtesse, the stand-in for the reader, understands, perhaps, the depth of this statement, that it is not just a cliché. The priest has given up the "possibility of happiness," of family, a wife, children, etc., for the "certainty of suffering," that is, the renunciation of "all that makes the rest of us love life," but that certain suffering is, for him, manageable because it is abstract (180, 175). Further, we can also see another kind of certain suffering: the fact of his parishioners' suffering, his share in their suffering losses of family members, etc. But this suffering, too, is manageable because it is indirect or abstract—because it does not touch him directly. The catch is that he may only experience happiness, too, vicariously: his experience of both joy and suffering is limited to indirect, vicarious experience through others' joy and happiness. He is not made for this world, so, he concludes, he must experience it from "the outside." This logic allows for all of his anxiety and "intolerable agony" to be "sublimated into sympathy and pity" for others: thus, his greatest burden becomes a gift, the heart of his ministry to others; likewise, his morbid narcissism is oriented outward toward others (180). His morbid self-focus is turned around into sympathy for other people.

The Comtesse, who has been listening the whole time, says, finally, "As for me, if I had not got my grandchildren, I don't think I should have the courage to go on living" (180). On one hand, she is reassuring the Priest that she understands because the logic of her survival in the face of the trauma (the loss of her son and daughter-in-law) is the same as his; on the other hand, the logic works for her the other way around: it is precisely her direct, concrete experience of love for her grandchildren, her life with them, that keeps her alive.

In a way, the Abbé Mauduit's adolescent trauma dramatically punctuates the end of his childhood; this coincides with the end of his self-centeredness and the beginning of an understanding that, only through reorienting his life toward others, would he be able to continue. And this seems, more or less, to have worked for him. Even as an old man, he is perceived as, maybe, too emotional, and he is still tortured by suffering, even if it is only vicariously experienced; he still fights the existential dread that has plagued him since childhood, but he has learned to deal with it by channeling it into his ministry, and so he survives. The old woman, the Comtesse, too, has transformed her suffering into the love for her grandchildren that keeps her alive.

The concept of trauma introduces an interesting paradox. Trauma, typically, describes the mental or psychological impression or memory of an unpleasant event in one's past (Storr 22). To parse the matter a little, traumas are experiences that are limited in scope, time, and place, but, for whatever reason, in the mind, they outlast the direct experience. They last and last, even when the individual wants to forget them. They defy a mind/body dualism: even though individuals experience the original event through their bodies or through their sense perception, the trauma wounds the mind, too. Life is rebuilt around the wounds of trauma. There is a certain degree of philosophical pragmatism to the priest's and the Comtesse's strategies for rebuilding: these are, simply, the acts of rebuilding that they must do to survive a life plagued with trauma. Perhaps this is among the "many things that do not occur to the young": traumas are ruptures in life that do not go away; they remain open wounds in the mind, the story suggests, but the mature individual is the one who learns to channel love through his or her wounds, to train the mind on others, so that the wound, though still gaping, opens the sufferer to the sufferings of other people.

"Just look at you": "A Hunger Artist" (1922) by Franz Kafka

As we discovered with our analysis of another of Franz Kafka's stories, "The Judgement," it can be difficult to understand exactly what Kafka's stories mean. His stories reach deep and, maybe, we even suspect that the author is, paradoxically, both trying urgently to communicate something and hiding whatever it is that he is trying to communicate. If you are like me, you feel the effect of Kafka's work before you really, intellectually, understand anything about it. Just as we may feel the confusion and anxiety in the "feedback loop" of reasoning at the beginning of "The Judgement," as Georg comes up with "lose-lose" option after "lose-lose" option as he thinks through how to navigate what to say in a letter to his distant friend, when we read "The Hunger Artist," we likely feel a number of things coming through that we do not, at first, quite understand. The narrator draws us into the perspective of the Hunger Artist and lets us feel his alienation, his dejection, his loneliness or isolation, his depression, his anger, his disappointment, and his dedication. If you are keeping a tally on these feelings, they are all "negative" except the last (and even the last one is oriented toward the negative in that, in this story, anyway, it seems to be at the root of the rest of them, so maybe we could reframe it as "stubbornness" for the sake of consistency). We likely come to the end of this story feeling pretty bad— and feeling bad *for* this protagonist. We might feel he was defeated from the beginning. After all, we know the story is about someone called a "hunger artist" (judging from the title alone), and the story starts out by stating, "In the last decades interest in hunger artists has declined considerably" (713). The narrator goes on to say that, in the past, it was possible to make a living as a hunger artist, but "nowadays that is totally impossible" (713). The guy does not have a chance!

Let's pause here and identify a couple of things.

(1) To the contemporary reader, this is probably a weird story about a weird subject. But Hunger Artists were real: there actually were performers who fasted "professionally" as displays of self-discipline, and there were Human Skeleton/Thin Man performers in carnival and circus side shows and "freak shows" (Nickell 101–105, Rothfels 158). So we can just take that as a fact of history and not get too side-tracked by the seeming oddity of what passed as entertainment in the past; it is a rabbit hole that goes very deep—and the people of the past would probably very well be surprised by what passes for entertainment in our day.

(2) Kafka himself around the time he wrote "A Hunger Artist" was quite ill. Among his letters is one from around this period in which he confesses to weighing a little over a hundred pounds in his winter clothes (he was six feet tall) (Friedlander 151). One of his friends described the last years of Kafka's life as "one long drawn-out suicide," saying that Kafka's tendency toward self-denial eventually killed him (and tuberculosis did not help either) (Grunfeld 188). Kafka died at only forty years old. All of this is to say that there are some obvious connections between "A Hunger Artist" and the author/artist himself. But, as I suggested with "The Judgement," in interpreting a piece of fiction, connections to author biography only go so far: if they enrich the interpretation of the story, then fine, but if all we can do is point out parallels

between the story and the author's life, then we are not really getting anywhere. Such connections just may be interesting, or they may be testaments to the impact of experience on art or something. Merely discovering a connection between the author's experience and a character's experience does not quite equal a valid interpretation—namely, because it is not really interpretation at all. We have to start with the story itself—the words on the page—and build from there. Then, if other details, like author biography or the history of odd entertainments or psychoanalytic theories (or whatever) can contribute something meaningful, we can bring them in.

Some interpretations of "A Hunger Artist" contextualize the story by reading it through Kafka's allegories and parables. Kafka did write a number of these sorts of works, but, to begin by limiting a work's scope by reducing it to a particular genre seems, to me, misguided. We may feel that there are allegorical or parabolic aspects in "A Hunger Artist," but, as I suggested with Nathaniel Hawthorne's "Young Goodman Brown," we do not necessarily have to allow such generic designations to control our interpretations. Let's take it as it is and see where the story takes us.

We can begin (again) with the point of view. The story is narrated in the third person, and on a first reading, we can observe that the narrator seems to know a lot about the cultural history of hunger artists; we can observe that the narrator seems to know a lot about this particular hunger artist—his actions, his thoughts, his feelings, etc.; we can also observe that, while the narrator focuses, mostly, on the hunger artist's internal life, the narrator also comments on the thoughts and feelings of other characters in the story as well. We probably, then, conclude that the narrator is omniscient, or all-knowing, that the narrator can dip into any character's head (even the very minor ones) and report on their thoughts and feelings as needed.

Let's push back on this idea for a moment. There are instances in the story that may challenge the conclusion that the narrator is completely reliable, and if the narrator is unreliable, then, regardless of its seeming omniscience, we, the readers, may be justified in questioning the information the narrator feeds us, a fact which we then should consider in our interpretation of the story as a whole. For the first several paragraphs, Kafka convinces us to trust his narrator, as he develops our empathy with the Hunger Artist—this heroic performer driven to perfect his, admittedly odd, art—and our enmity against the world around him that does not properly appreciate his gift, a world that judges him unworthy of their attention, a world that doubts him. At one point the narrator describes the paradoxical situation of the Hunger Artist:

> However, it was, in general, part of the fasting that these doubts were inextricably associated with it. For, in fact, no one was in a position to spend time watching the hunger artist every day and night, so no one could know, on the basis of his own observation, whether this was a case of truly uninterrupted, flawless fasting. The hunger artist himself was the only one who could know that and, at the same time, the only spectator capable of being completely satisfied with his own fasting [715].

As described here, the situation the Hunger Artist puts himself in, simply by being a hunger artist, is one in which the public's doubt regarding his skills is, to some degree, understandable, if not completely appropriate. So as much as this doubt wounds the Hunger Artist, it is natural to the situation. The narrator goes on to disclose that not even the Hunger Artist himself is satisfied with his fasting—even though he is the only person who is able to be satisfied with it:

> The reason he was never satisfied was something different. Perhaps it was not fasting at all which made him so very emaciated that many people, to their own regret, had to stay away from his performance, because they couldn't bear to look at him. For he was also so skeletal out of dissatisfaction with himself, because he alone knew something that even initiates didn't know—how easy it was to fast. It was the easiest thing in the world [715].

Let's resist drawing a conclusion for just a little bit longer.

In the paragraphs that follow these two passages, the narrator describes the carnivalesque culmination of a fast—how the Hunger Artist is limited to a forty-day fast, how he is stopped from fasting against his will. The narrator describes the fanfare and spectacle of the last day of the fast: there is a military band; there are doctors; there are young ladies to lead him out (715–716). The impresario has to go in the cage and pull him up because he refuses to stop fasting, which we are, apparently, to take as heroic, but he also seems like he is in pretty bad shape: he is unable to hold himself up; he cannot even hold his head upright; his legs drag on the ground (716). We learn a little later that there is evidence that sometimes by the fortieth day he must be put in bed, that he is "almost dead from exhaustion" (718). So, as confident as the Hunger Artist is that he could fast interminably, we are also being given information that demonstrates that that may not be so. Kafka is beginning to breach, just a little, the perimeters of the narrator's omniscience by exposing little cracks between the facts given and the sympathy with the Hunger Artist's inner world.

Further, the narrator may also be giving us other contradictory information. Concerning the "two young ladies," the story reports that, when they enter the cage to bring him out, they are "apparently so friendly but in reality so cruel" (716). But we see no evidence of their cruelty. If anything, we see these women deeply affected by the Hunger Artist's compromised state of being, and, so, by his art. They turn "pale as death" when they see him up close; they get flustered and look to others for help; one of them nearly faints, while the other bursts into tears (716–717). These women are anything but cruel. They are in shock.

The problem the attentive reader has at this point, after beginning to feel this disjuncture, is that the narrator creates an impossible situation: we are told one thing as if it is fact, and then we are given another set of facts in image-driven description that contradicts it. A little hole opens up in the story through this free indirect discourse, and now we must rerun the whole story back through that hole, asking, "How much can we trust this narrator?" How much spin is being put on the story to draw on our empathy with the Hunger Artist? The narrator suddenly seems less omniscient, less objective, and more a narrative agent working on behalf of the Hunger Artist himself. We probably begin to feel this before we reach this conclusion intellectually. In the episode immediately following the one I have just been describing, when the narrator discloses the Hunger Artist's increasingly gloomy mood and his rage at the suggestion that his sadness is related to his fasting and, finally, the measures the impresario takes to punish him for such outbursts, do we not feel less convinced about the interpretation that the impresario is intending to hurt the Hunger Artist (717–718)?

In a way, the spell seems broken—or at least we feel the distance between the facts reported and what now seems like the narrator spinning them to validate the Hunger Artist's feelings, whether those feelings are justifiable responses or not. Perhaps we look back to the moment in the story I mentioned previously, about the dynamics of doubt and the life of the artist, and see Kafka, quite literally, introducing doubt into the narrative through these moments of free indirect discourse, perhaps signaling to the reader to begin questioning things (715). Perhaps the Hunger Artist *feels* alienated, mocked, misunderstood, and unappreciated, all these humiliations he projects onto the public, but he also feels, to some degree, like a sham—which results in dissatisfaction with himself, which, somehow, results in him being more "skeletal" because it literally eats away at him—because fasting, for him, is the easiest thing in the world (715). The reader begins, then, to question the conclusion that the world is against the Hunger Artist and, perhaps, instead, should begin thinking about the idea that he is against himself. The culmination of the first sequence of the story is, essentially, a return to the idea that begins the story, and it seems more honest: it is a "lack of understanding," "a world of misunderstanding," that stands between the public and the artist—and perhaps also a rupture that opens up between the artist and himself. And it is this latter subject to which the second sequence of the story turns.

Almost all at once, the "crowd of pleasure seekers" loses interest in "fasting performances" (718). The impresario is unable to chase up much business, and the Hunger Artist has to contend with his pride and figure out some path for the future:

> What was the hunger artist to do now? A man whom thousands of people had cheered on could not display himself in show booths at small fun fairs. The hunger artist was not only too old to take up a different profession, but was fanatically devoted to fasting more than anything else. So he said farewell to the impresario, an incomparable companion on his life's road, and let himself be hired by a large circus. In order to spare his own feelings, he didn't even look at the terms of the contract at all [718].

He makes the most of this transition, though, and promises that, if "people would let him do what he wanted," "he would really now legitimately amaze the world for the first time" (719). And his new employers give him free reign to do so.

We, readers, see here the transition to a situation that allows the Hunger Artist to really shine, but, if we are paying attention, we also see the Hunger Artist's character anew: a predominating characteristic that, in the first sequence of the story, was explored through attention to the protagonist's dedication to his art and expressed in his feelings of alienation and humiliation under the eyes of, what turns out to have been, an interested and sympathetic audience, comes through in this new turn with a subtle twist: the Hunger Artist's pride. And it persists. It drives him crazy, for example, that he is placed near the animal cages, that the crowds push people past his cage, so that even those who momentarily pause to look at him are hurried along (719). Some misunderstand what his art is all about, and others just reject him outright: only little children vaguely seem aware that he is something special, but even they do not really care (720). He fasts in his best form for longer than he ever had before, and no one notices but him—and it is not enough. He wants to be noticed. He wants people to be impressed.

He wants them to recognize that he is special. But ultimately "no one, not even the hunger artist himself, knew how great his achievement was by this point, and his heart grew heavy": "the world was cheating him of his reward," of recognition (721).

But recognition for what? For fasting? That seems like a crazy expectation. But what else does he have? What else can he do? Nothing. He has nothing and can do nothing except this one thing. But this one thing is the basis according to which he elevates himself above everyone else. He, quite literally, makes a spectacle of his superiority to everyone else in the world. That sense of superiority develops into pride, and his pride drives him further and further inside of himself, filling him with indignation for everyone else, for the rest of the world, who will never fully comprehend him, will never fully appreciate him, will never be able to relate to him. But beneath this narcissistic view of his relation to the world is the nagging reality that he is not responsible for what makes him great. It is just the way he is, and he hates this too; it is eating away at him as much as the fasting does.

He finally seems to have a realization at the end of the story. He is forgotten—still fasting—in the back of his cage, which looks empty.

> They pushed the straw around with a pole and found the hunger artist in there. "Are you still fasting?" the supervisor asked. "When are you finally going to stop?" "Forgive me everything," whispered the hunger artist. [...] "I always wanted you to admire my fasting," said the hunger artist. "But we do admire it," said the supervisor obligingly. "But you shouldn't admire it," said the hunger artist. "Well then, we don't admire it," said the supervisor, "but why shouldn't we admire it?" "Because I had to fast. I can't do anything else," said the hunger artist. "Just look at you," said the supervisor, "why can't you do anything else?" "Because," said the hunger artist, lifting his head a little, and with his lips pursed as if for a kiss, speaking right into the supervisor's ear so that he wouldn't miss anything, "because I couldn't find a food which I enjoyed. If I had found that, believe me, I would not have made a spectacle of myself and would have eaten to my heart's content, like you and everyone else." Those were his last words, but in his failing eyes there was the firm, if no longer proud, conviction that he was continuing to fast [721].

The Hunger Artist repents of his pride, of his need for admiration, of his tendency to place himself on a pedestal above the rest. His fasting, he discovers, is no art at all. This was his greatest fear, the nagging pain that plagued him before—that, for him, fasting was easy. In the end, he accepts that fasting, for him, is existential or constitutional—that it is something about the way he is. It is not a sign of his superiority, of his talent for discipline or self-denial. It is simply a lack. It is an indication of something missing. He is not more, higher, or better than the rest. He is never satisfied, yet never hungry. He simply has no joy.

So, what is this all supposed to mean? Is that not what we are wondering the whole time? Is it a parable about the artist in relation to society? Maybe Kafka wants to say that the artist must realize her or his difference from everyone else. Maybe. Maybe Kafka wants to say something about the self-discipline required of an artist—a discipline which the rest of the world will never understand. Maybe that too. I do not know. What I am seeing, for sure, is something about pride. Perhaps the alienating impact of the life of the artist is a valid sentiment, and maybe artists are different from other people, and the other people will not always respect or understand them, but nothing about the artist's life gives the artist the right to pride, to elevating him- or herself above anyone else, whether other people understand the art or not. Pride is pride.

Pride and narcissism derive from projecting one's own dissatisfaction with oneself at other people. Pride insulates an artist from his or her own art; it puts the impetus on reception—on people's reactions, and people's reactions are based on shifts in public interests. People's interests are fickle. At one time they are drawn to the purity of privation, abstinence, and asceticism (and they go look at a Mark Rothko painting); at other times they may be drawn to the energy of wildness, action, and unconscious passion (and they seek out a Jackson Pollock). At one time they are drawn to a frail, quiet attempt to live against the grain of life and the pull of nature; in another turn of time, the fullness and vibrancy of nature is all they want. Sometimes they want a hunger artist, and sometimes they want a panther. But they do not understand their interest in one any better than their desire for the other—not any better than they understand their own desires for food or sex, for a kiss or a fight, for spiritual transcendence or a mindless thrill. Ultimately, Kafka seems to say, artists are driven by conviction—something that exceeds nature and runs deeper in them than they can understand, but it is something that they must explore, learn to accept, and practice with humility—even if no one notices—and even if it kills them.

So, like Maupassant's "Looking Back," Kafka's "A Hunger Artist" reveals something deep about the inner workings of narcissism. Specifically, these stories point to a very fine line between productive self-examination (in keeping with the Socratic imperative for one to examine one's life) that leads to some kind of revelation that orients the individual toward something other than the individual's own mind/self, whether the genesis of that examination begins with art or trauma (or consists of some combination of the two). Interestingly, both stories feature aspects of human life in which something like a Cartesian mind/body dualism seems to dominate: both trauma and willful starvation demonstrate the mind's ability to master bodily experience. In other words, in both trauma and willful starvation, the mind, in a way, works against the body by obsessive narcissistic self-examination. Each story in its own way resolves something about this situation by redeeming the "examined life," by finding a way to uproot the narcissism that eats away at the mind/self from within. The protagonist of our next story, W.B. Yeats' "The Tables of the Law," never learns such a lesson.

"To touch the Heart of God": "The Tables of the Law" (1897) by W.B. Yeats

The story "The Tables of the Law" was published on its own in 1897 after being rejected for publication with the cycle of stories with which Yeats intended it (Foster 176). (In the context of this story cycle, the references to the character Michael Robartes would make more sense; other stories from that group focus on Robartes, who is essentially a tangential name that is dropped in a couple of times in this story, which focuses instead on Owen Aherne) (Foster 176–177). Like Kafka's "A Hunger Artist," this story probably strikes the contemporary reader as pretty weird. It reflects the author's interest in (or obsession with) "spiritualism," or more broadly, mysticism. Yeats' biographer, Roy Foster, explains that this preoccupation among modern intellectuals (and Yeats himself) with mysticism, spiritualism, and occult practices (like magic, alchemy, secret societies, etc.) around the turn of the century emerges from a strange problem: the combination of the impact of science and reason on the "orthodox" practice of the Christian religion, resulting in skepticism, and the quasi-religious push among intellectuals for reanimating and reconnecting with cultural (in Yeats' case, Celtic) "spiritual" traditions, in lieu of religion, through folk tales, faerie stories, myths, and legends rich in meaning and symbolism through which their religious impulses and feelings could find satisfaction ("Yeats and Mysticism"). The result, in "The Tables of the Law," symbolizes that transition, even as it explores the dangers that such a move implies.

We are told the story by an unnamed narrator, who relays a cautionary tale about the excesses of the mind when it breaks free of the tethers of religious and social order. And we are left with questions. Is it the protagonist's obsessions that drive him through mysticism into darkness and dejection? Or does Aherne discover some real but mysterious forces that drive his quest to be the "Jesus" of this new gospel that results in his undoing? Or is it Aherne's pride and narcissism that push him into the new wisdom he wishes to teach to the world and his seeking self-importance that results in the story's dismal end in what, perhaps, is a vision or hallucination that allows the narrator to symbolize and encode the kind of wrong-headedness in which Aherne has lost himself?

With these questions in mind, let's jump into the story.

"The Tables of the Law" begins at a meeting of the two characters a decade before they reconnect in the second part of the story. This initial section begins with a question (technically two questions, but I will focus on the second, since the first one just justifies the second): "Why did you [Aherne] refuse the biretta, and almost at the last moment? When you and I lived together, you cared neither for wine, women, or money, and had thoughts for nothing but theology and mysticism" (392). A biretta is a kind of small, three-cornered hat that symbolizes the priesthood (among Roman Catholics, and some more traditional Anglicans and Lutherans). So the narrator is asking Aherne why he decided not to be a priest, even though he "had thoughts for nothing but theology and mysticism" (392).

We do not get a direct answer to this question, and before we get any kind of answer, the narrator gives us a lot of imagery and description regarding the kind of man Aherne is. The narrator guides our attention, first, to the play of light through a glass of red wine that gives the "impression of a man holding a flame in his naked hand" (392). Already, we are in weird territory if we think about this image. Fire has often been used to symbolize the human mind/spirit; it is the symbol of the Holy Spirit (tongues of fire on people's heads at Pentecost in the Book of Acts in the New Testament); it is also a prominent symbol in magic, and it is the activating principle in alchemy. If you have read the story, the Holy Spirit is, maybe, the one that seems like the best fit, given the rest of what is coming for Aherne, but we cannot altogether discount the connection to the human mind/spirit or to alchemy either. And, reading the very end of the story, perhaps we are drawn to the more satanic/demonic imagery associated with fire. Symbolic images are artistically useful in this way; they do not have to mean just one thing.

We read on and see the sort of respect that the narrator has for Aherne: he is a "supreme" human being, one who has "risen above, or has sunken below, the formalisms of half-education and the rational-isms of conventional affirmation and denial" and has turned away from "practicable desires and intuitions" and toward "desires so unbounded that no human vessel can contain them" (392–393). He is the sort of per-son who is "half monk, half soldier of fortune," who must "turn action into dreaming, and dreaming into action" (393). For people like Aherne, there is "no order, no finality, no contentment in this world" (393). So far, Yeats is making him out to be the intersecting point of a number of paradoxes.

Yeats seems to be really building this guy up in a very specific, though difficult-to-understand, sort of way. What does this mean? What do we see? We know this characterization is important; other-wise, why spend so much time and space on pre-developing this char-acter in such a short story? Let's read on a little further and see if any larger pattern emerges.

The next sentence or so tells us that Aherne has a philosophy of life—"half borrowed from some fanatical monk, half invented by him-self—that the beautiful arts were sent into the world to overthrow nations, and finally life herself, by sowing everywhere unlimited desires," an idea that, as yet, the narrator only knows as a paradox that Aherne had entertained since his youth, but which, we shall find out, has come to full fruition in his adulthood (393).

I think, now, we are beginning to see a fuller picture emerge. The narrator presents a dichotomous relation between paradoxical ten-dencies—that meaning in life, we could say, is split in two directions: one toward "practicable desires and intuitions" (let's call this "practical desires") and one toward "unbounded" desires (let's call this one "abso-lute desires"), one toward the ascetic life of the monk and one toward the untethered freedom of the mercenary: in short, one toward "law" (and the orthodox doctrines of the Church) and one toward "freedom" (and the symbolic, mystical desires of alchemy and mysticism). Accord-ingly, the "beautiful arts" represent the side of complete, or absolute, freedom (and the rest—unbounded desire, alchemy, mysticism, etc.). This seems like an enormous digression, that is, until we read on and go down the rabbit hole with Yeats into this mysterious world and its his-tory and philosophy/theology.

In response to the question about the priesthood, Aherne finally responds, saying he will *show* the narrator rather than try to explain it, so he takes him to his private chapel. The passage leading to the chapel is filled with beautiful art—art that, regardless of its domain (religious, erotic, etc.), sought "absolute emotion," art that depicted "souls trembling between the excitements of the spirit and the excitement of the flesh" (393). We should pause here, again, and unpack the significance. Yeats is giving us another way to understand Aherne's dualism—the philosophy of life that we are about to be given in the paragraphs that follow (which gets pretty deep)—but, in this architectural imagery, it is much clearer: all of this beauty, these images of excitement, of spiritual and fleshly enjoyment and freedom literally lead to and from the chapel, where one meets God. *That* is the message. And that is the message we are about to be introduced to through some very deep, weird, somewhat historical mysticism, which is explained in detail. But if we catch the imagery here, we have a template for what is about to happen.

Once in the chapel, the narrator draws our attention to a few essential items: the "square bronze box," which stands on the altar in front of a crucifix (and there is a lot about that box and what is inside, which we will get to shortly) and "two large empty tablets of ivory," which stand in the place of where "two marble tablets" containing the ten commandments once were, off to one side of the alter (and perhaps now we are beginning to see the connections to the title) (394–395). Now, if we know anything about the "liturgical traditions" (Catholic, Orthodox, Anglican, etc.) in Christianity, we will know that the altar is usually pretty sparsely set; things on the altar are there because of their significance. An alter might have a book of the Gospels, a crucifix or cross—some churches may include a "tabernacle" (a box in which consecrated "host" is kept); there might be icons, but even these are usually limited to Jesus and maybe Mary. So we are being given, in this description, more information about Aherne's theology. In place of the Bible or Book of Gospels is this book by Joachim of Flora (Aherne's new Gospel of the Holy Spirit)—it has literally replaced the Gospel of Jesus.

Again, what follows seems like another weird digression (but, by this point, we are beginning to understand that the whole story is composed of weird digressions): there is a close description of the bronze box and who designed it; there is a kind of genealogy outlining the transmission of the text from Joachim of Flora down through the ages to the present, each "generation" contributing his small part to its beauty. But even the narrator seems a little confused about why this book is so significant. He flippantly asks if the book's doctrine is just some "medieval straw-splitting about the nature of the Trinity" (395).

This bothers Aherne, perhaps, because, in a way, that is exactly what it is—but the significance of this "straw-splitting" is, for him, enormous. But what is the point of all of this information? It is that it both testifies to the impact this book has had on the lives of all whom it has touched, and it elevates Aherne himself, since he represents the culmination of this process of transmission: he sees himself as the prophet (the "Jesus") of this gospel of beauty, which has been passed down from one artist to another, and finally to Aherne, who will fully embody this wisdom, write its "secret law," and make disciples (394–395, 397). He sees himself as the Jesus Christ of the "Kingdom of the Holy Spirit" represented in this secret medieval manuscript (397).

Okay, that probably strikes us as an odd choice. "Why does this kingdom need a new prophet? Is the original Jesus not enough?" we, or the narrator, might ask. Aherne's answer is "No." There's a new gospel in town, and it is in Joachim of Flora's secret book. Some of this gets confusing because much of what Yeats includes here about Joachim of Flora (or Fiore) is true: more or less, everything except for the secret book is grounded in (nonfictional) reality (the rest of the stuff—the other title, his view that here was an "Age of the Father," an "Age of the Son," and a coming "Age of the Spirit" and so on—all of that stuff is part of the actual, historical Joachim's theology) (Placher 149–150). Aherne believes Joachim's secret (fictional) book is the new gospel of the Holy Spirit, and just like the "Age of the Son" replaced the "Age of the Father" (and the law of the Son fulfilled and replaced the law of the Father), the "Age of the Spirit" and the Law that goes with it has come and will, ultimately, replace the age and law of the Son—for some people.

That last bit (the "for some people") is the catch, one a little reminiscent of Nietzsche (whom we shall return to in a moment) (Foster 177). According to Aherne, Joachim taught that "those whose work was to live and not to reveal were children and that the Pope was their father; but he taught in secret that certain others, and in always increasing numbers, were elected, not to live, but to reveal that hidden substance of God which is colour and music and softness and a sweet odour; and that these have no father but the Holy Spirit" (397). These latter are the artists, poets, satirists, musicians, etc., whose art and lives *are* revelations of the Holy Spirit; therefore, they must be completely, absolutely free for beauty—to express and reveal the lawless beauty of God (397). No human or religious laws, no commandments, not even Jesus' commands regarding love and kindness, can constrain them. And Aherne sees himself as the prophet of this age, of this wisdom, and he will be the author of this secret law—the law of absolute freedom (hence the blank ivory tablets).

To go back to the very beginning, that is the reason why Aherne, at the last moment, did not become a priest. And after all of that, we are probably thinking, "Sorry I asked," and that seems to be what the narrator is thinking too. He says he "did not reason with him that night" because Aherne became so excited, and the narrator was afraid of angering him in such a state. The narrator thinks that not trying to convince Aherne of his mistake, however, was a sin. He concludes part one saying, "Since my conversion I have indeed done penance for an error which I was only able to measure after some years" (398).

Part II comes some ten years later. The narrator recognizes Aherne's face in a "lifeless mask with dim eyes"; he is a man "whose inner life had soaked up the outer life" (398–399). Aherne, after escaping the narrator once, finally agrees to speak with him, and invites him into his chapel again. Aherne prefaces the conversation by saying that his ideas turned out to contain "extreme danger" and "boundless wickedness" (399). Further, the passage to the chapel, which once was adorned with images of beauty, enjoyment, and transcendence, is now "choked with dust and cobwebs," the art all filmed in gray dust and "shrouded with cobwebs" (the words "dust" and "cobwebs" are combined three times in just one sentence, just so we do not miss the now forgotten and neglected images of beauty and freedom) (399). The new "tables of the law" are there, where the marble tablets containing the ten commandments once were (399). Interestingly, the narrator reads some of them but, apparently, finds nothing in them worthy of remarking upon. Instead, he focuses on happiness. He asks, "Has the philosophy of the *Liber inducens in Evangelium aeternum* made you very unhappy?" (399) (*Liber inducens in Evangelium aeternum*, remember, is the title of Joachim's secret book, which translates to something like "Freedom Leading to the Eternal Gospel") (399). Aherne's response is interesting. He says that, at the beginning, he was filled with happiness; he felt "divine ecstasy, an immortal fire" in all his passions, hopes, desires, and dreams—that he would touch the very "Heart of God" (399). But this all changed.

> I was full of misery; and in my misery it was revealed to me that man can only come to that Heart through the sense of separation from it which we call sin, and I understood that I could not sin, because I had discovered the law of my being, and could only express or fail to express my being, and I understood that God has made a simple and an arbitrary law that we may sin and repent! [400].

Chapter Five. *The Life of the Mind*

The narrator says that, after he delivered this speech, Aherne's body and posture portrayed more "dejection than any image I have met with in life or in any art" (400).

Aherne's predicament is very specific. Let's be careful not to miss it: he says that, because he is one of this special class of absolutely free artist-people (the new Jesus of the new gospel), he cannot sin (he either expresses his being or he does not—that is it). But the way to the "Heart of God" is through being forgiven for and redeemed from sin. So Aherne knows that his special status, which puts him a cut above the rest of humanity, also cuts him off from being unified with God. This means that, just like the original Jesus, Aherne is destined to sacrifice himself—his very soul—for this gospel because embodying its law puts him outside of "those for whom Christ died" (400).

Aherne's embodiment of paradox continues. His special status has a cost he had not thought of before. His belonging to the Holy Spirit severs him from the redemption of the Son, even if it frees him from the laws of the Father and the Son. Further, the absolute freedom and emotion and beauty is, here, expressed in dejection, that is, in the negation of these things. From the narrator's perspective, Aherne is *the* icon and emblem of absolute dejection, sadness, and rejection (maybe freedom, beauty, emotion—but definitely with a depressing spin). It is notable that, while the table of "secret laws" does not rate as important enough for the narrator to mention, the image of Aherne's complete dejection does. Further, this realization, along with the narrator's vision that follows, is enough to send him running for "spiritual and social order" (401). The vision is weird, too, but, regardless of its "reality" in the world of the fiction, the message seems clear: these "spirits whose name is legion and whose throne is the indefinite abyss" are the ones whom Aherne "obeys and cannot see," that as angelic and "spiritual" as Aherne *thinks* his calling is, in reality he is serving some demonic force (401).

All of this brings us back to the questions we started with. Given the narrator's framing of the story, I am inclined to see Aherne as an emblem, not only of dejection, but also of pride. In a way, it is only too consistent for Aherne, who sees himself as belonging to an elite class of artists for whom the moral and spiritual laws of the world or Christian orthodoxy do not apply, also to find a way to gain exceptional status, even among these elite, a status to rival, or even exceed, the status of Jesus.

This dynamic is a perfect, if rather pathetic, human mimicry of the fall of Lucifer, who, traditionally, was driven by pride to rebel against

143

God in an attempt to replace God. Such a connection would work well, interpretively, with the vision at the end of the story. But perhaps it implies a caution regarding "spiritual" pursuits, even in an era in which religion no longer provides the structure it once did: narcissistic pride can drive even those seeking only beauty, goodness, and truth. The "purity" of desire for, or the pursuit of, even noble goals is corrupted by claims to authority and status, perhaps, especially when that authority/status hides beneath the evangelical zeal to spread the good news. Even in a skeptical, secular age, pride is the "sin" that separates individuals from themselves, from one another, and from meaning by tricking them into thinking it is not pride, that their motives are pure. It is a mind game. Christianity or not, that is still the original sin. As "supreme" an individual as Aherne seems to be, his lack of self-awareness is shocking, primarily because he cannot seem to see past his own supremacy in the plans he has for spreading freedom to the world. He is reflective enough to discover that the dualisms into which religion divides life are really paradoxes, but he is not perceptive enough to see that his own division of humanity just turns back to a totalizing dualism that empowers and damns him all at once. His narcissism inflates his importance to such a degree that he has to be special both for being included and excluded at the same time.

A final thought brings me back to Nietzsche. Nietzsche, perhaps like Aherne, advocated for transforming human life, through "nobility and aesthetic values," into a work of art in a way that imagined art as altogether supplanting religion (Flynn 40–41). Accordingly, the new morality is one in which only "true individuals" (that is, like for Aherne, only *some people*) are truly free, able to create their own values, by assuming the prerogatives previously reserved for the divine (Flynn 40). His vision for the "free spirits" (what he called the "true individuals") associated with this new gospel, however, is based on the complete extirpation of Christian religion, of the "death of God," in their culture, their minds, and their imaginations (Flynn 40). It is, here, precisely, that Nietzsche and Aherne part ways. Whereas Nietzsche wants to elevate human potential to conceptual domains previously inhabited by the divine, his atheism precludes him from deifying humanity (though he does imagine a "superman"); Aherne's humanistic revolution is incomplete because he has not killed off his god, so he is left in dejection and sadness, a pathetic superman, who has seen and felt the ecstasies of his freedom, but who has also been severed by them from a God whose heart he still yearns to touch, whose bidding he thinks he is doing. He can only ever ride the fence between freedom and law at the center of the central paradox that defines his life. He can only ever be a sacrificial narcissist. We might observe that it is, perhaps, for this reason that the death of God, for Nietzsche, implies "demolition, destruction, decline, overturning," that the "old God" must be rooted out before the "horizon seems to us again free," before "every daring venture of knowledge is again permitted" (Nietzsche 110–111). This is not to say Nietzsche is right and Aherne is wrong (that, dear reader, is for you to judge for yourself, and I certainly see no reason why such a judgement needs to be between only these two options). My point is just that Aherne's path avoids the choice. And people who want to "have their cake and eat it, too" seldom become exemplars for anything good.

"You perceive?" "Pink Flannel" (1919) by Ford Madox Ford and "The Mark on the Wall" (1921) by Virginia Woolf

Whereas Maupassant's "Looking Back," Kafka's "A Hunger Artist," and Yeats' "The Tables of the Law" present carefully drawn pictures, mostly from the outside, of characters obsessed with and fixated on traumas, practices, or ways of life and sets of ideas, Ford's and Woolf's stories put us inside their characters' heads and, perhaps, give us an experience of "the life of the mind." The previous stories in this chapter also differ from these two on this account. The stories by Maupassant, Kafka, and Yeats, as odd as each story is, present narratives with discernable plots, presenting a character whose mind has carried him off—but at least the story relates this process in a recognizable form. The stories by Ford and Woolf may challenge even being defined as stories (perhaps we feel that the term "short fiction" often applied to short stories may be, technically, more appropriate here). If we try to summarize the plots of these two stories, what do we get?

In "Pink Flannel," a soldier in France cannot find a letter, and then he finds it.

In "The Mark on the Wall," a woman perceives a mark on a wall and takes a hundred mental paths as she thinks about what it is.

Neither story can really be said to have much of a plot. We would also be stretching things to say either story has the conventional properties of protagonist and/or antagonist. If we want to be honest, we might admit that, reading Ford's story, we get lost in the jumps between fantasy, dreamland, and the real world, and that, reading Woolf's story, we get impatient after the first page or so, after realizing that the story is going nowhere. These stories are experimental, and they definitely *feel* experimental when we read them. But, perhaps, if we read more patiently—and without prescriptive expectations for what a story *should* be and *should* do—we might find that these narratives do offer an interesting and provocative reading experience, just one that does not fit with all of the literary conventions we have been taught are "normal."

Maybe it will help to get a baseline on what is considered "normal" for literary fiction. Yes, to some degree "normal" is composed of some kind of literary object that can support the scrutiny of the literary-critical vocabulary we are accustomed to using (plot, character, setting, tone, style, theme, and so on), but even more basic than that is the idea that fiction is art, and art is representational, or "imitative" (another word for this is "mimesis"—that art is "mimetic"). Perhaps this sounds familiar: this is part of the discussion about how to define art with respect to its relation to nature that goes back at least as far as Plato and Aristotle, and it has really never gone away (as we discussed in Chapter One). To say that art is representational is to say that art is based, to some degree, on nature or reality, that art "re-presents" the stuff of real life in one form or another. If we are talking about literature, we might say that creative writers use words to construct images and concepts to develop people and places that, in one way or another, are "built" out of real life. We might flesh this out by observing that the easiest way for a writer to achieve this is by telling a story, by describing the world and the people in the world of the story in easily understandable ways, often using sense-based language, to make in the reader's mind a world full of colors, smells, objects, people, sounds, textures, and on and on—to paint a clear picture with words of this or that sequence of events with this or that person or people or whatever the case may be.

But what about the kind of art that messes with reality? What about impressionism, abstract expressionism, cubism, and the rest? Are they representing the real world? Most would say, yes, they probably are—something in real life—just not the way people have become accustomed to experiencing it. This is art that experiments with *how* to communicate its picture of the world to the viewer. This is art that may focus exclusively on one aspect of representation at the expense of others, that may try to cut reality up in ways that do not fit with the way we typically experience it. This kind of art may draw the viewer's attention to categories of perception itself, patterns of thought regarding how to categorize color and shape, motion and stasis, and so on. This is art that may be attempting to shock or shake us from our conventional, traditional modes of thought. And I think this is how we need to think about the stories by Ford and Woolf.

Both are experimenting with how to represent thought, the inner mental or psychological experience of a character. Most "normal" literature, even when describing a character's inner life, does so in a rational way and does so with a coherent progression of feelings, observations, thoughts, and conclusions—even when characters or events may be irrational. But is this the way we think? Do we think in rational examinations? Do we experience our feelings and drives in only reasonable ways: a leads to b, b to c, c to d, and so on? Are all of our inner thoughts so articulate and propositional as most literature presents them? Of course not. The literature of Ford and Woolf (and many others) is experimenting with a type of what we might call psychological or phenomenological realism, an "inner" realism that tries to demonstrate, to some degree, the largely patternless chaos and disorderliness of our minds, the seemingly limitless and unstoppable movement of the mind that hides within the stillness or measured action of the human body.

In "modernist" literature, this kind of experimental fiction gets called "stream of consciousness" writing. And it arose in the early 20th century around the same time as the philosophical mode of phenomenology shows up in the work of Edmund Husserl, and as Sigmund Freud and the early psychoanalysts begin therapies based on "free association" and the interpretation of dreams. All three disciplines, though, are, more or less, interested in the same thing: how the mind works, yes, but also a new view of the *deep* workings of the mind, beyond the rational, linear, progressive varieties that have been the focus of thinking on thought at least since the Enlightenment (Gay xx-xxii). For Husserl, the philosopher who developed phenomenology, the focus of philosophy becomes the "way things are perceived and informed by human consciousness," or "lived experience" (Childers and Hentzi 227). For Freud, free association, a process of quick replies to brief prompts or, alternatively, just spontaneously vomiting words as quickly as possible without censorship—in either case, attempting to side-step any rational thought about the arrangement or appropriateness of the words—was a way to get past the mind's reason-based defenses and into its inner workings (Storr 40). For the "stream of consciousness" writers, like Ford and Woolf, the point is to carefully present what inner processes may be like, which does not necessarily mean just "writing without thinking."

Philosophy and Fiction

They are artists, after all, so they are trying to achieve art as well, but art informed by these new ideas, art which operates according to a "psychological emphasis on processes of perception" and "provocative freedom" from presenting observations about factual reality (Saunders).

So what do we get?

With "Pink Flannel," Ford begins with a soldier, W.L. James: Ford writes that James "waved his penny candle round the dark tent and the shadow of the pole moved in queer angles on the canvas sides" (685). Perhaps we see in this opening line the controlling image of the story: a picture of something stuck in place (the tent pole) projecting its image in all directions, first here, then there, then over there, but the thing itself safe and stable in the center—perhaps like the letter itself, which we learn, by the end, is tucked safely away in a pink flannel pocket inside a booklet; perhaps we see James' mind (the mind, after all, has, seemingly forever, been imaged by fire) in this opening line casting shadows of the searched for object, first here, then there, then over there, unable to land solidly on the item itself. Or maybe it is just a way to get the story moving. Who knows?

We do get a small dose of drama in the next paragraphs. This letter is a letter from *Mrs.* Wilkinson (685), and it is regarding some kind of romantic affair with the soldier, James; he is concerned that the letter might be put to some "evil use," like being sent on to *Mr.* Wilkinson (686). So we have the makings of a romantic drama—an enticing incident that could be used to drive the plot of a story—but then we read nothing else about the matter. It is just a passing worry, one among many, that goes through James' mind as he continues searching his memory for where the letter could be. We could, conceivably, interpret this salacious detail as a tease from Ford: perhaps he knows the reader will latch onto this detail (because it is the sort of thing we are used to reading about—think of "The Storm" and "The Leopard Man's Story"). It keeps us reading on ("What will happen with this love triangle?"). But, by the end, we understand that this worry was just a fleeting concern, no more or less important than the rest.

Generally, I would guess that the impatient reader has an easier time with "Pink Flannel" than with "The Mark on the Wall." Ford's story, as experimental as it is, is well-paced and easy to read, though it may *feel* a little disjointed. It is even pretty "relatable": everyone has probably lost something special and looked everywhere for it (I think Jesus told a parable about such a situation, probably, because it, even then, was widely applicable); there is something universal about the

148

situation that is immediately understandable. But the pacing that moves the story along for the reader owes quite a lot to Ford's experimentation. The story unfolds amid time shifts, jumps from fantasy to reality, the movement into a revelatory dream or hallucination, leaps from one perspective to another. The reader is not "stuck" in a character's seemingly endless train of thought, as in "The Mark on the Wall." But, like Woolf's story, Ford does use one object, the letter, as the baseline. As much as the story flashes out in different directions, the letter does hold the rhythm for the entire narrative, just as the ambiguous mark on the wall serves the same function for Woolf.

Both stories also play with a toggling back and forth between sensory perception and thought. Ford presents the overwhelming stimuli of war (perception): the booms of bombs, the jarring rhythms of machine gun fire, the shouts of men—the soundtrack of battle. Interestingly, this soundscape is paralleled with relatively peaceful visions of a starry night through the triangular cutout in the top of the tent as James rests. This irony is doubled in the realization that the reader has, by the end of the story, that, as oppressive and frightening as the war obviously is, James seems to have become habituated to it—or perhaps he is so anxious about the lost letter that his mind is elsewhere and too consumed with his fantasies about what may or may not happen with Mrs. Wilkinson for him to bother himself with war. It is all just a backdrop to his real concern: a woman.

The close of the story and the denouement concerning the "pink flannel" itself is especially interesting, considering my introduction to these stories. James gets in his sleeping bag but cannot fall asleep, so he says a prayer to Saint Anthony, the patron saint of lost and stolen objects. And all of a sudden James is back in England; he is looking at a window as people pass by, women's skirts brushing him as they do, and Saint Anthony appears to him saying, "You perceive? Pink Flannel!" (688). And everything turns into the same "bluey pink" all around him (688). After a moment he *does* perceive. He wakes up and retrieves his letter from the book his fellow soldier had put into a particular pocket made of this "bluey pink" flannel (688–689).

What is the point? That he found the letter? Sure. That the contents of the letter from Mrs. Wilkinson were favorable to his plans and fantasy? Why not?

But more than these, I think Ford is demonstrating that this new view of the "mind behind the mind," as it were, the unexplored regions of the unconscious mind that he is experimenting with showing in "Pink

Philosophy and Fiction

Flannel"—the mind that is obsessive, associative, and non-rational in its operations, nonlinear in its processes, and largely imaginative, creative, and free-flowing—this mind works and solves problems in ways our rational, linear thinking cannot. We see this play out as James, in the opening of the story, goes through a rational process of elimination (he eliminates places where the letter could be based on whether he had certain articles with him at the time the letter was handed to him); he then examines the "chain of custody" (we could call it) as he ticks through who had the letter and when. All of these reason-based attempts fail him. It is his free-associating, dream-based, imaginative, and ridiculous unconscious mind that solves his problem through hints and riddles. But he gets the message. It works. Ford puts this new picture of the "dark side" of the mind on display and shows its usefulness, even as the portrayal also discloses its unruly nature.

Maybe we see Woolf's portrait of the new view of the mind doing something similar, even if "The Mark on the Wall" probably makes impatient readers wonder how much more of this they have to put up with. But if we are patient, careful readers, I think we find that Woolf does, in fact, lead us in a number of interesting directions. Further, Woolf demonstrates not just a directionless meandering of one's train of thought; she is also, to some degree, making observations about *how* we think, if we give ourselves the opportunity to let our minds wander and explore.

The whole story builds from a memory—but an indeterminate memory. It is a memory that must first be plotted or located precisely. She begins the story like this: "Perhaps it was the middle of January in the present year that I first looked up and saw the mark on the wall" (706). Okay, the narrator is attempting to orient the memory in time. The initial paragraph continues by bringing this "perhaps" to a more precise and definite articulation of the moment of the discovery of the mark:

> In order to fix a date it is necessary to remember what one saw. So now I think of the fire; the steady film of yellow light upon the page of my book; the three chrysanthemums in the round glass bowl on the mantelpiece. Yes, it must have been wintertime, and we had just finished our tea, for I remember that I was smoking a cigarette when I looked up and saw the mark on the wall for the first time. I looked up through the smoke of my cigarette and my eye lodged for a moment upon the burning coals, and that old fancy of the crimson flag flapping from the castle tower came into my mind, and I thought of the cavalcade of red knights riding up the side of the black rock. Rather to my relief the sight of the mark interrupted my fancy, for it is an old

150

fancy, an automatic fancy, made as a child perhaps. The mark was a small round mark, black upon the white wall, about six or seven inches above the mantelpiece [706].

We see the narrator continue to fix the memory in space as well, in the sequence of her physical actions, in the routine of the day, the other objects in the room, and so on. But the narration is also carrying us along her mental path: we move into the past, into a specific moment in the past, from the physical stimuli (that is, the perceptions themselves) to the mental pictures and thoughts that she associated with the objects of perception. The black and red of the burning coals inspire her "fancy" (or imaginative musing) of the red flag, the black rock, some knights (imagery that has been with her since she was a child, she says). Then she strikes upon the ambiguous mark. Its ambiguity is new; its appearance is surprising; it excites her mind. We see it in the next sentence: "How readily our thoughts swarm upon a new object" (706). And then she is off! If we pay attention to the sequence set up on the first page, then we are prepared for what follows.

And what follows is a sporadic, yet careful "free association," all of it deriving, in one way or another, from the mark on the wall. It is almost like a mental workout—an exercise routine. She starts with the warm up, the literal circumstances of the mark (maybe it is a mark made by a nail, perhaps by the people who lived in this house before), and then she blasts off into the sprint she will sustain throughout the rest of the piece, as she takes bigger mental strides of association, leaps that take her further and further away from the mark itself and into speculations about mysteries of meaning, into feelings that turn themselves into thoughts, from sheer perception to life itself and what it would be like to embrace the sheerness of living—of unconscious being that simply is life and thought that never ends. She moves from "the mystery of life; the inaccuracy of thought! The ignorance of humanity!" and she arrives at the speed of modern experience, "the rapidity of life, the perpetual waste and repair; all so casual, all so haphazard" (707). This drives her to meditate upon pure perception—living without thinking, not distinguishing trees from men, nor men from women—the pure experience of color, texture, light, and dark (707).

And then she returns to the mark on the wall. This is her reorientation point—the thing she returns to, almost like a refrain that provides the order for her as she flares off into speculation, serving the same function as the letter in "Pink Flannel." The cycle repeats, as she leaps from the literal (the tree outside the window) to abstract associations

Philosophy and Fiction

(Shakespeare, then botany, then the dynamics of self-consciousness and identity, then to the routines of Sundays, the rules of such routines, the role of men as authorities behind a culture's rules, and so on) (708–709). And she returns to the mark again, a return to center, to the point of orientation. Perhaps this is the mental equivalent of learning to fly, having to return to earth every now and again to regain one's confidence and stability. Or perhaps it is comparable to free jazz: there is always a grounding in the song, even if the solos take one on unexpected, improvisational journeys somewhere on the dark side of the melody.

But Woolf is also doing something with these improvisations: she arrives at ideas which, without the mark, she may not have otherwise, and many of these thoughts relate to the process itself. If we consider her remarks about pure perception or about identity: these are ideas related to the new view of the mind, connected with the deep regions of unconscious, pre-rational, nonlinear human thinking. She riffs on the inadequacy of knowledge. She writes:

> No, no, nothing is proved, nothing is known. And if I were to get up at this very moment and ascertain that the mark on the wall is really—what shall we say—the head of a gigantic old nail, driven in two hundred years ago, which has now, owing to the patient attrition of many generations of housemaids, revealed its head above the coat of paint, and is taking its first view of modern life in the sight of a white-walled fire-lit room, what should I gain?—Knowledge? Matter for further speculation? I can think sitting as well as standing up. And what is knowledge? What are our learned men save the descendants of witches and hermits who crouched in caves and in the woods brewing herbs, interrogating shrew-mice and writing down the language of the stars? And the less we honour them as our superstitions dwindle and our respect for beauty and health increases.... Yes, one could imagine a very pleasant world. [...] How peaceful it is down here, rooted in the center of the world and gazing up through grey waters [710–711].

She has effectively moved from knowledge to being (in philosophical terms, from epistemology to ontology), and in doing so she has combined her mind with Nature itself, no longer worried with what she knows, but now just drinking in the "satisfying sense of reality" (711). The rational mind yearns for certainty and knowledge, but deeper down, Woolf suggests, is existence itself, which we are part of, but which is also "other than ours" (712). She explores this "otherness" as a tree, as the natural perception affords; its life is rich and magnificent and long and (somehow) continues long after it is dead (712).

Woolf, in "The Mark on the Wall," presents the mind at work. If there is a point, it seems to be the process itself (it does not really matter what the mark on the wall actually is, though it may be interesting that the mark turns out to have been alive). The process provides the liberation of the mind: this is liberation from the rational and practical, from the utilitarian surface mind—the mind that only seeks knowledge by taking in facts, the mind worried about newspapers and war (712). The process allows the narrator to reach past *that* mind into the mysterious depths, into the unconscious thoughts that feed her dreams, her feelings deeper down—the thoughts behind the thoughts. And in flashing out and away from the self, the rational "I" or "ego," the mind discovers itself in the "everything else," the "otherness" in the world, in Nature, in being itself. Ironically, in orienting itself in a moment, contemplating the possibilities of a single object, the mind gets itself "unstuck," and finds itself in the "otherness" beyond the restrictions and categories it typically uses to make sense of the world.

Conclusions

These stories of the life of the mind drive toward the point at which the mind meets matter, the body, history, perception, and experience. Whereas philosophy and science tend to demarcate boundaries, to develop systems for organizing the order of our thought, our being, our perception, and so on, fiction attempts to put it all back together again. Why?

We can make an analogy to a deck of cards. Philosophy (and psychology and psychoanalysis) seems interested in thinking about the various ways the cards can be organized and described: by suit (spades, hearts, clubs, etc.), by rank (ace, king, queen, jack, etc.), by color (spades and clubs are black; hearts and diamonds are red, etc.), by aspects of shape and design, and so on. Fiction's interests lie elsewhere. Fiction wants to create. Fiction builds castles and pyramids from the cards; it makes pictures; it cuts them up and creates collages. Pattern and organization are still part of the picture, the collage, the castle, but these principles serve a different function, and sometimes what we think we know about what the cards are has to be thrown into question so we can combine them in new ways (on the analogy, by folding, tearing, cutting, drawing, splicing, gluing, burning, etc.). If fiction imitates reality (in whatever way), it has to "mess with" what we think we know about who and what and how humans are in order to portray them in their "natural" state, or some view or version of whatever that "natural" state may be thought to be. People do not, of course, literally, live in a house of cards, but people can make houses from cards and put a king or joker in them.

The stories examined in this chapter do something like this. They examine the mind-body dualism as one among the paradoxes of the human condition. "Looking back" demonstrates the reign of rationality and reason in a perfectly unreasonable, but understandably human, way, as an old priest tries to relate how he is emotionally deficiently composed for handling the basics of human life, and rather than trying to "correct" his thinking, we, like his friend, must accept him, try to understand him, relate our experience to his, and perhaps learn from him. Both "Looking Back" and "The Hunger Artist" portray adversarial relationships between the mind and body, but they also both demonstrate that this is just another way of saying that they depict oneself as, sometimes, one's own worst enemy. And when we read these stories, we are vicariously experiencing the realization that this is often at the heart of human misery, but that reaching such wisdom is both so very basic but so very important. "The Tables of the Law" demonstrates the same thing through a story in which the protagonist fails to reach this epiphany. Whether the hell he is destined for is, in the world of the story, real or imaginary does not really matter. If he is locked in an idea that both elevates and degrades him in order to convince him that he is special, then he is already in a self-alienating hell of his own making.

Further, these three stories conceive of the individual subject as a kind of specimen for study in a way that many of the other stories, so far, have not. All three characters are presented as isolated individuals, alienated from the social world around them, attempting to learn who they are in order to learn how they may relate to others. The tragic aspects of the stories come from their beliefs about how they perceive themselves, both how their minds are related to their bodies and how each one, as an individual, is related to everyone else, to the world, and/or to meaning. And the former seems to control the latter. Each one, in one way or another, believes that he is special, and each is crippled by the fear that what he believes is actually true. The individual subject, the self, in this case, is presented as a hopeless narcissistic paranoiac, one who has to figure out how to live with the likelihood that he is correct about his specialness.

The modernist authors seem to tend further toward a "ghost in the machine." The mind in these stories seems to float even freer of its body. But in both "Pink Flannel" and, especially, in "The Mark on the Wall," the spinning consciousness of the mind ends up putting the characters even more deeply in touch with their experiential lives. It is by going further within the mind that the characters seem to figure things out in the world of the body. James in "Pink Flannel" finds his letter by letting his mind drift into dreamland. The narrator in "The Mark on the Wall" perceives herself as a perceiving self, not as whatever her culture tells her she is: her mind puts her in touch with the world, with nature, with being as being. Could she be more integrated, mind and body, than simply as a "this" in touch with the "all this" around her?

The idea that the "unexamined life is not worth living" may just be a tautology. To some degree, we all must examine our lives in order to continue living at all. This is the basic paradox of the continuity (or discontinuity) of the self, the "I," the mind/soul, and the body, and everything else: I am not only mind or body, but neither am I wholly composed only of their combination—there is the "everything/one-else" with which I am in touch, with which I am connected, and so, which may, too, be part of who I am.

If we are going to go on living, we will have to go on examining what it means to live, piecing life together, organizing, describing, and creating. Perhaps this is why the ancient myths conceived of the mind (or soul) as a wanderer, Psyche, who falls in love with Eros, the god of sensual desire, the lover who puts her in touch with the body.

CHAPTER SIX

Love and Death

"The continuous work of life is to build death."
—Michel de Montaigne

Loving Death: Double Indemnity *(1936)* *by James M. Cain*

In Greek, the word for "passionate love" or "desire" is *eros,* while "death," in Greek, is *thanatos.* Each concept is also personified in ancient Greek mythology. Eros (Cupid is his Roman equivalent) is the son of Aphrodite (goddess of love) and Ares (god of war). Eros almost perfectly blends his parents' domains; he carries arrows to shoot at people to inspire love, and others to break the spell of love, or even transform it into hate. Thanatos (Mors is his Roman equivalent), god of death, is the brother of the god of sleep (Hypnos), son of Night (Nyx) and Darkness (Erebos). His relation to human life seems, appropriately, more determinative and absolute, and less capricious, less fickle, than Eros. But Thanatos is also more abstract: while he is frequently referred to in myth and legend, he very rarely emerges in embodied form (Sears 175–176). He is a shadow. As different as the domains of these gods may be, Eros and Thanatos do share a striking kind of indifference: Eros is often depicted with a blindfold (love is blind); Thanatos is something like a functionary, whose key role is merely a response to the length of one's life-thread (death treats everyone equally) (Sears 175–176). There are, of course, stories about tricking or manipulating them for this or that reason, but these gods' domains are universal: everyone loves and everyone dies. Contact with these gods is, thus, inevitable—and inevitably human.

If we dig into the worlds that these two deities symbolize, we may identify an interesting dichotomy in the gods and the human concepts they represent. Eros, of course, is where our English word "erotic"

Chapter Six. Love and Death

is derived from, and love, desire, sensuality, and sex, as much as they are romanticized, sentimentalized, and vulgarized, are, evolutionarily, directed toward the perpetuation of life. And death, Thanatos, the root of English words like "euthanasia" and (for poetry fans) "thanatopsis," clearly tends in the opposite direction. Humans become playthings in the hands of these gods: an impulse for Life drives us to one another in order to perpetuate itself (through reproduction); an impulse toward Death isolates and, ultimately, disintegrates us, returns us to our inorganic, composite parts (through decomposition). The struggle between these two forces is, accordingly, what life consists of, and James M. Cain's noir crime novel *Double Indemnity* portrays the intersection of these two domains in interesting, provocative, and disturbing ways, but it does so in a surprising context: the insurance business.

Fraud, Murder, and Intrigue

As with most crime novels, the plot of *Double Indemnity* is built around quite a lot of intrigue (secretive planning for bad deeds): a murder plot, insurance fraud, careful evasion of the authorities, manipulations of confidence, and so on. Put briefly, Walter Huff, an insurance man, meets Phyllis Nirdlinger, and the two fall for one another as they scheme to murder Phyllis' husband. The plan is perfect.

1. Take out an accident insurance policy, which contains a "double indemnity" payout for an accidental death on a train.
2. Kill Mr. Nirdlinger (not on the train), and then dump his body on the train tracks.
3. Walter, disguised as Mr. Nirdlinger, gets on the train, but hops off the observation platform of the moving train where they plan to dump the body.
4. Cover all the bases: witnesses (pull unassuming people into the scheme as needed), alibis (whereabouts of murderers are accounted for), nerve (keep up appearances of normalcy), audacity (act boldly when necessary).

The execution of the plan goes perfectly (they get a little testy with one another, but, other than that, it all goes off without a hitch). But it all still falls apart.

During their separation after the murder, Phyllis and Walter become suspicious of one another. Each one begins another relationship with someone else. Eventually, Walter devises a scheme to kill Phyllis, too, in order to get rid of the one person who can point the finger at him, and he plans to blame her death on the man she is seeing behind his back, a man who happens to be the ex-boyfriend of the woman with whom Walter is cheating on Phyllis. As he waits in a stolen car for Phyllis on the night he plans to murder her, she (literally) takes a shot at him instead. And the whole thing unravels, and everything is thrust into the open: the murderers are punished, and order is restored.

A Grim Courtship

Death haunts the story from page one. Walter relates how he first got into this mess, just trying to sell insurance. He went to the Nirdlinger "House of Death" on a whim because he was in the neighborhood and wanted to see about a renewal (1). Phyllis did not look like Death when he first saw her either: she looks like every other young, sweet-faced, blonde woman in southern California (3). Even though Walter knows she is up to something suspicious in their first encounter, he is drawn to her beauty, to her body; he is driven by desire. He feels that the deal is turning sour, that she wants something from him, and he knows better than most how not to get mixed up in a questionable situation, but as Phyllis flutters around him, Walter notices that beneath her pajamas was a body that, he says, would drive any man crazy (5). Three days later, Walter returns, knowing that there is something duplicitous about Phyllis, and this time the maid is gone, and the husband is out of town. She makes her pitch to him about accident insurance, which he has already told us is always suspicious, and, instead of dropping the whole thing and rejecting her, he kisses her, and she kisses him back (13).

Interestingly, his reflection on this moment is anything but erotic:

> I was standing right on the deep end, looking over the edge, and I kept telling myself to get out of there, and get quick, and never come back. [...]
> What I kept doing was peeping out over that edge, and all the time I was trying to pull away from it, there was something in me that kept edging me a little closer ... [15].

Walter returns to this image later, when Phyllis shows up at his apartment: he says he knew he should have shut the whole thing down, but "that thing was in me, pushing me still closer to the edge" (16). But instead of moving right in for another kiss (instead, that is, of being driven exclusively by Eros), Walter's first move is to push toward the murder—to let her know that he knows what she is thinking, and to volunteer his expertise and assistance in carrying it off. The shadowy figure of Thanatos surfaces. He says he will kill Phyllis' husband for her and for the money (20). She says she has no reason to kill her husband, that he is as good to her as any man can be to a woman; she does not love him, but he has never mistreated her (20). They talk on, and then Phyllis makes an odd confession. She says,

> But there's something in me that loves Death. I think of myself as Death, sometimes. In a scarlet shroud, floating through the night. I'm so beautiful, then. And sad. And hungry to make the whole world happy, by taking them out where I am, into the night, away from all trouble, all unhappiness [20].

They are a perfect couple. He has a death wish, and she identifies herself as Death. But it gets darker. In the next several pages, Walter describes a fully-formed murder plot (the one outlined above); he gives Phyllis a tutorial on how to commit the perfect murder. When class is over, and she is preparing to leave, Phyllis says, "Walter—I'm so excited. It does terrible things to me." Walter admits to feeling the same way, and they cannot help themselves: they kiss (26). I do not know how better to describe an intersection of Eros and Thanatos. Conceptually, it is paradoxical: Walter is, at once, drawn to her with both impulses: there is the sexual attraction, but there is also the darker, more abstract pull of the death wish, but she is the object of both—the one who embodies the object of both desires.

The Femme Fatale into Monstrous Feminine

In film theory and criticism there is a name for characters like Phyllis: *femme fatale* (a typical female character in a cinematic genre called *film noir*—literally, "black" or "dark" film) (Childers and Hentzi 112). The *femme fatale* is the "fatal woman," or the "agent of (evil) fate," and when she enters on the scene, "the hero's fate is sealed" (Zizek 192–193). The trope of the *femme fatale* is nearly ubiquitous in the noir genre. And Phyllis definitely emerges in *Double Indemnity* in this way, but, by the end of the novel, she has been transformed by Walter's narrative into something excessive—something that goes beyond such a definition.

After the murder, images and descriptions of Phyllis become increasingly monstrous. Even early on, she enters into Walter's story rather "spectrally" (she seems to "appear" out of nowhere), but, after the murder, Phyllis reenters the scene on the dark railroad tracks like a monster from a creature feature:

> I heard a panting. Then with it I heard footsteps. They would go fast for a second or two, and then stop. It was like being in a nightmare, with something queer coming after me, and I didn't know what it was, but it was horrible. Then I saw it. It was her. That man must have weighed 200 pounds, but she had him on her back, holding him by the handle, and staggering along with him, over the tracks. His head was hanging down beside her head. They looked like something in a horror picture [60].

Further, symbolically, we can see, here, Phyllis (the woman) and Death (in the murdered husband) depicted together, as one: this is everything Walter has been attracted to all wrapped up in one figure, the complete object of his desires—and it horrifies him. Perhaps it is not just the image and atmosphere that Walter finds so unnerving. Perhaps it is because, symbolically, the dead Mr. Nirdlinger on Phyllis' back represents Walter himself. He comes very close to realizing this at the end of the same chapter (a chapter in which he has just pretended to *be* Mr. Nirdlinger—more on that in a moment). He says that he had given in to her, that he had killed for her, and, in doing so, he had put himself in a position to be ruined by her because of what she had on him, and, now, he wants out: "That's all it takes, one drop of fear, to curdle love into hate" (64). And from that point on, Walter's story begins to drift toward demonstrating that he had been her unwitting victim all along.

As Walter's character begins to become more sympathetic, however, Phyllis becomes more horrifying, more monstrous, and in specifically feminine terms. Barbara Creed's term, the "monstrous-feminine" may be instructive here. Broadly, this idea develops from a theory for describing depictions of women in horror or of horror monsters with certain "feminine" characteristics, often associated with motherhood and maternity (68–69). When we learn of Phyllis' history, something like the "monstrous-feminine" seems right. We learn from Lola, Phyllis' stepdaughter, that Phyllis killed her (Lola's) mother (the first Mrs. Nirdlinger), and, of course, married Mr. Nirdlinger, thus, literally and symbolically, replacing the dead mother (Cain 87–88). And this maternal imagery becomes more and more monstrous as the concept of "mother" becomes obscene and inverted as inhabited by Phyllis: not only do we learn that she has been dating Sachetti (Lola's boyfriend), but also, in her previous career as a nurse, that she has murdered a number of little children (95, 127). So not only is Phyllis a mother seducing a man away from her daughter, but she is also a mother who takes children out of the world instead of bringing them into it—plus, she is a "false" mother, an imposter who has murdered her way into the role. These aspects, along with the creepy way she uses make-up to paint her face white, draw black circles around her eyes, and color her lips and cheeks red, and the red silk that transforms her body into something horrible and unhuman—makeup and clothing, here, both serving as symbolic markers of the "feminine" and both typically used to "beautify," to make one more "desirable"—fuse in Phyllis in an image of the monstrous-feminine that Walter compares to the figure of Death from Samuel Taylor Coleridge's *Rime of the Ancient Mariner* (101, 136). She is the perfect combination of desire and morbidity, of the impulse toward life inverted toward death (she does, after all, near the end of the novel, refer to Death as her bridegroom). She combines and embodies Eros and Thanatos.

The Serpent in the Self

Is Walter really any better? He wants us to believe he is, but he is in control of the narrative, since, in the world of the fiction, he is the author of the story. But we can see through the cracks. We know he is drawn to the danger that Phyllis represents, even before he knows what, exactly, that danger is. He feels something in him pulling him toward her, and it does not seem to be lust alone (16). The problem is that the desire is mixed up with something deeper and darker that he does not even completely recognize or understand in himself; instead, he refers to it as "that thing" that is *in* him (14–15, 16). By the end of the story, Walter wants to convince the reader that he has been taken in by Phyllis but, now, has seen the error in his ways. He wants to seem honorable, demonstrating it by looking out for Lola's safety as he makes his deal with Keyes (130). And Keyes seems to buy this; he says as much to Walter in the hospital room: "You just got yourself tangled up with an Irrawaddy cobra, that's all. That woman—it makes my blood run cold just to think of her" (124).

Walter's feelings for Lola (Mr. Nirdlinger's daughter, Phyllis' step-daughter) provide some interesting fodder for further analysis of his character. At the beginning of Chapter 11, Walter dispassionately discusses his plan to kill Phyllis, and within two sentences he describes his feelings for Lola. He even compares and contrasts his feelings for the two women. He says his feelings for Lola were nothing like what he felt for Phyllis, who inspired some "unhealthy excitement" that took hold of him (102). The situation with Lola was something altogether different: she brought out in him a "sweet peace"; they could be together for hours without even speaking, and then they would exchange a glance, and the purity of that sweet, peaceful moment would be sustained (102).

We know that Walter is only so cognizant of his own feelings, but this description is interesting. We know that Lola is nineteen years old and that Walter is thirty-four—but, even so, this is yet another woman he thinks he loves, but Walter calls her a "girl" (Phyllis is only ever described as a "woman"). Further, his feelings for Lola appear not to be sexual; in fact, he is careful to distinguish them from the "unhealthy excitement" with which he responds to Phyllis. Oddly, perhaps, his description of how he feels about Lola seems largely paternal. In fact, every interaction Walter has with Lola is markedly paternal: he gives her a ride to the drugstore to meet up with her (age-appropriate) boyfriend (he even offers them some money); he helps out the boyfriend with a loan; he feigns interest in the boyfriend's dissertation (30–31, 32–35, 37–38). Even when she comes back after her father's murder (a matter of a week or so), she is still treating him like a father figure, asking him for advice, complaining about her break-up with Sachetti, venting about her stepmother (85–90). Let's see how far this goes.

Walter began replacing Lola's father from the beginning of the narrative, almost accidentally, by replacing Mr. Nirdlinger for Phyllis. We should not overlook that Walter checked Phyllis' boxes, too. Phyllis makes clear that she is interested in Walter erotically, and as a voluntary agent for her death obsession (13–20). So he is a stand-in both for Mr. Nirdlinger and for her other "bridegroom," Death (134). But Walter also willingly plays both roles. In addition to the murder plan displaying Walter's clever scheme for bilking his company out of thousands of dollars, it also shows, literally, what is happening with Walter's character symbolically. He dresses, just like Mr. Nirdlinger, in a blue suit; he fashions a cast to wear on his ankle; he wears a pair of horn-rimmed glasses, just like Nirdlinger (47). After he kills the man in the car, he performs the role of Mr. Nirdlinger, right down to putting the dead man's half-smoked cigar (an object with possible phallic significance) into his own mouth, walking with Phyllis to the train, limping past the travelers, and kissing her goodbye (51–57).

Walter symbolically occupies Nirdlinger's roles when he "becomes" him. In a way, this makes the ludicrous shift from Phyllis to Lola *more* credible because it is not a shift at all: it is just the other side of the role he has put on (it is just confused). Further, still, once Walter commits to loving Lola and hating Phyllis, his scheme operates in exactly the same way, demonstrating literally what he is doing symbolically. His plan is to frame Sachetti, so he performs as Sachetti (who, ironically, is now dating Phyllis); he drives around in Sachetti's car; Lola even mistakes him for Sachetti (111–112, 127). But Walter's roles contract into one disturbing monster, just like Phyllis,' the process is just less noticeable, since Walter is the one controlling the narrative: he becomes illicit "husband" (Mr. Nirdlinger), stand-in "father" ("daddy" Nirdlinger), pretend "teen lover" (Sachetti), and "agent of death"/murderer (Death), all wrapped up in one. He is a monster as horrible as Phyllis; he is just less accomplished.

Psychos and Psychoanalysis

Phyllis' accomplishments are yet another interesting touchpoint in *Double Indemnity*. And, here, we can perhaps begin to ask about what the novel says as an artifact of its era. Phyllis is, of course, quite accomplished at murdering: her tally of successful murders (that we know about) is, by the end of the book, ten, plus an attempt on Walter (Sachetti found five cases before the three little children, plus the first Mrs. Nirdlinger and Mr. Nirdlinger himself)—and she is only thirty-one or two. We also know that Phyllis was a nurse, and not just any nurse, but one of the top nurses in the city, and the chief nurse at her last job (88, 125). She is cunning, intelligent, educated, sexual, manipulative, powerful, and she is beautiful and not shy about showing it off. For the sake of comparison, Lola, however, the other major female character in the novel, is presented as innocent or naïve, uneducated, impulsive, earnest, pure, devoted, emotional, girlish, trusting, pretty, playful, and meek. If we wanted to draw broad conclusions, we might say that, as provocative and indecent as the novel probably seemed in the mid–1930s, when it was published (Bradford 29), it reinforces a very conventional view of the "ideal" woman and castigates, not just as "bad," but as horrible and dangerous—as a force that is, literally, destroying the traditional American family, and, thereby, threatening civilization itself—those characteristics associated with feminism, or even just the independent, modern working woman, generally.

We might be able to connect this grand-scale picture of the threat the "monstrous-feminine" presents to civilization through the concepts we began with—and by taking a tip from Keyes about reading more "modern psychology" (Cain 124).

In unpacking the significance of his theory of the "death instinct," Sigmund Freud writes,

> If we are to take it as a truth that knows no exception that everything dies for internal reasons—becomes inorganic once again—then we shall be compelled to say that "the aim of all life is death" and, looking backwards that "inanimate things existed before living ones" [qtd. in Storr 66].

Freudian psychoanalyst Anthony Storr suggests that what Freud is saying here is that "since the inorganic precedes the organic in the history of our planet," then the death instinct "can only be a striving towards a state before life itself existed" (66). Freud, thus, had come up with a "dualistic scheme in which all the phenomena of mental life could be ultimately traced to the interaction of, or conflict between, two drives, or instincts": Eros and Thanatos (67). Sound familiar? Freud claims that the aim of Eros is not sex alone, not just the unity of two individuals, but to "establish ever greater unities and to preserve them thus—in short, to bind together," while the aim of Thanatos is not death alone, but "to undo connections, and so to destroy things," ultimately, to "lead what is living into an inorganic state" (qtd. in Storr 67). This all sounds very abstract, but Freud clarifies things: civilization is a "process in the service of Eros, whose purpose is to combine human individuals, and after that families, then races, peoples and nations, into one great unity, the unity of mankind," while Thanatos, the aggressive, death drive, works through the "hostility of each against all and all against each" to "oppose this programme of civilization" (qtd. in Storr 68).

The problem, for Freud, in *Civilization and Its Discontents*, is the same problem we see embodied in both Walter and Phyllis in *Double Indemnity*, namely, that "this aggressive instinct is the derivative and the main representative of" Thanatos, the death drive, "which we have found alongside of Eros and which shares world-dominion with it": the "meaning of the evolution of civilization" is in its playing out of the drama of "the struggle between Eros and Death, between the instinct of life and the instinct of destruction as it works itself out in the human species" (111). We can see this drama play out on a small scale in the relationship between Phyllis and Walter, as Eros becomes Thanatos and vice versa, as the family is undermined by the role confusion they introduce into its relations, as relationships outside the family are corrupted as both Phyllis' and Walter's erotic impulses carry their aggression beyond. But the novel does present a male-dominated story to a patriarchal culture, one whose grasp on power is threatened by the possibility of feminine power, so the dominant threat is "encoded" in the monstrous-feminine character of Phyllis. My point, however, is that, if we look hard enough, we can see the cracks in this façade: Walter, too, presents this monstrous duplicity that chews away at human bonds, hollows them out, until they begin to resemble his own vacuous heart, as Richard Bradford observes in his study, *Crime Fiction*, noting the gradual fragmentation of Walter's character and confidence, leaving a hollow man "no longer convinced of anything, including who he is" (31).

And maybe it is not just the two of them.

More Than Just Business

Phyllis's motivations, as strange and morbid as they seem, are projections through Walter, an unreliable narrator if there ever was one. Even if she is motivated by the "thanatic-erotic" combination ascribed to her, she is also driven by a more familiar desire: money. And so is Walter, of whom we can say the same things. But, whereas both Keyes and Walter ascribe Phyllis's motivations to something like "evil" or, more charitably, pathology (Cain 124–128), Walter is more forthcoming, and, in addition to the psychoanalytic motivations we have already discussed, we still need to analyze the depth and source of Walter's training in the insurance business.

Earlier I pointed to the surprising speed and facility with which Walter devised a nearly perfect murder scheme, but we need to remember that he did not just dream it up out of nowhere. From the first page of the novel, Walter discloses that the insurance business is about manipulation, from getting in the door (1) to getting a feel for a deal in progress (5) to reading and controlling a potential client (7, 25). He explains, at length, the corrupting influence the business has had on him:

> You think it's a business, don't you, just like your business, and maybe a little better than that, because it's the friend of the widow, the orphan and the needy in time of trouble? It's not. It's the biggest gambling wheel in the world. [...] You bet that your house will burn down, they bet it won't, that's all. What fools you is that you didn't *want* your house to burn down when you made the bet, and so you forget it's a bet. That don't fool them. To them a bet is a bet, and a hedge bet don't look any different than any other bet. [...] They know there's just so many people out there that are out to crook that wheel, and that's when they get tough [26, emphasis in original].

So far in this monologue, Walter describes the business as a duplicitous institution that takes easy bets against the occurrence of unlikely events. The industry functions according to a threefold scheme: maintain the positive public optics, take people's money hand-over-fist on easily winnable wagers, and threaten people who try to turn the system in their direction through fraudulent claims. Walter's characterization of the company is that the insurance business is based on *legal* fraud, on cheating people out of money; it is organized crime with a human face, and the one thing a mafia does not like is being cheated. But his description becomes darker yet.

> I know all their tricks, I lie awake nights thinking up tricks, so I'll be ready for them when they come at me. And then one night I think up a trick, and get to thinking I could crook the wheel myself if I could only put a plant out there to put down my bet. That's all. When I met Phyllis I met my plant [27].

Here, early in the novel, Walter, essentially, is confessing that he thought he was manipulating Phyllis, using her for his own dark fantasy, a fantasy constructed around the cynical, antisocial pessimism he had internalized after fifteen years of treating people like marks, dollar signs, and threats. He says as much: "I had seen ... so many awful things people had pulled to crook the wheel, that that stuff didn't seem real to me anymore" (27).

Even if this is a justification for his actions, it does testify to the corrupting influence of the business, one Keyes confesses to sharing near the end of the book, explaining his disappointment with Walter. Keyes admits that he had liked Walter, even though, from his perspective in the insurance business, all of humanity looks morally sick or venal, which makes it hard to like anyone at all (123). No wonder they got along so well.

As much as we might be drawn to the interpretation that Walter's explanation allows him to save face, when we look past all of the intrigue and sexual melodrama and, instead, at the business politics in the story, we see something pretty consistent with—and maybe a little worse than—what Walter describes. The company's initial response to the Nirdlinger death is to do just about anything so it does not have to pay. This, perhaps, is to be expected, since a business, of course, makes money by taking in as much money as possible and paying out as little as possible (even if that sounds slightly cynical). But the company is also able to work around proper, legal channels: for example, Walter relates that the company has a special relationship with the coroner's

Chapter Six. Love and Death

office, and, through this relationship, the company obtains a secret, illegal autopsy rather than risking the legal option (67). The president of the company, Mr. Norton, makes an argument for Nirdlinger's death being a suicide, regardless of the improbability and insensitivity of such a conclusion (68–69). More disturbing, still, is Keyes' speech about the statistical analyses of suicides, the records and tables kept by the insurance industry to advise agents and investigators in assessing probability, risk, and fraud (70–71). The business response is cynical, and acquiring a secret autopsy is clearly illegal and personally intrusive, but, once the company's suspicions find some purchase, it gets very tough indeed (26).

After Walter is shot in the final chapters of the book, but before it becomes clear that it was Phyllis who shot him, Lola and Sachetti are suspected of being involved, which implicates them in the death of Mr. Nirdlinger, too, which thereby makes them suspects of insurance fraud as well. Keyes' theories start spinning: he connects Sachetti through the car loan, and he is quick to go after Lola for the murder. He says, "you think it funny, that a girl would pull something like that on her own father. But it's happened. It's happened plenty of times. For fifty thousand bucks it's going to happen plenty of times again" (119). This is an interesting justification, but if we consider it analytically, we also see another potential problem. The situation that Keyes is describing, that people, given the opportunity, would kill their own fathers for fifty thousand dollars, is, of course cynical and pessimistic. But we should also observe that the only reason such an opportunity exists is because the insurance business has dreamed up this scheme for them—that no one would have such an opportunity if the company had not offered a double indemnity clause that awarded so much money for a death under this peculiar set of circumstances. It is not only cynical and pessimistic in its view of human nature; worse, the company is completely irresponsible, knowing what it claims to know about the extremes to which people will go because of greed, to dangle such a payout before them. But the company does it for money: capitalistic greed outweighs social responsibility.

Worse, yet, are the extremes to which the company is willing to go to hold onto the fifty thousand dollars and to save face with the public. Keyes, before Walter comes clean about murdering Nirdlinger, sets out the plan for how to deal with Lola and Sachetti: "A little help from the cops, a few treatments with the rubber hose, something like that, and sooner or later this pair is going to spill it. Especially the girl. She'll crack before long.... Believe me this is what we've been waiting for" (120). Again, Keyes suggests illegal interactions with public officials, but he even goes so far as to suggest that torturing the pair will get the business the information it needs so it will not have to pay the claim. He even seems to relish the ease with which a beating with a rubber hose will break a teenage girl—and this is even too much for Walter (which is saying something) (120).

Finally, in order to save the company the public embarrassment of a situation in which Walter, its star salesman, is on the front page of every newspaper around, Keyes is delegated to give Walter a special deal: if he plays nice and writes a statement confessing to Nirdlinger's murder, the company will set him up on a steamer out of the country, which will offer him a chance to escape; it, of course, makes the same offer to Phyllis (129, 133). Keyes takes precautions; if Walter reneges on the deal, Keyes will deny everything, and he will have proof that no such deal was ever offered (130). Again, the company is working outside of legal and proper channels of civilization, outside of any kind of business ethics, outside of the law, outside of basic morality, in order to save itself some bad press. Further, it is setting free two criminals, one of whom has murdered at least ten people already.

So, what are we to make of all of this? In a way, it fits perfectly with everything else, especially with the framing Freud gives to Eros and Thanatos. But the criticism is more biting. Of course, seeing the grotesque combination of Eros and Thanatos, one ever peeking out from behind and corrupting the other in the match-made-in-hell that is the relationship between Walter and Phyllis is disturbing, provocative, and scandalous. This merging of illicit sex, antisocial desire, suicide, murder, and confusion provides the shock the novel produced when it was first published. But the dark, shadowy role played by business in *Double Indemnity* provides an incisive comment on the insurance company, but, even more broadly, on business/corporate culture itself, or even on capitalism as a whole. Corporate culture thrives on impelling people toward greed and fear, the novel seems to say. It trains people to perceive others as numbers, marks, dollar signs, or threats. In the extreme view of corporate culture given in the novel, the company is *the* dominant force, the most powerful institution in society, more powerful than the laws, the courts, or the other public social institutions. It provides the context in which people can be traded or sacrificed for dollars; it creates and encourages repulsive relationships; it requires and/or rewards aggression, manipulation, greed, and suspicion: it thrives on "the hostility of each against all and all against each," which, according to Freud, spells the opposition of the "programme of civilization" (qtd. in Storr 68).

Death-Drive: The End

In the last chapter, as Walter sits talking with Phyllis on the steamer, just before the end, Walter describes Phyllis one last time, as he sees again the sweetness in her smile that drew him in when he first met her, before she dresses up in her bride of Death garb to end it all: "I thought of the five patients, the three little children, Mrs. Nirdlinger, Nirdlinger, and myself. It didn't seem possible that anybody that could be as nice as she was when she wanted to be, could have done those things" (137).

Two concluding observations:

1. Is this not also the dynamic we see given to the company in the novel? Both Phyllis and the company present a façade, a public face, and underneath is something dark, repulsive, aggressive, and ugly. Why does Phyllis pose such a threat throughout the novel? Perhaps because she rivals the company at its own game.

2. The same goes for Walter. He, very cleverly, steers us away from himself by focusing on the strange paradox of love and death he sees in Phyllis. Or maybe it is not clever. Maybe he just believes it. Maybe he is still that blind to his own motivations, to his own desires, to his own corruption. In his list of Phyllis' victims, he included Mr. Nirdlinger (whom Walter actually killed) and himself. Maybe, finally, Walter is even better at this than Phyllis. Besides, as Walter himself says, "I'm a salesman, if I'm nothing else" (25). He has, after all, been selling us a story the whole time, and it is a story he himself is already buying.

CHAPTER SEVEN

The Ends of Fiction and Philosophy

"Every movement reveals us."—Michel de Montaigne

Morality, Madness, and (Un)freedom

The examination of fiction through philosophy (and vice versa) in this book reveals the following conclusions.

First, over and over again, a trend emerges, ultimately, toward ethical or moral philosophy, and often toward moral failure and ethical ambiguity. In outlining the themes according to which this study was organized, I intentionally avoided this domain, opting instead for "Social Cont(r)acts" since it limited the subject considerably, but the stories seem to have led toward moral considerations regardless. Upon reflection, however, we cannot be too surprised by this. Ultimately, fiction precludes abstraction. It forces ideas into actions, into human moral agents who confront one another, the world, and themselves. Even the headier of the stories we examined, like Yeats' "The Tables of the Law," or the fantastic ones, like Wilde's children's stories, put ideas into behaviors, concepts into characters and worlds and relations—they activate philosophy in an invented world for the reader to perceive, and perhaps to judge, their value. So, of course, thinking philosophically about fiction guides us toward reflecting on morality.

Another, perhaps surprising, major trend is human *unreason*, or reason gone awry. This aspect arises in various interesting ways. There is the "mad logic" of Poe's protagonists, which presents obvious and dramatic examples of this theme. But there are numerous subtler variations as well, like the "transcendental emotionalism" of Calixta in Chopin's "The Storm," the "gendered" logic of "How I Killed a Bear," the disintegrated reasoning in "The Remarkable Case of Davidson's

Eyes," the "encultured" (or ideologically circumscribed) reasoning of "Mateo Falcone" or "The Judgement," among others. We also see, perhaps more along the lines of "reason gone awry," corrupted reason, still logical in its way, but (paradoxically) *un*reasonably so, in "The Tables of the Law," "Looking Back," and "The Hunger Artist." Finally, in "Pink Flannel" and "The Mark on the Wall," where logic turns associative and irrational, there is an interesting parallel to the irrational, symbolic, sometimes sentimental fantasy reasoning of the "religious" stories, from "The Lightning-Rod Man" and Irving's and Hawthorne's Devil stories to Wilde's morality fables. And, again, we might conclude that this is only too human. Reason is aspirational, an ideal human faculty which is liable to corruption, degeneration, and so on, but it is also a human tool, a (not *the*) mode of human thinking, which, when fit together with other philosophical or "theoretical virtues" (clarity, consistency, truthfulness, etc.), functions admirably well, but which can be used for other, perhaps, mad, vile, immoral, etc., purposes as well (Beebee and Rush 66).

Finally, this exploration of philosophy and fiction points toward the dynamic relations of freedom and unfreedom. In fiction we see shadows of ourselves in characters, but they share our sense of ourselves: they seem to think they are free, but the mere fact of our consideration of them locked, as they are, in "closed" narratives, demonstrates their unfreedom. What we call plot is, for them, fate. This reveals some kind of "metafictional" aspect to the relation of philosophy and fiction. We may process the possibility of meaning and our relation to it by considering the intersection of these domains, but neither fiction nor philosophy can pronounce exactly what that meaning consists in—or even promise that it is really there. In the end, even our deepest reflections, whether fictional or philosophical, can only reach for possibility, the shadow of the meaning that *may* actually be there. Somewhere. We may write about the cave, the chains, the shadows, the light; we may reason through what it would be like to be free. But none of it means that we are actually free, nor what it would really mean if we were.

Slippery Subjects

Literature and philosophy are "slippery subjects": they both evade clear definition; both are rhizomatous. So it is not so surprising that fiction and philosophy, amid their tangling and spreading tendrils, stretch out and touch one another, or that this contact results in interesting, provocative connections. We can observe, too, that they share an immense common object: namely, human beings, in all their complexities and contexts. Their relation to their object, however, is trickier.

Perhaps we can say, broadly, that fiction relates to life metaphorically. A metaphor, essentially, "characterizes an action, concept, or object in terms used to denote something else, often quite different," but, at the same time, a metaphor also "implies a comparison" between the two, even though the relation is "not articulated *as* a comparison" (Childers and Hentzi 185). If we frame this figure of speech philosophically, then, for our purposes, fiction characterizes human life in the terms of specific narratives, often quite different from and obviously more specific than, life itself is, but these stories imply a comparison to what it means to be human, even though they do not typically articulate the nature of that comparison. Perhaps this is just a carefully stated way of saying that art imitates life. But maybe not. In seeing fiction as metaphorically related to life, the art resides in the manner of the imitation. The art, at once, acknowledges as the basis of its being the dissimilarity and its comparison to life: in other words, fictional art acknowledges that it is fiction, that it both shrinks from and embraces life, that it both imitates and exceeds life, that it has everything to do with what it means to be human—and that it is also both more than and less than that. Like all art, fiction is a human attempt to understand humanity. Is this not a pursuit of wisdom, a manner of examining human life, something like philosophy?

Philosophy has the same goal, but its first impulses are different. Helen Beebee and Michael Rush, in *Philosophy: Why It Matters*, write that "philosophy matters because it seeks and promotes understanding and clear thought and because it is practically helpful, intrinsically interesting, and culturally and historically significant" (1). This succinct thesis for philosophy points to its primary impulses: understanding, clarity, practicality, usefulness, intellectual satisfaction, significance. Philosophy (most of it, anyway) seeks clear understanding through the practical use of reason. Like art, or perhaps we should say, *as* an art, philosophy, too, is a human attempt to understand humanity.

In a way, philosophy and fiction seem made for one another: fiction speaks of life in metaphors, and philosophy speaks of life by unpacking and clarifying. But the relation, as we have seen, goes the other direction, too. Philosophy informs human life, so fiction packs philosophy (and more fiction!) into the gap between what is meant and what is said. So, in relating to one another, both fiction and philosophy are always already relating to themselves through and to the other (and on and on the circle goes), in a never-ending dialogue that "makes things matter" (Eagleston 8).

Works Cited

Andersen, Kurt. *Fantasyland: How America Went Haywire: A 500-Year History*. Random House, 2017.

Aquinas, Thomas. *Aquinas on Nature and Grace*. Edited by A.M. Fairweather. John Knox Press, 1954.

Arata, Stephen, ed. *H.G. Wells: The Time Machine: A Norton Critical Edition*. Norton, 2009.

Aristotle. *Metaphysics. Introduction to Aristotle*. Edited by Richard McKeon. Random House, 1947, pp. 237–296.

"B. F. Skinner." *Department of Psychology, Harvard University*. psychology. fas.harvard.edu/people/b-f-skinner. Accessed 10 December 2020.

Bakhtin, Mikhail. *Rabelais and His World*. Translated by Helene Iswolsky. Indiana UP, 1984.

Bate, Jonathan. *English Literature: A Very Short Introduction*. Oxford UP, 2010.

Beebee, Helen, and Michael Rush. *Philosophy: Why It Matters*. Polity, 2019.

Bergonzi, Bernard. "Wells the Myth-Maker." Arata, pp. 190–201.

Bertens, Hans. *Literary Theory: The Basics*. Routledge, 2004.

Berthoff, Warner. Introduction to "The Lightning-Rod Man," by Herman Melville. *Great Short Works of Herman Melville*. Edited by Warner Berthoff. Perennial/Harper & Row, 1969, p. 187.

Blackburn, Simon. *Think! A Compelling Introduction to Philosophy*. Oxford UP, 2001.

Bradford, Richard. *Crime Fiction: A Very Short Introduction*. Oxford UP, 2015.

Butler, Gillian, and Freda McManus. *Psychology: A Very Short Introduction*. Oxford UP, 2000.

Butler, Jon, Grant Wacker, and Randall

Balmer. *Religion in American Life*. Oxford UP, 2003.

Cain, James M. *Double Indemnity*. 1936. Orion, 2005.

Cantor, Paul A., and Peter Hufnagel. "The Empire of the Future: Imperialism and Modernism in H.G. Wells." Arata, pp. 229–242.

Castle, Gregory. *The Blackwell Guide to Literary Theory*. Routledge, 2007.

Childers, Joseph, and Gary Hentzi, eds. *The Columbia Dictionary of Modern Literary and Cultural Criticism*. Columbia UP, 1995.

Chopin, Kate. "The Storm." Daley, pp. 411–416.

Craig, Edward. *Philosophy: A Very Short Introduction*. Oxford UP, 2002.

Creed, Barbara. "Kristeva, Femininity, Abjection." *The Horror Reader*. Edited by Ken Gelder. Routledge, 2000, pp. 64–70.

Critchley, Simon. *The Book of Dead Philosophers*. Vintage, 2008.

———. *The Faith of the Faithless: Experiments in Political Theology*. Verso, 2012.

———. *Memory Theater*. Other Press, 2014.

———. *Notes on Suicide*. Fitzcarraldo Editions, 2015.

———. *On Humour*. Routledge, 2002.

Daley, James, ed. *100 Great Short Stories*. Dover, 2015.

Darwin, Charles. "The Origin of Species and The Descent of Man." Webb, pp. 167–180.

De Botton, Alain. *Status Anxiety*. Vintage International, 2005.

Descartes, René. *Discourse on Method & Meditations on First Philosophy*.

Works Cited

Translated by John Veitch. CreateSpace, 2011.

Dickens, Charles. "Nobody's Story." Daley, pp. 111–116.

DuBois, Ellen Carol, and Lynn Dumenil. *Through Women's Eyes: An American History with Documents.* 3rd ed. Bedford/St. Martin's, 2012.

Dunston, William E. *Ancient Rome.* Rowman & Littlefield, 2011.

Eaglestone, Robert. *Literature: Why It Matters.* Polity, 2019.

Eagleton, Terry. *Why Marx Was Right.* Yale UP, 2011.

Emerson, Ralph Waldo. "Art." 1841. Webb, pp. 582–585.

Ferry, Luc. *A Brief History of Thought: A Philosophical Guide to Living.* Translated by Theo Cuffe. Harper Perennial, 2011.

Flynn, Thomas. *Existentialism: A Very Short Introduction.* Oxford UP, 2006

Ford, Ford Madox. "Pink Flannel." Daley, pp. 685–689.

Foster, R.F. *W.B. Yeats: A Life: The Apprentice Mage.* Oxford UP, 1998.

Freud, Sigmund. *Civilization and Its Discontents.* Translated by James Strachey. Norton, 2010.

Friedlander, Saul. *Franz Kafka: The Poet of Shame and Guilt.* Yale UP, 2013.

Gay, Peter. *Modernism: The Lure of Heresy, from Baudelaire to Beckett and Beyond.* Norton, 2008.

Gioia, Dana, and R.S. Gwynn. Introduction. *The Art of the Short Story.* Edited by Dana Gioia and R.S. Gwynn. Pearson-Longman, 2006, pp. 3–6.

Gonzalez, Justo L. *The Story of Christianity: The Reformation to the Present Day.* Harper San Francisco, 1985.

Greenblatt, Stephen, et al., eds. *The Norton Anthology of English Literature: The Major Authors.* Norton, 2013.

Grunfeld, Frederic V. *Prophets Without Honour: Freud, Kafka, Einstein, and Their World.* Kodansha, 1996.

Harvey, Van A. *A Handbook of Theological Terms: Their Meaning and Background Exposed in Over 300 Articles.* Touchstone, 1992.

Hawthorne, Nathaniel. "Young Goodman Brown." Daley, pp. 54–66.

Henderson, Heather, and William Sharpe, eds. *The Victorian Age.* Longman, 1999.

Homer, Sean. *Jacques Lacan.* Routledge, 2005.

Hospers, John. *An Introduction to Philosophical Analysis.* 4th ed. Prentice-Hall, 1997.

Huntington, John. "*The Time Machine* and Wells's Social Trajectory." Arata, pp. 222–228.

Inwood, Michael. *Heidegger: A Very Short Introduction.* Oxford UP, 1997.

Irving, Washington. "The Devil and Tom Walker." Daley, pp. 14–24.

Jung, Carl G. "Approaching the Unconscious." *Man and His Symbols.* Edited by Carl G. Jung. Laurel, 1968, pp. 1–94.

Kafka, Franz. "A Hunger Artist." Daley, pp. 713–722.

_____. "The Judgement." Daley, pp. 636–646.

"Kate Chopin: 'The Storm.'" *The Kate Chopin International Society.* katechopin.org/the-storm/. Accessed 29 November 2020.

Kennedy, X.J., and Dana Gioia. *Literature: An Introduction to Fiction, Poetry, Drama, and Writing.* 11th ed. Longman, 2010.

Klein, Étienne. *Chronos: How Time Shapes Our Universe.* Translated by Glenn Burney. Thunder's Mouth, 2005.

London, Jack. *The Call of the Wild.* 1903. Dover, 1990.

_____. "The Leopard Man's Story." Daley, pp. 465–468.

_____. *White Fang.* 1906. Dover, 1991.

_____. "The White Silence." Daley, pp. 427–435.

Lovejoy, Bess. *Rest in Pieces: The Curious Fates of Famous Corpses.* Simon & Schuster, 2013.

Luckhurst, Roger. "The Scientific Romance and the Evolutionary Paradigm." Arata, pp. 525–259.

Machiavelli, Niccolò. "On the Exercise of Power (from *The Prince*)." Webb, pp. 340–345.

Maupassant, Guy de. "Looking Back." *50 Great Short Stories.* Edited by Milton Crane. Bantam, 2005, pp. 175–180.

McKeon, Richard. Introduction to

Works Cited

Metaphysics. Introduction to Aristotle. Edited by Richard McKeon. Random House, 1947, pp. 238–240.

Melville, Herman. "The Lightning-Rod Man." Daley, pp. 117–122.

———. *Moby-Dick.* 1851. Barnes and Noble Classics, 2003.

Mérimée, Prosper. "Mateo Falcone." Daley, pp. 25–36.

Montaigne, Michel de. *The Complete Essays.* Translated and edited by M.A. Screech. Penguin, 2003.

Moshfegh, Ottessa. *Death in Her Hands.* Penguin, 2020.

Myers, Tony. *Slavoj Žižek.* Routledge, 2003.

Nickell, Joe. *Secrets of the Sideshows.* U of Kentucky P, 2005.

Nietzsche, Friedrich. "God Is Dead (1887)." Webb, pp. 109–111.

Paine, Thomas. *The Age of Reason.* 1896. Merchant, 2010.

Palmer, Donald. *Does the Center Hold? An Introduction to Western Philosophy.* Mayfield, 1991.

Placher, William C. *A History of Christian Theology: An Introduction.* Westminster Press, 1983.

Plato. "Apology." *Five Dialogues: Euthyphro, Apology, Crito, Meno, Phaedo.* Translated by G.M.A. Grube. Hackett, 2002, pp. 21–44.

———. *Republic.* Translated by C.D.C. Reeve. Hackett, 2004.

Poe, Edgar Allan. "The Cask of Amontillado." Daley, pp. 88–94.

———. "The Philosophy of Composition." *The Norton Anthology of Theory and Criticism.* Edited by Vincent B. Leitch. Norton, 2001, pp. 742–749.

———. "The Tell-Tale Heart." Daley, pp. 83–87.

Robertson-Lorant, Laurie. *Melville: A Biography.* U of Massachusetts P, 1996.

Rollyson, Carl, and Lisa Paddock. *Herman Melville A to Z.* Check Mark, 2001.

Rothfels, Nigel. "Aztecs, Aborigines, and Ape-People: Science and Freaks in Germany, 1850–1900." *Freakery: Cultural Spectacles of the Extraordinary Body.* Edited by Rosemarie Garland Thomson. New York UP, 1996, pp. 158–172.

Rousseau, Jean-Jacques. "On the Origin of Inequality." Webb, pp. 451–456.

———. *The Social Contract. The European Philosophers: From Descartes to Nietzsche.* Edited by Monroe C. Beardsley. The Modern Library/Random House, 1988, pp. 321–364.

Ruland, Richard, and Malcolm Bradbury. *From Puritanism to Postmodernism: A History of American Literature.* Penguin, 1991.

Russell, Bertrand. *The History of Western Philosophy.* Touchstone, 1972.

Saunders, Max. "Ford Madox Ford (1873–1939): Biography." *The Ford Madox Ford Society.* http://www.fordmadoxfordsociety.org/fords-biography.html. Accessed 15 October 2020.

Scruton, Roger. *A Short History of Modern Philosophy: From Descartes to Wittgenstein.* Routledge, 2002.

Sears, Kathleen. *Mythology 101.* Adams, 2014.

Shorto, Russell. *Descartes' Bones: A Skeletal History of the Conflict Between Faith and Reason.* Vintage, 2008.

Sir Gawain and the Green Knight. Translated by Brian Stone. Penguin, 1974.

Storr, Anthony. *Freud: A Very Short Introduction.* Oxford UP, 2001.

Stromberg, Roland N. *European Intellectual History Since 1789.* Prentice-Hall, 1981.

Urmson, James O. "Plato and the Poets." *Plato's Republic: Critical Essays.* Edited by Richard Kraut. Rowman & Littlefield, 1997, pp. 223–234.

Warner, Charles Dudley. "How I Killed a Bear." Daley, pp. 218–224.

———. *In the Wilderness.* 1878. CreateSpace, 2018.

Warner, Charles Dudley, and Mark Twain. *The Gilded Age: A Tale of Today.* 1873. Penguin, 2001.

Webb, Igor, ed. *Ideas Across Time.* McGraw-Hill, 2008.

Wells, H.G. "The Remarkable Case of Davidson's Eyes." Daley, pp. 358–367.

———. *The Time Machine.* 1895. Bantam, 2003.

Wilde, Oscar. "The Happy Prince." Daley, pp. 291–299.

Works Cited

———. "The Selfish Giant." Daley, pp. 300–303.

Wittgenstein, Ludwig. *The Blue and Brown Books: Preliminary Studies for the Philosophical Investigations.* Harper, 1965.

———. *Tractatus Logico-Philosophicus.* Chiron, 2016.

Woolf, Virginia. "The Mark on the Wall." Daley, pp. 706–712.

"Yeats and Mysticism." *In Our Time.* BBC Radio 4. 31 January 2002. https://www.bbc.co.uk/programmes/p00548b3.

Yeats, W.B. "The Tables of the Law." Daley, pp. 392–401.

Žižek, Slavoj. *Enjoy Your Symptom! Jacques Lacan in Hollywood and Out.* Routledge, 2001.

Index

Index